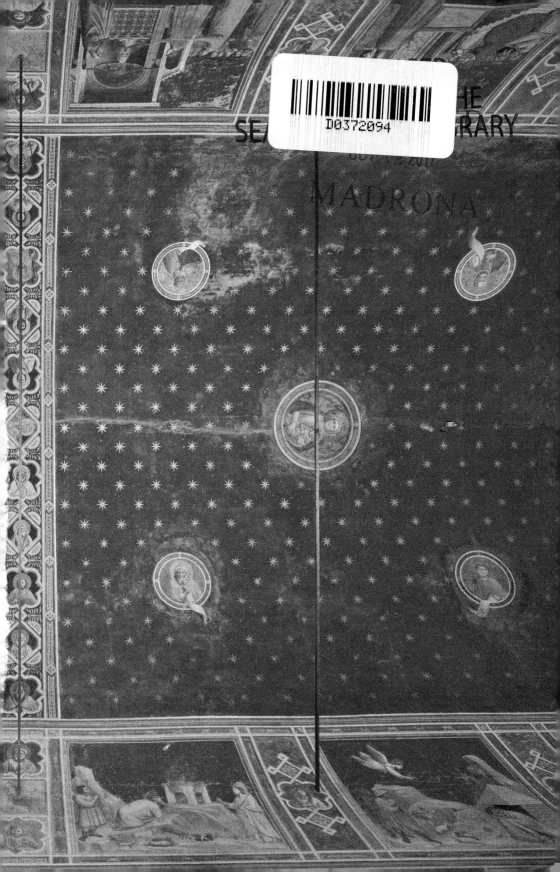

Overleaf: Ceiling of Scrovegni Chapel, Padua
Bridgeman Art Library

by thomas cahill

also by thomas cahill

the hinges of history

We normally think of history as one catastrophe after another, war followed by war, outrage by outrage—almost as if history were nothing more than all the narratives of human pain, assembled in sequence. And surely this is, often enough, an adequate description. But history is also the narratives of grace, the recountings of those blessed and inexplicable moments when someone did something for someone else, saved a life, bestowed a gift, gave something beyond what was required by circumstance.

In this series, THE HINGES OF HISTORY, I mean to retell the story of the Western world as the story of the great gift-givers, those who entrusted to our keeping one or another of the singular treasures that make up the patrimony of the West. This is also the story of the evolution of Western sensibility, a narration of how we became the people we are and why we think and feel the way we do. And it is, finally, a recounting of those essential moments when everything was at stake, when the mighty stream that became Western history was in ultimate danger and might have divided into a hundred useless tributaries or frozen in death or evaporated altogether. But the great gift-givers, arriving in the moment of crisis, provided for transition, for transformation, and even for transfiguration, leaving us a world more varied and complex, more awesome and delightful, more beautiful and strong than the one they had found.

—*Thomas Cahill*

the hinges of history

nan a. talese
anchor books

A DIVISION OF RANDOM HOUSE, INC.
NEW YORK

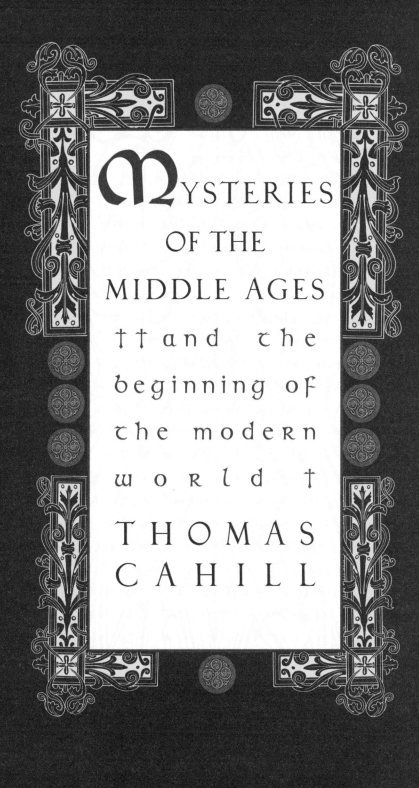

Mysteries of the

Middle Ages

✝✝ and the
beginning of
the modern
world ✝

THOMAS
CAHILL

FIRST ANCHOR BOOKS EDITION, MARCH 2008

Copyright © 2006 by Thomas Cahill

All rights reserved. Published in the United States by Anchor Books, a division of Random House, Inc., New York, and in Canada by Random House of Canada Limited, Toronto. Originally published in hardcover in the United States by Nan A. Talese, an imprint of The Doubleday Broadway Publishing Group, a division of Random House, Inc., New York, in 2006.

Anchor Books and colophon are registered trademarks of Random House, Inc.

Pages 328–330 constitute an extension of this copyright page.

The Library of Congress has cataloged the Nan A. Talese edition as follows:
Cahill, Thomas.
Mysteries of the Middle Ages : the rise of feminism, science, and art from the cults of Catholic Europe/Thomas Cahill.—1st ed.
p. cm.—(The hinges of history ; v. 5)
Includes index.
1. Civilization, Medieval. 2. Women—Europe—History—Middle Ages, 500–1500. 3. Science, Medieval. 4. Art, Medieval. I. Title. II. Series: Cahill, Thomas. Hinges of history ; v. 5.
CB.351.C22 2006
909.07—dc22 2006044545

Anchor ISBN: 978-0-385-49556-1

Author photograph © Barbi Reed
Book design by Terry Karydes (from the original series concept by Marysarah Quinn)
Map art by Virginia Norey
www.anchorbooks.com

Printed in the United States of America
10 9

e là m'apparve, sì com' elli appare

subitamente cosa che disvia

per maraviglia tutto altro pensare,

una donna soletta che si gìa

e cantando e scegliendo fior da fiore

ond' era pinta tutta la sua via.

and there appeared to me—as can befall

so suddenly a thing that drives away

all other thought by wonder magical—

a lady alone who went along her way

singing and plucking flower upon flower,

which painted all the path that before her lay.

contents

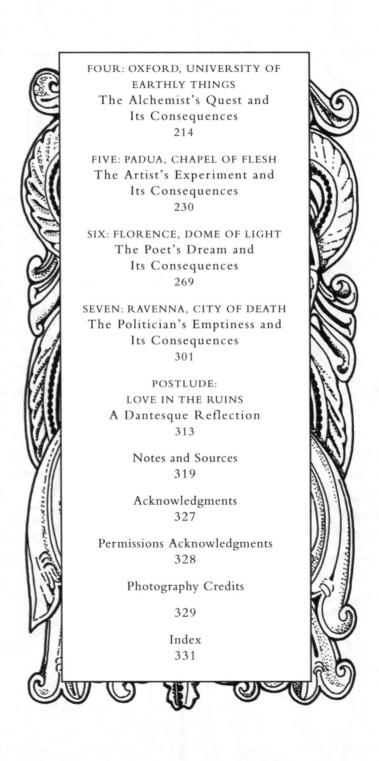

list of illustrations

maps

charts

illustrative art

list of illustrations (continued)

Mysteries

OF THE

MIDDLE AGES

†† and the

beginning of

the modern

world †

a chaucerian invitation

At night was come in-to
that hostelrye
Wel nyne and twenty in a companye,
Of sondry folk, by aventure y-falle
In felawshipe, and pilgrims were
they alle . . .

S O DOES GEOFFREY CHAUCER describe the convening—at the Tabard Inn in Southwark on the southern bank of the River Thames—of twenty-nine pilgrims. The next day they would ride southeast from London to Canterbury, "the holy blisful martir for to seke [seek]." For in the year 1170, Canterbury had been the scene of the martyrdom of Thomas Becket, the unbending archbishop of Canterbury, slain by four knights in service to King Henry II. The martyr's bones were kept in a jewel-encrusted shrine in the cathedral where he had been murdered, and from them was believed to emanate miraculous healing power. All over England people prayed to Becket, invoking his intercession with God "whan that they were seke [sick]," as Chaucer tells us. Those who were cured of their maladies would then make their promised pilgrimage to Becket's bones.

All across Europe, a pilgrimage in company with others was a life-defining event and one of the principal satisfactions of a well-tuned life. A man or woman went on pilgrimage in thanksgiving for a favor granted or to ask a member of the court of Heaven for something greatly desired or as penance for sins committed. But even a penitential pilgrimage was full of incidental pleasures. The pilgrim joined with other pilgrims for safety and companionship, and each pilgrimage offered its promise of adventure. One was, after all, traveling farther into the world than one had ever ventured before. Most medieval wayfarers had never gone beyond the nearest market town, so every pilgrim could look forward to marvelous sights and strange encounters. Whether you journeyed to a national shrine like Canterbury, to an international destination like Santiago de Compostela in Spain, or to the most exotic goal of all, the Holy Land itself, you would have enough stories to tell on your return to fill what remained of your span of days.

Especially from your fellow pilgrims, mostly people previously unknown to you, you could expect to receive an unparalleled learning experience. For these were people from other places, places you had never seen, who had life stories quite unlike the ones you were familiar with. "A crowd is as exciting as champagne to these lonely people, who live in long glens among the mountains," John Millington Synge once wrote of rural Irish folk, who had managed even in his day to maintain many medieval customs and who still bore a medieval mind-set. Not all medievals lived in long mountain glens, but most lived among what would seem to us but a handful of other humans. So though pilgrimage was a religious duty, it also became a glorious—and sometimes picaresque—experience.

I invite you on a pilgrimage, dear Reader. Come along with me (and many others) to places we have never seen before and to people we could otherwise never have expected to know. We are surely sundry folk, as Chaucer would have called us, and we shall meet sundry folk even more exotic than ourselves. "By aventure"—by happenstance—we have fallen into fellowship.

In the Prelude that follows we must spend a little time in late antique Alexandria, for it was a place of cultural percolation that would have untold influence on the making of the Middle Ages. Then in the Introduction, we shall quickly navigate the intervening centuries from the death of antiquity to the budding of the high Middle Ages. Do not be troubled if all this seems far removed from our principal quest. By starting in late antiquity and then by turning, however briefly, to the uncertain beginnings of the medieval period, we learn by contrast: how different are the seeds from the soil that nourished them, how splendid will be the flowers compared with the seeds. And like a hearty breakfast taken at the Tabard, these early courses will stand us in good stead as we venture forth in Chapter One to the solemn and merry mysteries that will constitute our chief employment.

alexandria, city of reason

the great confluence

*The soul takes nothing with
her into the other world
but her education and culture.*

—PLATO

LEXANDRIA WAS THE MOST
Greek of cities. Situated in the
alluvial delta where the life-
giving Nile meets the dolphin-
torn Mediterranean, it had been
commissioned by Alexander the
Great as his very own civic apotheosis. And though the young
world-beater did not live long
enough to see even one of its
buildings rise from the mud of the

delta, his corpse was transported here—shunned by the obscurantist priests of Egyptian Memphis, who feared his restless spirit would bring them bad luck—and here did the body, at least, of Alexander find rest in the late fourth century B.C. within the massive mausoleum called *to sōma*, Greek for "the Body."

The city that materialized around the tomb was almost impossibly grand. It had not grown like most cities as an unplanned thicket of huddled *quartiers*, dense with fetid air and insalubrious shadows. Rather, it was laid out in a reasonable pattern, not unlike such later cities as Paris and Washington, and it seemed to classical eyes to embody the principle of rationality. "The first thing one noticed on entering Alexandria by the Gate of the Sun," exclaimed one tourist of late antiquity, "was the beauty of the city. A line of columns processed from one end of it to the other. Advancing along them, I came to the place that bears the name of Alexander, and there I could see the other half of the town [divided from the first half by the broad Canopic Way], which was equally beautiful. For just as the colonnades stretched out ahead of me, so did other colonnades now appear at right angles to them." Grids, right angles, generously proportioned boulevards radiating from dignified monuments, punctuating colonnades at regular intervals—expansive, mathematical, open to the bright sun, and all assuring the ancient visitor that here at last he had reached the harbor of balance and tranquility, the architectural and social expression of *Logos*, of Thought Itself.

For the ancients, Alexandria, cultural successor to war-devastated Athens, became in the third century B.C. the great City of the Mind; and for all the untroubled urbanity of its polished surfaces, it buzzed noon and night with theory, disputation, and intellectual engagement. Its first ruler, Alexander's companion-in-arms Ptolemy—Soter (or Savior), as he styled himself—had not particularly meant to create such a cerebral center. He meant only to consolidate and extend the power of his realm of Greek Africa, the rough third of Alexander's empire that had fallen to him (just as Greek Asia and Greek Europe had fallen to others among Alexander's generals). Ptolemy was of course hardly unaware of the status that accrued to him on account of his ownership of Alexander's body, as sainted a relic as the ancient world possessed. (He had in fact kidnapped it during its funeral procession.) And he knew perfectly well how much his power would be enhanced by the creation of a great urban stage set.

Ptolemy Soter founded the Mouseion, parent of all subsequent museums, nerve center of philosophy, mathematics, literature, and a dozen other scholarly pursuits. Within its vast domain was the multilingual Library containing, it was said, all the books that had ever been written.[a] Among the varied enterprises housed in the Mouseion was a faculty of engineering that made possible the Pharos, the Lighthouse, which stood in the harbor on a limestone island and was one of the Seven Wonders of the World. It rose more than four hundred feet into the sky, and its ground floor alone was divided into three hundred separate workrooms and offices. "To the imagination of contemporaries," wrote E. M. Forster, "the Pharos became Alexandria and Alexandria became the Pharos. Never, in the history of architecture, has a secular building been thus worshipped and taken on a spiritual life of its own. It beaconed to the imagination, not only to ships at sea, and long after its light was extinguished memories of it glowed in the minds of men."

There is even tantalizing, if fragmentary, evidence that the Pharos may have been topped by a telescope. (If so, lenses were a Greek invention, lost well before the Pharos fell to ruin under the Arabs and rediscovered in the thirteenth century of our era.) The Ptolemys would rule safely and ruthlessly till Cleopatra VII, unable to secure the throne for Ptolemy XV, her son by Julius Caesar, died with an asp at her breast, her only way of avoiding the humiliation of submitting to Caesar's conquering successor, Octavian, who

[a]   The original Library, called the Mother, was much enlarged under Ptolemy Soter's son and heir and was thereafter called the Daughter. The Library was burned three times, first in 47 B.C. by Julius Caesar (who accidentally set fire to some storerooms in the course of a battle), then deliberately and more extensively by a Christian mob toward the end of the fourth century of our era, and finally in A.D. 642 by the forces of Caliph Omar. At its greatest extent it may have contained considerably more than half a million separate texts—which astonishing abundance alone accounts for its legendary status throughout the ancient and early medieval world.

would style himself Caesar Augustus and take the title Imperator, Rome's first emperor.

Would that we could spend a little time with Cleopatra, a woman as unafraid to play power politics as the boldest of men. She was an exemplary Alexandrian, devoted to the pleasures of Eros, the Greek god of Love, whose lissome image stood in every verdant courtyard and was reflected in every glistening pool. ("Who sculpted Love and set him by the pool, / thinking with water such fire to cool?" went a popular song that had been penned in his spare moments by the head librarian.) Nor was this last queen of Greco-Egyptian Africa ever less than realistic about the things she must do to retain her throne. But she knew that in Octavian she was up against an opponent who, unlike the avuncular Julius Caesar or the besotted Mark Antony, would accord her no mercy, for he was, in Forster's words, "one of the most odious of the world's successful men." Knowing exactly when all was lost, she departed as gracefully as she had reigned; and Egypt was absorbed into the Roman Empire.

Fascinating Cleopatra has little to do, however, with our story, a story of cultural evolution that will take us from one age to another. Indeed, the political dramas of the high and mighty made scant impact on Alexandria's intellectual life, which proceeded uninterrupted under each of the many Ptolemys, then under each of the many Caesars. Scholars and sages were drawn to the city from all over the civilized world: first Greeks; then Greek-educated Romans; then provincial philosophers and mystagogues of several varieties—Persians, Indians, Jews, and last of all Christians. The imperial safety, the effortless wealth, the stately pace, the clarity of light, the geometric symmetry, the characteristic Greek ambience of inquiry all acted as correlative inspiration to their own enterprises: the labeling of reality and the calm, dispassionate ascent to truth.

About 300 B.C. a man named Euclid landed in the harbor, as if from nowhere, and became the founding father of Alexandrian (and world) geometry, without which the city could never have been built in the monumental manner for which it became famous. Euclid's thirteen

books of *Elements* would serve as the basis for all ancient building pro-
grams; and even though the books were lost to non-Arabic Europe till
the twelfth century, thereafter Euclid's proofs would sustain European
geometry right through the nineteenth century. At the end of each neat
proof, superlogical Euclid carefully added the Greek *"hoper edei deixai"*
(which was to be proven). This tag, especially in its Latin abbreviation—
Q.E.D., for *quod erat demonstrandum*—has ever after been the conventional conclusion to demonstrations of logical reasoning.

Euclid in his fussy orderliness, however, was the exact opposite of a
celebrity personality, and because of this only a single anecdote has survived him. When one frustrated reader, Ptolemy Soter himself, high-
handedly demanded a shortcut to understanding the difficult *Elements,*
Euclid replied tersely that there is "no royal road to geometry." And so
the life of Alexandria continued on its parallel tracks, the one royal, the
other intellectual.

Other Alexandrian scholars of the third century B.C. were hardly less
enterprising than Euclid. The physician Erasistratus practiced vivisection
certainly on animals, possibly on human criminals, and came close to
discovering the circulation of the blood. Long before Freud, he recognized that nervous breakdowns usually had a sexual component. The geographer Eratosthenes, a younger contemporary of Euclid, was certain
that the earth was round; and by measuring shadows at midsummer in
various locations, he was able to calculate the circumference of the
globe, coming within fifty miles of the actual figure. His *Map of the
World,* though inexact, shows three continents and names everything
from Ireland to Sri Lanka. His successor, Claudius Ptolemy (perhaps a
relative of the royal family), is responsible for the "Ptolemaic theory"
that the sun revolves around the earth, the theory that would be held as
dogma by the medieval church and against which the great Galileo
would come to grief. Another scientist, Aristarchus of Samos, who collaborated with Claudius Ptolemy at Alexandria, suggested that, just
possibly, the earth might revolve around the sun. Unfortunately and
accidentally, Aristarchus's works perished, while Ptolemy's survived and

so came, in time, to be awarded quasi-scriptural authority, an honor attained in the Middle Ages by a fair number of surviving Greek treatises.

But however important scientists were to the look and pleasure of the city, general philosophers were the quintessential Alexandrian intellectuals. They were all of them children of Plato, the great philosopher who had taught at Athens in the early fourth century B.C., a lifelong bachelor who never engendered a child of his body but had philosophical children everywhere. Plato has made chapter-length appearances twice before in this series[b] because his influence on the Western world is unequaled. Here we must at least acknowledge his principal disciple, Plotinus of Alexandria, who lived in the third century A.D. and whose philosophy, dubbed "Neoplatonism," was a guiding light to an immense variety of thinkers, both pagan and Christian.

Though Plotinus studied at Alexandria and moved to Rome in midlife, he was born in neither place. He would never tell anyone where he was born, and no one could ever discover it. He said that his birth, that is, the occasion of the descent of his immortal soul into his embarrassingly corruptible body, had been—like all human births—a moment of ineffable catastrophe and would not bear discussion.

Despite the high esteem in which Plotinus was held in the ancient world, much of what he had to say is hard to sit still for today. Like Plato and most of the later Greek philosophical tradition, Plotinus believed that all the Greek stories about the multiplicity of gods were no better than nursery tales. If the universe was to make sense, God must be (somehow) One. And Plotinus believed, along with Plato and many others, that we would all be better off without our bodies, which are made of matter, which is the principle of unintelligibility. The immortal soul, however, that spark of divinity imprisoned in the foul mud of materiality, yearns to shuffle off this mortal coil and fly back to the One.

---

b Plato is an important subject in *How the Irish Saved Civilization,* Chapter II ("What Was Lost: The Complexities of the Classical Tradition"), and the chief subject of *Sailing the Wine-Dark Sea,* Chapter V ("The Philosopher: How to Think").

Though many things may be posited of Plotinus, nittygrittyness is not one of them. He is more lofty, more abstract than Plato, just about as sublime as sublime can be—and his prose, unlike Plato's, can be virtually impenetrable. Still, he's clearly in the Platonic tradition. When we read in Plato those gorgeously sensuous passages that scorn the material world—"beauty tainted by human flesh and coloring and all that mortal rubbish"—we can easily identify the magisterial source of Plotinus's anti-material loftiness. Even though Plato's belittling of the flesh is in tension with his love (and perhaps even craving) for fleshly realities, and even though such tension is bleakly absent from the writings of Plotinus, there can be no question that Plato is Plotinus's intellectual father.

The Greek-sponsored philosophy of scorn for the flesh, articulated by Plato and further aerated by Plotinian sublimities, will leave indelible marks first on Jewish, then on Christian, attitudes. For both Jews and, later, Christians will come to live within the prevailing Greco-Roman cultural context; and it is virtually impossible for minority cultures to avoid absorbing and internalizing the principal values of the majority culture in which they move and breathe, whose language they speak and whose vocabulary becomes the currency of daily life. At the same time, it should be noted that the Greeks and the Romans (who took over the Greek philosophical inheritance more or less intact), though dismissive of the philosophical value of human flesh, reveled in the full panoply of its fleeting pleasures in ways that would remain markedly alien to the Judeo-Christian tradition. The statues of nude Eros that stood up everywhere in Alexandria and the lubricious lyrics about him were testimony to a god whose presence everyone took for granted. Sex, sex of all kinds, was everywhere. Give in. What, for heaven's sake, would be the point of battling a god? You can't win, so go where your desire takes you. Just bear in mind that—at the philosophical level—such *rencontres* have no Ultimate Significance.

The Jewish moral tradition, like its younger sibling, the Christian, could not easily embrace this strange dichotomy that gave centrality to Eros in art and song while trivializing its importance philosophically. For Jews and Christians, all human actions were consequential, brimming with moral implications. At the same time, many Jews of the last centuries B.C. found themselves exceedingly attracted to Greek culture and especially to the novel idea of the soul that had its origin in Plato and his predecessors.

The Jewish worldview, like other primeval worldviews, assumed that death was the end: when the body died, you died. Period. Both ancient Jews and ancient Greeks left room for a shadow world beneath the earth, where the insubstantial shades of what were once living men and women drifted like smoke. The Hebrews called this underworld Sheol, the Greeks Hades, but it was in essence the same place. Both cultures may have adapted their "Hell" from a similar shadow world that the even more ancient Mesopotamians had imagined; or it may simply be the normal way for early peoples to envision the shadowy existence of those who have been buried underground. What was important to the Jews was life, not death (which no one can do anything about, anyway). Live according to the laws of God, and you will live well and long.

What then of the martyr, the one whose life is artificially shortened by his devotion to God, the one who is, say, executed by a God-hating tyrant? Are death and the gloom of Sheol his only rewards? Surely not. Out of such concerns arose the later Jewish idea of bodily resurrection—one's return "in the flesh" by an act of God at "the end of days"—which would become central to primitive Christianity.

But if we are to look forward to physical resurrection at the end of time, what may we say about the personal identity of the dead person in the meanwhile? If he cannot have utterly ceased to exist, where is he? It is here that the Plato-sponsored idea of the soul comes in so handy. "The souls of the just are in the hands of God," concludes the Book of Wisdom, written by an Alexandrian Jew in the century before Christ, written not in Hebrew, the sacred language of the Jews, but in lively, contemporary Greek. This Book of Wisdom, which masqueraded under the title "The Wisdom of Solomon," wrapped itself in the mantle of tradition, even though it was very much of its moment, the granddaddy of all spirituality books, a sort of "How to Love God and Still Be Cool by the Pool," a book that shows you how to be faithful to Judaism while impressing your hip Greek neighbors with the right lingo.

The Jewish community at Alexandria, probably as old as the city itself, boasted the largest Jewish population in the ancient world. In the third century B.C., under the second Ptolemy—Ptolemy Philadelphus (or Loving Brother)—a historic assembly of Jewish scholars had been convened on Pharos Island. Their task was to make a Greek translation of the Hebrew scriptures for deposit in the great Library. Thus would the insights of this singular monotheistic religion begin to be shared with the whole world. Several legends would afterwards accrue to this unusual enterprise: there were seventy-two scholars who took seventy-two days to complete their translations; and each, working separately, came up with the exact same translation.

But however it was actually composed, the translation, called the Septuagint (or Seventy, after the approximate number of translators), turned into a best-selling sensation throughout the Greek-speaking world, not only among the many diaspora Jews who could no longer read Hebrew but even among gentiles in search of a more rigorous and satisfying spiritual way. Though few of the latter underwent circumcision or abided strictly by Judaism's tedious dietary rules, they were welcomed to Jewish worship and study as "Godfearers" and "sons of Noah." From their ranks many—probably most—of the first gentile Christians would be recruited. By the time Christianity appeared, editions of the Septuagint usually included the Book of Wisdom as well as a few other late compositions. This expanded version of the Septuagint, its books shuffled somewhat to coincide with Christian presupposi-

c These late compositions—principally Esther, Judith, 1 and 2 Maccabees, Wisdom, Ecclesiasticus (or Ben Sira), Baruch, Tobit, and three additions to Daniel that are extant only in Greek—have been accounted differently by different religious communities in the course of Judeo-Christian history. The church fathers of the fourth century A.D., who issued the first definitive "canon" of the Bible, regarded all of them as divinely inspired, as the Orthodox and Catholic churches continue to do. Later Jewish and Reformation traditions accept only Esther (in a shorter—and older—Hebrew version) and consider the other compositions "apocryphal." The order of books within the Bible could not be fixed till after the invention of the codex (or bound book, as we still know it), since before that time writings were kept not in order within a single volume but in a cabinet of multiple scrolls. But even in the days of Jesus, centuries before the codex, "The Torah [or Law of Moses] and the Prophets" was the common phrase for referring to the Hebrew scriptures. What was neither Torah nor Prophets was included among the nondescript

tions, would then become known throughout the dawning medieval world as the "Old Testament."**c**

Before we begin to consider the impact that Christianity made on the Greco-Roman mindset, there is one more instance of Greek-influenced Judaism we should have a look at, in many ways the most elegant and influential. Philo Judaeus (Philo the Jew) was born at Alexandria in the last decades of the first century B.C. and died toward the middle of the first century A.D. Unlike his elder contemporary, the anonymous author of the Book of Wisdom, Philo was no popularizer. His extant works—and we by no means possess everything he wrote—run to thirty-five volumes in their annotated French edition. And though he commented on many subjects in the course of his impressive literary career, his main thrust was to expound on the sacred texts of the Septuagint in such a way that their stories and assertions would be rendered immune from Greek ridicule.

For though there was throughout the late classical world much admiration for Judaism among both Greeks and Romans, Greek tongues were sharp, Greek logic was quick to seize on anomalies and contradictions, and Greek comedians delighted in parodying folkloric inanities and provincial narrow-mindedness. In not a few passages of the Septuagint, translated from exceedingly ancient (and foreign) texts into the sometimes clumsily Semitized prose of immigrant translators—what could sound like Molly Goldberg Greek to an educated ear—critics found considerable material for satire.

Philo's main device for turning Greek ridicule to admiration was allegorical interpretation. The talking serpent of Eden, for instance, is not meant to be a snake, silly. Rather, as might be the case in one of Aesop's fables, it is the evil principle of pleasure. (Were you really so unsophisticated as to misunderstand *that?*) Moreover, God's curse upon this principle, claimed Philo,

"Writings," as the third (and last) division of the scriptures. These are the three divisions still maintained in order in Jewish Bibles. Christian Bibles, however, place the books that Jews count as the Latter Prophets at the end of the "Old Testament," so that these may more easily be read as prophesying the coming of Jesus, whose story appears immediately afterwards at the beginning of the "New Testament."

is appropriate: "Earth shalt thou eat all the days of thy life" [Genesis 3:14]. For the food of the body brings pleasures of earth; and rightly so, it would seem. For there are two things of which we consist, soul and body. The body, of course, has been formed from the earth, but the soul belongs to the upper air, a shard detached from the Deity: "For God breathed into [Adam's] face a breath of life and man became a living soul" [Genesis 2:7]. It accords with reason, therefore, that the body, made from earth, has food like unto itself, which earth provides, while the soul, partaking of ethereal being, has, rather, ethereal and divine food, for it is fed by knowledge in its various forms and not by the meat and drink that the body requires.

The "living soul" of Genesis 2:7 is a literal translation of *psyche zoe,* the Greek phrase employed in the Septuagint, which is the Hellenic-flavored version of Genesis that Philo is quoting. The words used in the original Hebrew, however, are *nephesh hayyah,* which mean only "living [that is, moving, breathing] being." The Hebrews of the period in which Genesis was written down (perhaps ten centuries before Philo) had no notion of a soul—and Philo, so far as we can determine, had no Hebrew.

So the Greek of the Septuagint enables Philo to stake out an implicit claim that the very earliest passages of Genesis, the first of the Five Books of the Law of Moses, already employ the lofty Platonic distinctions of body and soul. In Philo's telling, Moses even becomes the teacher of Plato and of the entire Greek philosophical tradition! For Philo, no proof of this amazing connection was necessary, since the texts themselves reveal that such must be the case. The Greeks, having no way of critiquing this fanciful claim, tended to give it credence.

Thus, over the course of Philo's many books, the Hebrew and Greek traditions shed light on one another and become, at last, inextricably intertwined. The extensive Greek vocabulary explicates difficult, sometimes previously inexplicable passages in the scriptures, clothing even barbarous incidents in refined Hellenic draperies. The Hebrew stories and the astonishing assertions of the God of Moses lend their memorable pithiness and rude strength to the airy speculations of the Greeks.

But Philo, prolix and rambling as he often is—a writer who never met a digression he didn't love—is ultimately no compromiser. Greek philosophy is all well and good, but only insofar as it can be reconciled to Moses. The softening of biblical stories by means of allegorical interpretation should be taken just so far:

> It is quite true that the Seventh Day is meant to teach the power of the Unoriginate and the nonaction of created beings. But let us not for this reason abrogate the laws laid down for its observance, and light fires or till the ground or carry loads or institute proceedings in court or act as jurors or demand restoration of deposits or recover loans, or do all the things we are permitted to do on [other] days.

The Sabbath of Moses is to be kept strictly, not allegorically. Circumcision, though it "does indeed portray the excision of pleasure and all passions, and the putting away of the impious conceit under which the mind imagined that it was able to beget by its own power," is not to be merely symbolic; it requires the cutting of the foreskin.

Otherwise, there is no genuine symbol, just empty waffling. Philo is no Jewish Unitarian; he is a deadly serious apologist for his ancient religion, one who understands the Greek context so well that he can use its language fluently and convincingly, while never leaving the central tenets of Judaism unprotected.

All the same, Philo adopts (and adapts) many Greek philosophical categories. God is indeed the One of which nothing may be known or said—except that he *is,* which is why he gave his name to Moses as *ho on* (He Who *Is*). By his Word (*Logos,* in Greek), as Genesis tells us, God created the world. Philo even calls the Logos a "second god" and God's firstborn. And Philo perceives even a third level in God, the Powers by which he acts in the world. Philo's Logos and Powers, therefore, play the role of mediators between the unknowable One and mankind.

If Philo, more than any other figure, found the means to reconcile Judaism and Hellenism, he was also—without knowing it—an extraordinary intellectual channel that linked Judaism, Hellenism, and the Christianity that was to come. For the somewhat sketchy Trinity of Persons that Philo discerned in the Hebrew Godhead will cascade into the future, not only influencing the thought of Plotinus but forming the theoretical framework for the Christian Trinity.ᵭ Philo's writings seemed so alien to later Judaism that they had no impact on rabbinical thought and were lost to intellectual Judaism till well into the Renaissance. For Christians, however, Philo would become an honorary "father of the church." In Byzantine copies of his works, he is often designated as "Bishop Philo," even though there is no hint in any of his writings that he ever heard of the Palestinian offshoot of Judaism that would come to be called Christianity and that remained in his lifetime a hunted, marginal sect.

ᵭ The Trinity is commonly regarded among Christians as deriving exclusively from the inspired revelation of the New Testament, especially the "trinitarian" passages in John's Gospel and, more sparingly, in Paul's letters. But these few passages, though suggestive, cannot yield anything like a systematic theology of the inner life of God. The early Christian apologists needed to rely on Philo's more elaborate philosophical scheme in order to begin to make coherent sense of the hints they found in the New Testament. Philo's Logos and Powers undoubtedly owe much to the philosophy of the Stoics, but to explore this connection would take us far afield.

Though Philo lived only into the early first century A.D., we know more of him than of the mysterious Plotinus, who flourished two centuries later. Philo was born to an exceedingly wealthy Alexandrian family. His brother Alexander was probably chief customs officer for Egypt's eastern border and guardian of the empress dowager's Egyptian properties. Alexander even made a loan to the Jewish king Agrippa I and plated the gates of the Jerusalem Temple in silver and gold. Alexander's son, who became an apostate from Judaism, served as procurator of Judea, then as imperial prefect of all Egypt, and finally—to his shame—as chief of staff to the emperor Titus during the Roman seige of A.D. 70 that leveled Jerusalem, the sacred city his father had so lovingly adorned.

Uncle Philo, however, always a protector of his fellow Jews, journeyed in old age to Rome in the year 40ᶜ to beg the then-emperor not to outlaw the Jews of Alexandria, who found themselves unable to join in emperor-worship. The emperor in that year was the vindictive, delusional Caligula, who believed himself a god. Plucky Philo was lucky to escape the confrontation with his life. But Caligula seems to have (at least briefly) entertained Philo's argument—that the Jews of Alexandria were unswerving in loyalty to the emperor even if their religion forbade the worship of a, um, human being—because it was so deftly presented. In the end, however, the god-emperor could not accede to such a demotion of himself. And the pogrom, instigated against the Jews of Alexandria by Greeks who were jealous of the Jews' soaring financial successes, raged on till Caligula was assassinated the following year. His imperial successor, Claudius, decreed a halt to the violence and affirmed the rights of the Alexandrian Jews, though they would never again find themselves on an equal footing with citizens of Greek ancestry.

ℭ Henceforth, the text will designate B.C. dates as such; A.D. dates will be left undesignated.

In a world of competitive strivers, each of whom meant to excel all others, envy and *Schadenfreude* were the warp and woof of daily experience, and collective violence—one group determined to get rid of another—was a common occurrence in the life of Greco-Roman cities. The ancient Greek ideal of combative personal excellence, combined with more primeval urges to familial and tribal dominance, almost ensured the periodic eruption of urban riots and interethnic carnage—and this despite the fact that late classical philosophy stressed that the good life must be a life devoid of uncontrollable passion. *Apatheia* was the thing to strive for; and though the word turns into *apathy* in English, its original Greek meaning is "passionless balance, calm equipoise." But, hey, not everybody was a philosopher.

The Greeks had gone through several stages in their approach to human emotion. In the ancient lore, the passions that overcome us, especially anger and lust, are gods that possess us and that we must submit to. But at least from the sixth century B.C.—from the time of Plato's predecessor, Pythagoras—there was an alternative doctrine, taught by a minority of Greek sages who saw uncontrollable passion as an antisocial evil and insisted it was possible to overcome such passion by a strict regimen of life, which could be mastered by dedicated disciples. Such disciples gathered in communities under a revered teacher and practiced techniques of self-denial that enabled their will to control their emotions. To us, such quiet, introspective communities would have seemed rather like monasteries (and there is even some reason to think that the earliest of them, the Pythagorean conventicles of Sicily, may have been modeled on the practices of Indian religious movements, such as late Hinduism and early Buddhism, that invented the world's first monasteries).

There can be no doubt, however, that the vast majority of men and women have never been particularly attracted to monasticism in any form. Pythagorean and Platonic communities, as well as the Stoic communities that developed later—about the time Jewish scholars were gathering at Alexandria to translate their holy books into Greek—were the object at times of awe but often of hostility from ordinary people who found spiritual asceticism alien or even unattractive. Most people knew in their bones that *they,* at any rate, would never gain control over their emotions and could only respect or resent those who claimed to be able to do so. The tranquil apathics, for their part, could be chilly and contemptuous toward ordinary people and their flotsam-and-jetsam lives.

Though we may view the self-denying practices of this minority through the lens of later monasticism, picturing the apathics as pagan monks and nuns, there is no way to view the generality of Greco-Roman sexual attitudes through any lens in our modern repertoire. For one thing, Death was so present to the ancients that his name resounded through their streets with numbing frequency. The average life span was twenty-five years, and only four men in a hundred—and far fewer women—lived to celebrate their fiftieth birthday. Infants and children expired like fireflies in the night. This was a society, in the words of Peter Brown, "more helplessly exposed to death than is even the most afflicted underdeveloped country in the modern world." For the population to remain stable, let alone grow, each woman had to produce five children in the course of her short life; and since not all women would prove fertile or long-lived enough to do so, others had to make up the deficit in the death-defying task of population replacement.

Only when we take into account the constant presence of Death can we come to understand the uses of sex among the ancients. The Jewish obsession with generativity—God's primeval command to Adam and Eve to "be fruitful and multiply," God's promise to Abraham that his seed would be countless as the stars in the sky—finds many echoes in the classical world, where the principal role of an upstanding man was to engender children of his body and protect their lives insofar as he could, while the role of a woman was to bear those children and rear them to adulthood. But whereas the Jews developed a fairly straightforward morality of sex—men are obliged to marry and perpetuate the race, women to be obedient and faithful—the Greeks and Romans inhabited a society that came to permit somewhat more elastic options.

Ethnicity as such had none of the mystical meaning for Greeks and

Romans that it had for Jews, enjoined to raise up God-fearing children for Israel. Obligation for Greeks and Romans was not to the nation but to the city. The free adult male, if he meant to be of any consequence, was required to exhibit in his stately carriage and resonant voice the natural sense of command, the graced aura of unquestioned authority that triggered knee-jerk submission from all lesser beings, whether lower-class males, women, children, horses, hounds, or slaves. In an age free from all media magic—the tricked-up images of television and advertising, the spin doctors controlling the way we perceive our leaders—a man was more likely to be who he seemed to be, the ensouled body that presented itself to our senses. His physical presence either exuded authority or did not. It was harder to hide behind Wizard of Oz manipulations.

By means of genuine leaders, human magnets who actually drew others to themselves by the visual and aural magic of corporeal attraction, the *polis,* the city, the impressive civic entity that the Greco-Roman world saw as its greatest achievement, could be saved from sundering and chaos. The city was not unlike the human body, fragile, tempted to excess, vulnerable to disease. Its unpredictable swings and irrational tides needed to be kept in check by a spiritual principle, a Logos of its own— the controlling male intelligence.

The human body, an iffy thing, easily undone, was yet the acme of the beauty of the cosmos. No wonder that a male on the cusp of full manhood was the loveliest thing in the universe, repeatedly portrayed in statuary and fresco, "the beauty of the world, the paragon of animals," desirable by all, whether female or male (though completely possessable by none), whose hot blood beat against the walls of his body, seeking release, turning to white foam and spurting from his engorged penis—"a human Espresso machine," as Brown calls him. The first spurt of the adolescent male was celebrated by his family at the Roman Feast of the Liberalia on March 17. It was, of course, but the first of many, for the achieved male body was a furnace of fire that required repeated release from inner pressure.

The female body, on the other hand, was visibly deficient. In her mother's womb, the female had received insufficient heat, so she was softer, more liquid, underdone. Periodic menstruation proved that she was not fiery enough to burn up her excess liquids, which would nonetheless come in time to supply the nurturing wetland for the hot male seed that must be implanted within her. Were it not for this providential usefulness of her excess, we would have to conclude that she was simply a mutilated male, wrote Galen, the Greek physician of the second century whose pronouncements would exercise unparalleled influence over natural philosophy and medical practice well into modern times.

(Because the treatises of Galen and other Greek physicians would come at last into the hands of medieval healers like Hildegard of Bingen and Roger Bacon, Greek is still the technical language of Western medicine.)

Galen was full of convictions. He knew only too well the differences between men and women. Why, hadn't his own father been "the most just, the most devoted, and the kindest of men," the model Greco-Roman paterfamilias? "Mother, however, was so very prone to anger that sometimes she bit her handmaids!" That Father's gracious calm might have issued from his civic and domestic omnipotence, whereas Mother's irascible outbursts might be laid at the door of her total powerlessness, would never have occurred to Galen, who was convinced (as were most of his readers ever after) that he knew just about all there was to know about Nature, whether physical or psychological.

Physicians like Galen counseled their patients to moderation (one could spurt too often), even to periodic celibacy (in the case of athletes who needed to bank their fires for the contest ahead), but never to a life of complete sexual renunciation.[f] Before a male took up the

f   Nor were women encouraged to a life of virginity, the exception being priestesses at important shrines, who tended to "have menstrual difficulties and grow fat and ill-proportioned" (according to Soranus, a Greek gynecologist, contemporary with Galen and like him active at Rome). But consecrated virgins were often released from their vows at some point. Rome's Vestal Virgins, for instance, were allowed to marry after thirty years of duty, even if the record is blank as to how many of these lumbering lovelies attracted spouses. At any rate, though discovery of the loss of virginity in an on-duty Vestal was cause for her to be buried alive, none of these women had ever been consulted about whether she wished to be virginal. She was basically a kinder, gentler human sacrifice, her virginity an apotropaic relict of prehistoric propitiation of the gods.

duties of full citizenship, he was allowed to discharge his excessive heat as he wished, so long as he didn't, in Cicero's words, "undermine [another citizen's] household"—by adultery with the citizen's wife. Once he became paterfamilias in his own right, his sexual affairs—usually with house slaves of either sex, whose bodies he owned—needed to be carried on discreetly. Condemnation of those who were openly and carelessly self-indulgent was a matter not of morals but of breeding. For to spend too much time tending to the needs of one's body "in much exercise, in much eating, drinking, much evacuating the bowels, and much copulating" was, in the severe opinion of Epictetus the Stoic, who died a few years before Galen was born, "a mark of lack of refinement."

Ancient Greek science and Greco-Roman philosophy, though replete with insights and discoveries that have served mankind, were partly dependent on the biases of their practitioners, as no doubt are science and philosophy in any age of the world. Ancient medicine, in particular, depended on the observations of highly prejudiced, supremely privileged males, who alone were free to speak aloud and who wrote all the books—from high-minded marriage manuals (in which well-born wives were seen to be sufficiently educable by thoughtful husband-instructors as to be given eventual control over their households) to scurrilous pornography (in which low-born women were seen to be throwaway playthings). But the focus of attention was never a female of any sort but the urbane man of affairs, whose bounden duty was to orchestrate the pageant of his domestic life with such taut refinement and graceful superiority that he could be trusted to go on, according to Plutarch's stuffy *Maxims for Marriage,* to "harmonize state, forum, and friends."

Pleasure, seldom an articulated motive among ancient Jews, was of conscious importance to Greeks and Romans, for whom visual, gustatory, and tactile pleasures were both the lifetime work of many artisans—architects, artists, musicians, chefs, trainers, masseurs, and courtesans—and the subjects of extensive philosophical commentary. Hardly puritanical, Greco-Roman caution about sex concerned the possibly all-consuming tyranny of pleasure, not its extirpation. But when in the second century we reach the first Christian treatises on sex, we are shocked to hear a new tune altogether. Clement of Alexandria, urban gentleman, Christian convert, and Galen's contemporary, concedes that the best pagans have had admirable goals: "The human ideal of continence—as set forth by the Greek philosophers, that is—teaches one to resist passion, so as not to become its slave, and to train the instincts in the pursuit of rational goals." All well and good. But, adds Clement on behalf of his fellow Christians, "*our* ideal is not to feel desire at all."

By Zeus, how's that?

Like Philo, Clement is a religious apologist, setting forth arguments meant to convince readers of the superiority of his way over other courses of life. Just as Philo had borrowed concepts from pagan philosophy and interpretive techniques from pagan literary criticism, Clement borrows from pagan manuals of manners. Christians had been tarnished with every slander imaginable: they were cannibals (because of the Eucharist), practitioners of free love (because of their custom of embracing one another warmly), atheists (because of their refusal to sacrifice to the gods). Clement's task is to show that Christians are even more refined and high-minded than the most exquisite pagan.

The compleat Christian's manners are impeccable: he does not slobber over food nor "besmear [his] hands with the condiments," nor is he ever "amazed and stupefied at what is presented," however "vulgar" and extravagant the dishes may be, for he has already partaken of "the rich fare which is in the Word." You can always recognize the true Christian by his admirable comportment: he eats and drinks but little and "commits no indecorum in the act of swallowing"; his burps are inaudible, his farts undetectable; he wouldn't think of laughing—too coarse, altogether—but smiles his gentle smile. His chin is never greasy. If "attacked with sneezing" or with hiccups, the Christian does not "startle those near him with the explosion and so give proof of his bad breeding" but "quietly transmits" his sneeze or hiccup "with the expiration of the breath, the mouth being composed becomingly, and not gaping and yawning like the tragic masks." "Snorting" is unthinkable. The Christian woman is no "ape smeared with white paint," nor does she "season the flesh like a perni-

cious sauce" nor dye her hair yellow as if she were some Northern barbarian "nor stain her cheeks nor paint her eyes."

"In a word, the Christian is characterized by composure, tranquility,
calm, and peace," writes Clement. In a word, my religion is classier than
your religion—and the Christian alone fulfills the Greco-Roman ideal
of the balanced, always-in-control public man, steadily reigning above all
fitfulness. As a householder, he shrewdly oversees his extensive properties, knowing that Christ did not intend that he sell everything he has
and give it to the poor, even if that's what Jesus actually said in the
gospels. (He was being metaphorical, of course. He meant only that one
should not set one's heart on the things of this world.) Naturally, the
ideal Christian has done his duty by the city and engendered children of
his body, but in old age he devotes himself as a wise church elder to
higher things, having put away the passions—though he may be permitted just a cup or two more of wine in the evenings than would be appropriate for the hotblooded young.

Clement is easy to caricature and even to dislike—till we take notice
of what he was fighting against. For impassioned movements were
swirling around the Christian church that struck Clement as even more
barbaric than a Greek lady dyeing her hair yellow. The Encratites (or
Retaining Ones or Those Who Do Not Spill Over) had given up sex altogether, believing that only in this way could they bring the world to an
end and usher in the Second Coming of Christ. They were sweaty, ignorant, underbred, and intolerant and had brought their peculiar notions
with them from the hinterlands of (God help us) Syria. But as convinced
fundamentalists often do, they impressed simpleminded souls with their
simple rules: give up sex, go to Heaven. Their way, if taken up wholesale
by Christian communities, would, as Clement saw it, result only in
Christianity's extinction.

The Gnostics were at the other end of the spectrum, always whispering among themselves about secret knowledge available to the select few,
teachings Jesus had passed on only to his most intimate associates that
treated of the evil nature of creation and the evil hopelessness of the

ALUMNI OF ALEXANDRIA

POLITICIANS	DEATH
alexander the great, FOUNDER	323 B.C.
ptolemy soter, FIRST RULER, FOUNDER OF THE MOUSEION AND THE LIBRARY	283 B.C.
ptolemy philadelphus, SECOND RULER, COMMISSIONER OF THE SEPTUAGINT	246 B.C.
cleopatra VII, LAST RULER (TILL THE ROMAN CONQUEST)	30 B.C.

MATHEMATICIANS AND SCIENTISTS	DEATH
euclid, MATHEMATICIAN	early third century B.C.
erasistratus, PHYSICIAN	mid-third century B.C.
eratosthenes, ASTRONOMER, GEOGRAPHER	C. 194 B.C.
claudius ptolemy, ASTRONOMER, GEOGRAPHER, AUTHOR OF THE PTOLEMAIC MODEL OF THE UNIVERSE	C. 178 B.C.
galen, PHYSICIAN	A.D. 99

PHILOSOPHERS AND THEOLOGIANS	DEATH
philo, JEWISH SCRIPTURE SCHOLAR AND PHILOSOPHER	C. A.D. 45
clement, CHRISTIAN PHILOSOPHER	C. A.D. 213
origen, CHRISTIAN SCRIPTURE SCHOLAR AND THEOLOGIAN	A.D. 254
plotinus, PAGAN PHILOSOPHER	A.D. 270
arius, HERETICAL CHRISTIAN THEOLOGIAN	A.D. 336

CHURCHMEN	DEATH
athanasius, BISHOP, OPPONENT OF ARIUS	A.D. 373
cyril, BISHOP, INCITER OF MOB VIOLENCE	A.D. 444

human body. Why, did you know, Jesus hadn't even been human, just appeared to take on flesh, not unlike a Greek god? Christ the Logos, after all, could never have united himself to the, ugh, material world. The Gnostics, too, tended to favor total abstinence from sex, though rather less vociferously than the Encratites; at times it seemed as if they favored doing whatever you liked, so long as you didn't get caught. Whatever the case—and it was difficult to know exactly *what* the heads-in-the-clouds Gnostics were talking about—neither Gnostics nor Encratites were interested in the wonders of the world as it was: the sun-dappled familial peace and richly embroidered civic life that were the protected pride of Greco-Roman civilization. Both groups would gladly look upon the collapse of the world that Clement loved, and it was as much against them both as against the slandering pagans that he took up his quill.

9 Stoic philosophy was attractive to both Jews and Christians because it tended toward monotheism and opposed images of the divine. Furthermore, it emphasized classless human kinship, the divine element in each person, and the importance of ethical behavior and even (to some extent) social justice. The philosophy of the Epicureans, whom the Stoics saw as enemies, was deplored by Jews and Christians for its denial of divine providence and exaltation of pleasure as "the beginning and end of living happily." Though Epicureanism was subtler than its historical caricature, there's no getting around the fact that Epicureans would have been useless as martyrs.

In the eyes of Clement, who had been raised a Stoic and continued to teach characteristically stoical attitudes after his conversion, Christianity was available to save the best of Greco-Roman life and make it even better.[9] But his view was soon to become a minority one. His successor as head of Alexandria's famed Catechetical School was an earnest scholar in his early thirties, Origen, a contemporary of Plotinus who, like him, believed in the eternal preexistence of the human soul but who wrote with a clarity and precision Plotinus could not touch. Origen, a theological prodigy, wiped the floor with the airheaded Gnostics. But the tenderhearted young man also believed that at the end of time even the most evil of beings—the bloodiest tyrants, Satan himself—would be redeemed, a position unacceptable to orthodoxy. Origen was, for all his clarity, an emotional extremist: at

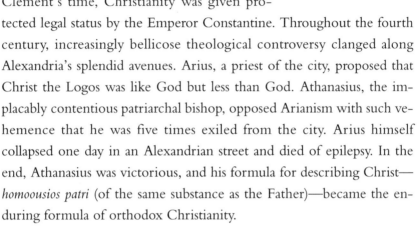

twenty, he had had himself surgically castrated, a fearful violence against the erotic self that could claim no place in Clement's poky philosophy. Worse was to come.

In the year 313, less than a century after Clement's time, Christianity was given protected legal status by the Emperor Constantine. Throughout the fourth century, increasingly bellicose theological controversy clanged along Alexandria's splendid avenues. Arius, a priest of the city, proposed that Christ the Logos was like God but less than God. Athanasius, the implacably contentious patriarchal bishop, opposed Arianism with such vehemence that he was five times exiled from the city. Arius himself collapsed one day in an Alexandrian street and died of epilepsy. In the end, Athanasius was victorious, and his formula for describing Christ— *homoousios patri* (of the same substance as the Father)—became the enduring formula of orthodox Christianity.

Before the fourth century was out, Christian vigilantes attacked the Temple of Serapis, center of the city's pagan cult, and in the process destroyed countless volumes of the great Library that were stored in the cloisters surrounding the buildings of the Temple. (Ah well, but the demonic Temple was destroyed, that was the main thing—and, anyway, most of the books weren't worth reading, don't you know.) In 415, a wild-eyed army of illiterate, black-cowled monks filled the streets of Alexandria like so many crazed bats, "human only in their faces." In a sense, they were the prototype for all the mobs of religious fanatics that sweep through history. One of their number had already stoned the imperial prefect and been canonized for his deed by Cyril, Athanasius's successor as holy patriarch.[b] Now they encountered Hypatia, a philosopher and mathematician, on her way home from lecturing at the Mouseion. She was a pagan teacher, an unescorted woman; she did

[b] Rigid, unrelenting, intolerant leaders of the Greek church like Athanasius and Cyril would one day serve as models for certain Muslim clerics, once Islam had ushered in the next wave of religion to the Greek East, known to us today as the Middle East.

not bow to their beliefs. She lured impressionable young Christians to her lectures; she consorted with Jews; she had dared to speak against the patriarch. She practiced who-knows-what obscenities. They dragged her from her carriage and into the cathedral, where they stripped her, gouged her eyes out, skinned her alive, and tore her to pieces with jagged tiles ripped from the mosaics.

By this time, the Gnostics had been read out of the churches, some of Origen's teachings had been condemned either as pagan philosophy or as Arian heresy, and the ancient ideal of the city as bastion of balanced reasonableness was long buried. But in the spectral, screeching monks, the Encratites had triumphed.

ROME, CROSSROADS OF THE WORLD

how the Romans became the Italians

Rome was not built in one day.
—TRADITIONAL SAYING

IKE PARIS FROM THE TIME OF Napoleon III to the eve of the Second World War, Alexandria was for many years the place to be, the "City of Light" in every sense. But as with all shining cultural capitals, it gave way at last to a new star. By the time of Clement, Alexandria had already lost much of its glow as men on the move, like Galen, abandoned the declining cities of the Greek East[a] and were drawn inexorably west to Rome, the immense upstart that had become the capital of the world.

[a] Alexander the Great had created what was called "the Greek East," comprising greater Greece (Greece as it is today with the additions of the southern Balkans and the European territory

now occupied by Turkey), Greek Asia (from the east coasts of the Adriatic and the Mediterranean to the Indus), and Greek Africa (Egypt and some noncontiguous territories that lay along Africa's Mediterranean coast west of Egypt but that did not include the lands of ancient Carthage, where Latin came to be spoken). What became "the Latin West" began as Latium (modern Lazio), the territory surrounding the city of Rome, and came to comprise most of the Italian peninsula, Istria (modern Italy's extreme east and most of Croatia), Illyria (the rest of the former Yugoslavia), Gaul (modern France), the Iberian Peninsula, north Africa, and eventually parts of Germany, Switzerland, the Low Countries, and southern Britain—that is, the Roman Empire at its farthest extent. By 1054, the year of the final division between Greeks (who were now Orthodox) and Latins (who were now Catholic), the Latin West had grown to include all of Europe except Greece and the Orthodox Slavic countries.

Rome began as the insignificant market town of a Latin-speaking tribe of sharp-eyed, closemouthed herdsmen and farmers who settled around a ford in the River Tiber, prospered in their cultivations, and flourished in their populations. The Latins overwhelmed another tribe, the Sabines, abducting their women, and were in turn overwhelmed by a more advanced people from the north, the innovating Etruscans, who gave their name to Tuscany and who, though they adopted the language of Rome's inhabitants, expanded the rustic town by means of Greek-inspired public works new to the older populations: the draining of marshes, extensive pavement, city walls, and large buildings of brick and stone. The tidy but impressive result was *Roma quadrata,* a square, walled city whose combined population found itself in a position to capture territory far beyond its borders, which made Rome in short order the force that controlled central Italy. Besides their territorial acquisitions, the Romans steadily increased their inventory of slaves, the sinewy, silent muscle of their economy.

The political structure of this new power was composed of Etruscan kingship, an advisory council of clan chieftains called *Senatus* (or Meeting of Elders), and a tribal assembly of citizens. This structure would come to be called *Res Publica* (Public Thing), later elided—by the general Latin tendency to soften sequences of consonants—into *Repubblica*. But this designation veiled the purpose of Rome's political machinery, which was operated on behalf of the leading families. In time, the role of the Senate would gain in prestige, the kingship would be replaced by an elected executive of two consuls, and the citizen assembly would wither, retaining in the end little more influence than a mob in the marketplace.

More important than the nature of the Roman political establishment, however, was the Roman temperament, an admirable stability born of relentless practicality and common sense, combined with an openness to innovation, provided the innovation was of obvious service to a practical goal. And there was but one goal, really: unspectacular but steady increase in the wealth of Rome's leading families (and, to a lesser extent, of all her citizens) by means of territorial expansion. Never in human history has real estate been more highly prized.

By gradual conquest, the city became master of the Italian peninsula; by the beginning of the second century B.C., she had added Spain, northwest Africa, southern Gaul, Sicily, Sardinia, and Corsica to her possessions. Naturally adept at military strategy and expert at administration and accounting, the Romans ruled their new possessions frugally and reasonably; and ever more wealth flowed to the mother city from taxes and trade. As coin poured in, so did exotic goods and people, as well as provincial families bent on keeping a house in town so that they too might sup on the excitement of urban life. The result was an enormously expanded Rome, always rebuilding her walls at further distances from the original settlement.

But in the shadow of Rome's explosive building program a new underclass was massing, clueless, all but homeless, far more dispossessed than any slave, and easy prey to demagogues. This new proletariat included gamblers who had lost their togas in the acquisition game, fools who had spent their modest estates on evanescent luxuries, and the perennial urban poor, adept at pickpocketing, stings, and rackets but otherwise unemployable, demanding public welfare. Though the old aristocracy continued to recite its devotion to the ancient Roman virtues of order and thrift, this new class possessed but one virtue, its votes, which it sold happily enough to public figures, contentiously cutthroat in the great race for riches. Class warfare ensued, as representatives of the

Populares and the Optimates—I could almost write Democrats and Republicans—struggled over the direction of the Roman Republic, each politician pretending to represent what was best for Rome, all the while grabbing whatever additional wealth he could lay his hands on. As stoical Cicero moaned over each new scandal, *"O tempora! O mores!"* (What times these are! What morals!)

The upshot was a civil war, then another, then a third, all fought within the first century B.C. In the end, the Republic was "saved" through its elimination and replacement by a new political order in which all power was vested in one man, Caesar Imperator (Commander-in-Chief, thence Emperor), whose empire would soon stretch from the border of present-day Iran in the east to Scotland in the west, from the entirety of north Africa in the south to the River Rhine in the north. The first emperor, Augustus, [b] ruled for more than forty years, setting the style for his many successors. He built the marmoreal Rome that lives in memory (and in not a few still-standing shrines and monuments, public spaces and private palaces); he accepted the honors of a god and was received as such throughout the imitation-Romes of his far-flung empire, where the most impressive buildings were often temples dedicated to Divine Caesar. ("Great is Caesar: God must be with him!") Not for a moment was he distracted from his main purposes: the efficient administration of his vast bureaucracy, carrying the emperor's awesome presence to every corner of his territories, and the collection of his taxes.

Augustus died in the second decade of the first century, when Jesus of Nazareth was still an unknown teenager in a dark corner of the empire. By the second century—the time of Clement and Galen—Rome had reached its zenith. Too large and diverse to be as perfect as Alexandria, it was the New York of the ancient world. Because it attracted would-be winners from everywhere, there was no food or face, no

b Caesar Augustus, originally named Octavian, was adopted as son by his uncle Julius Caesar prior to the older man's assassination. Rome's first dictator-for-life, Julius Caesar was well on his way to becoming emperor but was never in fact awarded the title. Octavian upon his adoption assumed his uncle's name, Caesar. The Senate, in awarding this second Caesar the new (and supposedly temporary) title *imperator*, also bestowed on him the honorific *augustus*.

costume or custom you could not find here. If it existed somewhere in the known world, there was an example of it in the streets of this city, crossroads of the world, teeming with a population of more than a million souls, four times that of any other ancient metropolis. If you could make it there, you could make it anywhere. And if your luck ran out, you could molder in obscurity in one of the crammed and crumbling tenements that teetered noisily over narrow alleys far from the august monuments of the city's imperial center.

Lunching one day at a favorite trattoria and watching a variety of convivial Roman families enjoy their afternoon meal and their companions at table, I wondered how the ancient Romans had ever turned into the modern Italians. Unlike many other ancient stocks, the Romans are more or less the same people they were in the time of the Caesars. Whereas the once dark-haired Irish are today much mixed with Viking genes (as the red–gold hair of many testifies), the British with Celtic, Italian, and especially German genes, and the Greeks with the genes of the Turks and the South Slavs, the Italians of today are the direct descendants of those who inhabited the Italian peninsula in the centuries before Christ, in the centuries of the Caesars, in the days of Dante, of Michelangelo, of Garibaldi, of Fiat, Loren, and Armani. More southerners (with their undoubted African, Greek, Arabian, and Norman genes) have moved north; and the gene pool of the Lombards and other Germanic tribes shows itself in the honey-colored hair, pale skin, and towering height of a few northerners, but the faces of the vast majority of Italians are the same faces that peer at us from ancient portraits in marble, metal, mosaic, wax, fresco, and coral. As an observant American friend resident in Rome remarked recently, "Only this morning I saw Julius Caesar strolling across the piazza."

But if the Italians still look like their ancient counterparts—with their small feet and expressive hands, their well-knit bodies, their healthy skin, their shining black hair, their large noses and knowing faces, their profoundly brown eyes, their sense of personal presentation—their souls have changed considerably. These, after all, were the military geniuses who conquered the world and crucified without remorse any troublemaker who dared get in their way, who enjoyed nothing so much as an afternoon watching slaves slaughter one another in the arena or an outdoor evening frolic lit by human torches. Those soulful brown eyes were once as glazed with vindictive cruelty as human eyes have ever been.

And yet today flags of peace fly everywhere—rainbow flags petitioning for *PACE* against a skyblue field. To protest George W. Bush's imperial adventure in Iraq, Italians organized the largest antiwar demonstration in world history, as many as three million protesters (by some estimates) crowding into the streets of Rome (whose normal population totals somewhat less than three million), stopping all traffic while trying to reach the event's announced center, the enormous piazza in front of Rome's cathedral of San Giovanni in Laterano. Most had to abandon their goal and so stood singing, dancing, and waving their flags wherever they found themselves throughout the labyrinthine streets and sunlit squares of Rome. It was a day on which one could believe in human solidarity.

Italy was one of only three nations—the others being Bulgaria and Denmark—whose country-wide program to hide Jews from the Nazis still provokes admiration. Alone among the nations, the Italians had no prominent political or religious figure to lead them toward these brave acts of salvation. In Denmark, the king did his best to protect Jewish citizens; in Bulgaria, the Orthodox patriarch collaborated with leading politicians to save the entire Jewish population of the country. The wily Italians, who were led by a fascist dictator and a silent pope, nonetheless saved eighty percent of their Jews by using every underhanded stratagem they could think of. Their effective goodness, it must be admitted, is compounded as much of an ancient cynical realism—what Carlo Levi called the "ironic pride" of the Romans—as it is of an acquired love of God and man.

As the historical record shows, it was the Italian state of Tuscany that first conceived of banning all judicial executions (as well as torture!)—on November 30, 1786, two centuries before elimination of the death penalty became an item on international agendas. Today, Italy leads the world in opposition to that cruel form of retribution; and state-sponsored executions, scarcely reported elsewhere, are front-page news. Whenever another country signs the international moratorium on the death penalty, the Colosseum, universal Roman symbol of man's inhumanity to man, is lit in the night by redeeming spotlights, as are famous civic monuments throughout Italy and, with Italian encouragement, monuments from Brussels to Buenos Aires. Members of the Italian Community of Sant'Egidio have repeatedly befriended death row inmates throughout the world, many of whom have sealed those friendships by requesting that after their executions their ashes be interred in Italy.[c] Throughout the Italian peninsula, Sister Helen Prejean, the American death row nun who wrote *Dead Man Walking,* is a media figure, attracting rock-star-size crowds of young people.

The dark side of Italy—from the Mafia to Mussolini—is so well-known that it needn't be advertised here. All countries have their darkness and their light. Less well-known to outsiders, however, is the tender sympathy that blows through Italy like a gentle breeze and that still fights elsewhere for breath and life.

How did the Romans become the Italians? I hope this book as a whole will answer the question and demonstrate as well how an Italian *vita nuova* coursed beyond the borders of Italy and lifted other nations. But the overture to an answer—a kind of melodic sketch of the grand opera to come—lies in the obscure centuries that

[c] I have more personal experience of this request than I would wish. A dear friend, Dominique Jerome Green, was executed by the state of Texas on October 26, 2004. By the time of his death, after years of solitary confinement in a tiny cubicle on death row, Dominique was probably as much a saint as a human being can hope to be, a man of deep humanity and expansive forgiveness. It is unlikely that he was guilty of the crime he was convicted of, murder in the course of an armed robbery with three other (then) teenagers. He was surely guilty, however, of being poor and black. The one white participant in the robbery was never charged with any crime; and as we all know, there are no millionaires on death row, nor will there ever be. In death Dominique has been awarded the dignity he was denied in life: at his request, his mortal remains have been interred not in Huntsville's brutal burial ground but in the shadow of the beautiful basilica of Santa Maria in Trastevere, the very spot where Christianity first took root in the imperial city of Rome.

stretch from the initial Christianization of the pagan Romans through the dankness of the Dark Ages to the sprouting of a fresh and vibrant sensibility in the early twelfth century, which marks the beginning of the high Middle Ages. For the remainder of this Introduction, permit me to identify just a few of the buds that open tentatively between the fourth century and the twelfth, presaging the amazing rebirth of the twelfth, thirteenth, and early fourteenth centuries that will be the subject of the rest of the book.

In the early fourth century a new emperor, Constantine the Great, secured his position against all rivals and made himself into the first Christian to occupy the imperial throne. How Christian Constantine was is a matter of conjecture: he seems to have continued to pay homage to his father's patronal god, the Unconquered Sun, and was not baptized till he lay on his deathbed in 337. But his Edict of Milan, issued in 313, established religious freedom throughout the empire and ended the persecution of Christians, which till that time had broken out occasionally like a recurring contagion, claiming lives and creating martyrs. Constantine, whatever his beliefs, was a practical military man who wished to eliminate unnecessary conflict of every kind and to rule as unified a populace as possible. In deference to Christian feeling, he proscribed the shameful ordeal of public crucifixion, which was known to have been inflicted on the Christian God-Man four centuries earlier and had remained till Constantine's day a favorite Roman method of enforcing popular quiescence. He even made the detested cross his royal symbol—as unusual a thing to do as would be, say, a governor of Texas electing to wear a tiny electric chair or a poison-filled hypodermic needle on a chain around his neck.

While Constantine was hardly a squeamish fellow, his dramatic contribution to the easing of punishment and the relaxation of retribution within the Roman state could only have far-reaching consequences. Throughout the empire, Christian bishops, politically suspect figures in the pre-Constantinian centuries, were now invited into partnership with state officials for the great Roman enterprise of maintaining law and order. They lost no time in pressing for further gains: the outlawing of the bloody games and murderous gladiatorial displays that the Romans counted as their chief entertainments. Soon enough the bishops would be petitioning for an end to all manifestations of pagan sensibility— public prayers and processions, nude athletic contests, the casual mixing of naked men and women in the baths, even philosophical dialogues between pupils and pedagogues (who were often pedophiles)—that had long provided Greeks and Romans with public spectacle and private diversion.

The office of bishop (*episkopos,* Greek for "superintendent"), though an invention of the Christian church in the late first century, was modeled on the traditions of Roman government, heavily dependent on alpha males to apply the laws and keep the peace. Each bishop ruled over a "diocese"—originally a secular Greco-Roman term for a provincial administrative district. As time went on and Roman administration collapsed in Western Europe under the increasing pressures of incursions by Germanic barbarians, the bishop would often be the only Roman official left in a given locality capable of implementing a body of law and custom that could reestablish social peace and guide the new barbarian ruler (and the mixed population of Romans and barbarians that he now ruled) toward a rational political settlement.

In the time of Constantine, however, the barbarian threat still sounded like faraway thunder. In addition to his lightly worn Christianity, Constantine would be remembered chiefly for his dramatic change of imperial residence. He didn't care much for Rome, too huddled and pluriform for his tastes, so he established a New Rome in the small Greek city of Byzantium on the southwestern shore of the Bosphorus. It was an excellent choice, for the site commanded Europe and Asia on opposite shores, was virtually impregnable, yet stood wide open to trade. Though Western Europe began to fracture into a puzzle of barbarian kingdoms little more than a century after Constantine's death, the Byzantine Empire would remain in the hands of Constantine's successors for ten centuries more—till in 1453 Byzantium, now a golden

N.
NORTH SEA
NORSE
Swedes
Lapps
Getes
Balts
Picts
Irish
Jutes
Angles
Danes
Frisians
Saxons
Lombards
Siling Vandals
Franks
Thuringians
Burgundians
Rugians
Alemanni
Marcomanni
Quadi
Asding Vandals
Gepids
Atlantic Ocean
Roman
Rome
Mediterranean Sea
Latin-speaking
Greek-speaking
Berbers
Roman Empire

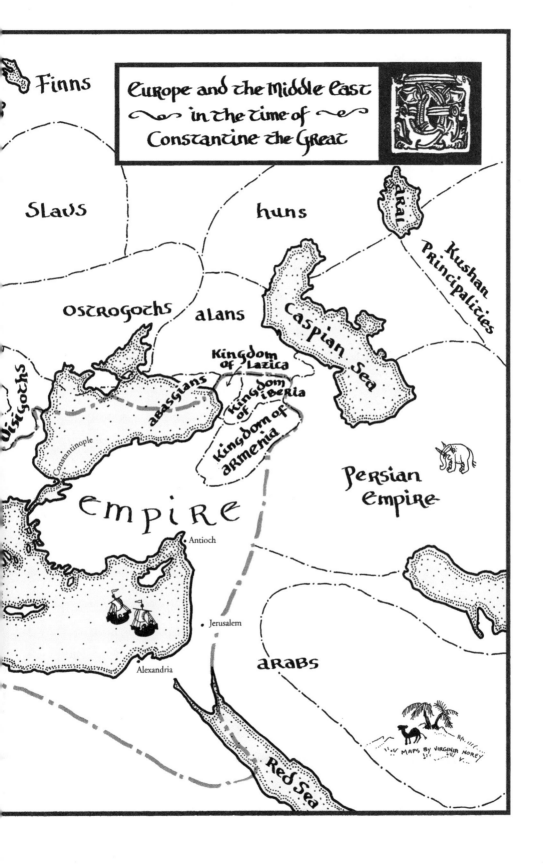

Finns

Europe and the Middle East
~ in the time of ~
Constantine the Great

Slavs

Huns

ARAL

Kushan
Principalities

Ostrogoths

Alans

Caspian Sea

Kingdom
of Lazica

Visigoths

Abasgians

Kingdom
of
Iberia

Kingdom of
Armenia

Persian
Empire

Constantinople

Empire

• Antioch

Jerusalem •

Arabs

Alexandria

MAPS BY VIRGINIA NOREY

Red Sea

ↄ The pope, to begin with, was not in any sense head of the church. He was just bishop of Rome, one of several dioceses thought to have been founded by apostles and therefore especially ancient and venerable. The head of the church was Christ, as the New Testament pellucidly states. If the church could be said to have an earthly head, it was Constantine, who styled himself "the Thirteenth Apostle" and whose express confirmation the popes needed for their elections to be considered valid. The popes addressed the emperor with the same obsequious formality as everyone else; and the very appellation "pope" (or "*papa*") was not reserved to them but was used widely in addressing bishops and even priests. Though this account—for simplicity's sake—employs the word *pope* only for the bishop of Rome, the reader should bear in mind that such exclusive usage is anachronistic.

capital called Constantinople, fell to the Turks, who called it Istanbul.

When Constantine left Old Rome, he left the old capital to the pope, who quickly took on imperial perquisites and donned imperial panache. The pope and his brother bishops,ↄ however, would soon need whatever smoke and mirrors they could command to dazzle the barbarians in what was to become a centuries-long struggle. The withdrawal of the emperor, and with him a significant portion of his armed forces, from Western Europe meant that Italy and the other western provinces were far more exposed to barbarian assault than they had ever been before. At the same time, the barbarians just beyond the border of the empire were experiencing an exploding population and the ensuing famine conditions that would make their overflow into Roman territory inevitable. To some extent, the popes—the good ones, at least—would have no choice but to take on the role of emperor, certainly insofar as the protection of Italy was concerned.

During the fourth century, however, the rumble of barbarian thunder could be ignored while Rome, gifted with lavish donations from the now-distant emperor, rebuilt itself into a Christian shrine, no longer possessing the living presence of the emperor but rather the saving relics of dead apostles and martyrs. Rome had long been deemed *civitas aeterna,* meaning that this marble-fronted colossus, its roots sunk in myth and legend, could never fail to rule the world. Now, under an elaborate program of church construction—to consecrate the bones of such slaughtered apostles as the New Testament figures Peter, Paul, and

Priscilla and the grisly martyrdoms of such unyielding aristocratic ladies as Cecilia, Sabina, and Domitilla—the city was transformed into an earthly gateway to everlasting life, the Eternal City that it still is, focus for worldwide Christendom, font of ambiguous religious authority, and irresistible magnet for pious, free-spending pilgrims as well as for awed, if secular, tourists. From a Roman cleric's point of view, worldly failure had been transmogrified into heavenly success; from a municipal accountant's point of view, it was a very smart move.

The atmosphere of ancient political power now combined with the spectacle of continuing religious authority; and it would prove an impressively durable, not to say fertile, combination. "Most great cities," writes the Princeton historian Theodore K. Rabb, "get only one shot at a golden age. Rome is the chief exception, an Eternal City not least for having hosted repeated outbursts of remarkable creativity." From Virgil to Cavallini, from Fra Angelico to Michelangelo, from Bernini to Fellini, outsized creative geniuses have flourished along the banks of the stinking Tiber, always managing to serve up from Rome's cultural depths surprising delights to a bedazzled world.

For centuries to come, the Italian church and the Byzantine emperor would continue to influence each other, even if at each interaction the distance between them seemed to lengthen and the wall separating the Latin West from the Greek East grew ever thicker and more impassable. But besides this gradual estrangement (with its lasting historical consequences),℮ there looms the more profound question of why the ancient Ecumene, East and West, turned Christian in the first place. Why did the classical Greeks and Romans abandon their ancestral altars, bury forever their old gods—mighty Zeus-Jupiter, shining Apollo, lust-inducing Aphrodite-Venus, bountiful Demeter-Ceres, darkly provocative Dionysos-Bacchus, and all those other age-old, larger-than-life presences—and turn in prayer to a bloody worm of a man nailed to a cross?

Conventional analysis customarily points to

℮ For more on the gradual schism that divided East from West and for the role of the papacy in that process, see my *Pope John XXIII,* which contains a useful overview of papal history that cannot be repeated here.

Constantine as the catalyst for this remarkable conversion. Everyone, after all, knew that Christians were in the emperor's good graces and that upward social mobility might now depend on being part of the Christian club. Well, yes, that's a fair enough description of what happened in the fourth century; but it hardly explains the position the church had already achieved by the time of Constantine's accession. Over the course of three centuries Christianity had gone from being a minuscule sect of Judaism—itself a decidedly minor religion—to serving as the favorite whipping boy of psychopaths like the emperor Nero, to acting as a refuge for more and more disaffected Greco-Romans, whether runaway slaves, working-class artisans, housewives, or (at last) well-connected aristocrats.

Christianity's claim that all were equal before God and all equally precious to him ran through class-conscious, minority-despising, weakness-ridiculing Greco-Roman society like a charged current. It is no wonder, really, that the primitive church seemed an almost fairyland harbor to women, who had always been kept in the shadows, and to slaves, who had never before been awarded a soupçon of social dignity or political importance. What is truly remarkable is how many aristocrats joined the still-illegal Jesus Movement in the course of the second and third centuries. Unlike the well-born opportunists of the fourth century who joined in the train of Constantine and his family, the Christians of earlier centuries were, by and large, distinguished by their sincerity and courage. They were seekers after truth who had gone quite out of their way to find it and then held to it despite the many inconveniences and even dangers that membership afforded.

There were no social scientists to count heads and take polls in the time of Constantine, but it seems obvious that such a down-to-earth fellow, such a realistic politician, would never have been tempted to join the ranks of a marginal sect or even a larger movement that was too obviously not of this world. If from a philosophical viewpoint Christianity offered Constantine internal consistency, it also offered him a practical vehicle for uniting the empire in common cause. The old gods, at war with one another, had already proven themselves unbelievable to the intelligentsia, and even for many simple souls pagan worship had devolved to little more than empty rote. Christianity was a religion that could outlast its adversaries—and that already boasted among its members many of the most reliable and upstanding people in the empire. If it did not claim a majority, it was inching ever closer to that goal. To Constantine it was obvious: Christianity was his ready-made instrument, the medium for revivifying the flagging spirits of an increasingly cynical populace and the bullhorn through which the imperial Thirteenth Apostle could speak to his subjects on God's behalf.[f]

But what was the internal consistency that had drawn so many devotees? Was it only the—admittedly extraordinary—lure of spiritual equality? Was it that Jewish monotheism, now repackaged in its open-door Christian format, answered the previously unanswerable challenges to polytheism that had been posed by Greek philosophy? It was these things, for sure, and no doubt many others as well. But, above all, what gave Christianity its remarkable inner cohesion was the figure of Jesus Christ himself. Nor is it necessary to be a believing Christian to appreciate the immense strength that this stupendous character lent to the new religion.

[f] Constantine's intervention in church affairs was hardly an unalloyed good. But I find myself at odds with purists who regularly insist that he ruined Christianity by making it part of the power structure. There was no way that this increasingly powerful movement could have remained on the cultural sidelines. But following imperial approval, Christianity's besetting temptation, to which it has repeatedly succumbed, has been to use its political power for evil ends, even as it has justified its actions by the need to protect the church as an institution. We should not for this reason wish to deprive Christianity of its power as (at times) a uniquely positive social force, which has been employed to lasting effect at significant historical moments—as in our time, for instance, by such "establishment" Christian figures as Dr. Martin Luther King Jr., Archbishop Oscar Romero, Dom Helder Camera, Mother Teresa, and Archbishop Desmond Tutu—in behalf of the powerless on four different continents.

The depiction of Christianity in the popular thriller *The Da Vinci Code* as a fraud perpetrated by Constantine not only is preposterous to any reader with a modicum of

historical knowledge but rests on melodramatically anti-Christian assumptions. The book's further premise that the Catholic Church sends out Opus Dei hit men to murder anyone who has stumbled on the truth is a straight-forward anti-Catholic libel. And its notion that Jesus fathered progeny by Mary Magdalene is a fantasy lacking the least historical support.

Anything new must be received into the old. Buddhism, for instance, was received into an ancient Indian religious context, so much so that, in its vocabulary and outlook, it came to be understood as a kind of Reformed Hinduism. Similarly, the early attempts by Christian intellectuals to come to grips with the new revelation were largely limited by the mind-set of Greek philosophy. To one looking backwards from the twenty-first century, Clement of Alexandria seems as much a Greek philosopher (of negligible importance) as he does a Christian. His outlook might be more easily adopted by a Stoic of his own day than by a Christian of ours; and while only a few Christian leaders of our day would be able to muster much sympathy for the repressive, howling monks who murdered Hypatia, the sixth-century patriarch of Alexandria was comfortably at home among their fanatical obsessions, which amounted to a sort of dumbed-down, if baptized, version of Plotinus's anti-carnal philosophy.

For all that, the Christians of late antiquity understood that they were holding something new by the tail: they may not have been able to make out the full contours of the fabulous beast, but they had no doubt that it was alive and scarily larger than themselves. Almost from the moment the persecutions were past, Christians began to argue heatedly about Christ: who exactly was he? and how do we explain his role in the great scheme of things? Their undying disagreements over the nature and function of this figure were so fierce and unyielding that for us—at so great a distance from their concerns—they illuminate little about Jesus as we might come to understand him today, but they do serve to underscore the obvious fact that he was utterly central to ancient Christianity.

The proposed solution to the quarrels, hammered out by bishops meeting in a series of councils (called "ecumenical" because they were thought to represent the whole Christian world), was that Jesus, though human—having "taken flesh" in the womb of his mother, Mary—was God's Word *incarnate*. This Word of God had always existed, for he was the Second Person of the divine Trinity. The First was God the Father, and in this guise God had spoken to the prophets of Israel. The Second was God the Son, God's own Word by the utterance of which he had brought the universe into being, as related in the Book of Genesis. The Third was God the Holy Spirit, who acted in time—who, for instance, had brought about the miraculous conception of Jesus and who animated the church, the Assembly of Christians, in its pilgrimage through history.

The consequences of such rarefied, Greek-inspired thinking would shape the subsequent history of Christianity—and, therefore, of the Western world—like no other theological statements ever made. It is not surprising that Greek Christians, enamored of subtlety, would continue to gaze upon this construct and fashion it into the focus for all their theology and prayer. If Christ was both God and man, did he have two natures with two separate intellects and wills? If so, how did these natures communicate with each other? As God, he knew all things; as man, his knowledge was necessarily limited. In the gospels, Jesus does not seem always to know what will happen next, so did God keep things from himself? As man, Jesus was capable of committing sin. Since all human beings commit sins, what, if anything, stopped Jesus from becoming a sinner?

Such speculations ensured unending controversies and ever-multiplying theological-political factions throughout the Greek world. Often enough, the controversies were so strident that considerable blood would be shed, sometimes spilled by slogan-reciting mobs of simple-minded monks. But in their secluded monasteries and chapels, monks and other clerics turned the esoteric into the palpable: the still point of Christian contemplation became the unapproachable Trinity, and invocations of the Trinity became essential to liturgical prayer. "Holy God,

Holy Mighty, Holy Deathless," sang the chanters in their tripartite prayer as clouds of spiced incense billowed heavenward. "Let all mortal flesh keep silence / And with fear and trembling stand / Ponder nothing earthly minded." Ponder the ineffable and bow before the mystery.

For practical, can-do Romans, this was a bit much. Roman Christians found Greek distinctions tiresome, and the endless theological disputes occasioned by those distinctions made them cross-eyed with weariness. Yes, yes, Jesus is both God and man; now let's move on. And the liturgies of the East, in their attempts to evoke the ineffable, certainly put one in mind of eternity, for they seemed just about endless. How many *Kyrie eleisons* is that damned deacon going to make us warble before he brings this litany to a conclusion?

For Romans, liturgy was not a mystical end in itself. What the Greeks called the Sacred Liturgy, the Romans called *missa* (or mass) after the deacon's last words, "*Ite, missa est*" (Go, you are dismissed). If that sounds to you as if their main interest was in getting out of church as soon as decently possible, you wouldn't be so very far from the truth. Public prayer is not an end in itself, only part of a Christian life, a caesura of recollection; fortunately, it comes to an end and we are sent back to our lives. In fact, we come to this prayer not for some unspeakable spiritual high but to renew ourselves for further work in the world. We don't even need always to chant the Eucharistic celebration or bother ourselves with arranging elaborate processions of vested acolytes or choke the air with incense. Sometimes, we can even celebrate a short, stationary, said mass, a *low* mass, with just one officiant and a handful of worshipers—which pared-back arrangement the Greeks thought an abomination. Such stylistic differences between East and West implied significant differences in theological perspective.

Instead of getting off on the unutterable Trinity, Roman Christians found their attention drawn to the most down-to-earth aspect of Trinitarian doctrine: the Infleshing, the Incarnation, the Making of the God-Man. What, they asked themselves, are the practical consequences—to human beings—of the Word becoming flesh? From this question will flow, with some notable divagations, the main course of what was to become Western Christianity.

Despite the aspirations of so many mystical Greeks, human beings are not disembodied spirits. What should matter to us is not so much the inner life of God—and whatever *that* may be, the truth is that not one of us knows squat about it—as the impact of divine revelation on our own lives. The only point at which we can sensibly connect with the Trinity is the point at which, as John's Gospel puts it, "the Word became flesh and pitched his tent among us." If God became man and took on our weakness, our pain, even our death, these things can no longer be the woeful embarrassments we have always conceived them to be, for they are now shot through with his grace and elevated by his willing participation in them. If God became man, lived an earthly life as all of us do—suckled, sweat, shat, wept, slept, loved, feared, bled, died—but also rose and returned to Heaven, the same route has been opened to all of us, to all "mortal flesh," now impregnated with divinity. Our despised humanity entitles us, for it is now the humanity of God.

How are we to follow such a path? The four gospels of the New Testament tell us how, for each recounts the story of Jesus's earthly pilgrimage from a somewhat different personal angle—the angle of each writer—and in this story Jesus shows us the Way, the way to live our lives so that we may reach the same conclusion his life reached, eternal union with God. "No one has ever seen God," states John's Gospel, for, like Plotinus's One, he-she-it is in himself-herself-itself unknowable. There is nothing you can assert positively about God (including gender) that is secure from falsehood. But, says Jesus conclusively in the same gospel, "If you know me, you will also come to know my Father. Henceforth you do know him—for you have seen him." The face of the Father-God that we have seen is his *ikon,* his veritable image in flesh, Jesus.

And what shall we say of this face of God turned toward us? Only that it is compassionate beyond all imagining, willing to live, suffer, and die for each of us, so compassionate that it excludes no one, not even the most stupid, the most craven, the most outrageous, the most corrupt.

9 For a far more complete treatment of the impact of Jesus on Western civilization, see the third volume in this series, *Desire of the Everlasting Hills: The World Before and After Jesus.* Readers of the series will note how much the original identity of Jesus as the Christ (or Messiah)— an identity proclaimed by the first Christians and necessitated by a Jewish conceptual framework— has given way to the identification of Jesus as Word/Son of God—an identification necessitated by a Greco-Roman conceptual framework. By the time of Constantine, Jesus was already shedding his Jewishness; and the Greek word *Christos* (Christ), meaning "Anointed One," a translation of the Hebrew *mashiach* (messiah), had become in effect Jesus's surname. It is unlikely that many Christians gave much thought to the meaning of this title or to the origin of Christianity as a form of Judaism.

What must we do to follow the face of God? Jesus tells us in Matthew's Gospel: "You must . . . include everyone, just as your heavenly Father includes everyone." No one is negligible.[9]

It would be arrogant to claim that Roman Christians understood this business better than Greek Christians. Both were working from the same gospels and the same basic creed. It is a question not of evangelical understanding or credal positions but of cultural emphasis, of almost gustatory preference. If Greeks preferred to contemplate the Trinity, Romans preferred to celebrate the Incarnation. If Greeks, more theologically precise, understood the *Anastasis,* the Day of Resurrection, to be the supreme Christian feast, Romans agreed in principle— but in practice they came to prefer Christmas, the feast of Christ's birth, the supreme celebration of his humanity. In fact, the Romans invented Christmas. For the Greeks, the first celebration of Christ's infancy was not Christmas Day but January 6, the *Epiphania,* or Showing Forth, the feast of the infant Jesus's recognition by the Persian magi who seek him out in Matthew's Gospel.

There is a telling passage in the Roman Martyrology, the record kept by the Roman church to commemorate the acts of Christian martyrs (and, eventually, of other saints) and to ensure that their valorous deeds would never be forgotten. It is a curious, ramshackle collection, full of information and misinformation, fact, legend, and supposition, the work of many anonymous hands over many centuries, some contributors more scrupulous than others. It grew over time to voluminous proportions, and its thumbnail *vitae sanctorum,* its daily entries on the saints to be commemorated at mass the following day, were read aloud in monastic refectories during the evening meal.

The most eloquent entry in the whole unwieldy collection is for the birth of Jesus, a summation of salvation history that presages the colorful tableaux of seminal scriptural moments that would one day shine from the many-paneled windows of stained glass in the great cathedrals of the high Middle Ages. Though some of the dating in the entry appears fanciful to us, it was based on the best calendrical calculations of late antiquity, both Hellenic and Hebraic. In his rolling cadences, the writer means to summon all the dignity of his pagan Latin inheritance; in his simplicity, he foreshadows the mystery plays, those tinseled, tumbledown scriptural pageants that guilds of workmen would one day perform in every town square; in his extravagant use of capital letters, he is already entering into the playful, childlike spirit of illuminated manuscripts. The entire entry consists of a single periodic sentence. As in all such sentences that have come down to us from classical antiquity, this one builds in a triumphant crescendo, like a chorus by Handel. Its most significant words are those that end its final three phrases:

THE TWENTY-FIFTH DAY OF DECEMBER

In the 5199th year since the creation of the world,
when in the beginning God made heaven and earth;
the 2957th year since the Flood;
the 2015th year since the birth of Abraham;
the 1510th year since Moses
and the going forth of the People of Israel from Egypt;
the 1032nd year since David's royal anointing;
in the 65th week, according to the Prophecy of Daniel;
in the 194th Olympiad;

the 752nd year from the Foundation of the City of Rome;

the 42nd year of the Rule of Octavian Augustus, all the world
    being at peace,

in the sixth age of the world,

JESUS CHRIST,

eternal God and Son of the eternal Father,

desiring to sanctify the world by his most merciful coming,

being conceived by the Holy Spirit,

and nine months having passed since his conception,

IN BETHLEHEM OF JUDA WAS BORN,

OF THE VIRGIN MARY MADE MAN—

the Birthday of our Lord Jesus Christ according to the flesh.

He is born! He is human![b] He is made of flesh and blood! Such concrete, happy, almost merry statements were to have more impact on the shaping of Western Christendom than all the airy musings of the Greeks. As the Eucharistic prayer of the Roman rite proclaims, this Jesus is "like us in all things," adding only the necessary qualifier "but sin." He is Emmanuel, God-with-us, God-for-us, God never distant, God on the side of humanity.

To say these things with the sheer élan they inspired in Christians of the dawning Middle Ages is to find oneself very nearly singing a Christmas carol. "Tomorrow shall be my dancing day," sings the Second Person of the Most Exalted Trinity in an English carol in which he contemplates his coming Incarnation, his "dancing day." It is a song to be sung on Christmas Eve:

[b]   In the original Latin, the phrase I have translated "made man" is *factus homo,* which bears no hint of sexism, since Latin has a separate word for "man" in the sense of "male," *vir. Homo* designates a human being.

Tomorrow shall be my dancing day:
I would my true love did so chance
To see the legend of my play,
To call my true love to my dance:
Sing O my love, O my love, my love, my love;
This have I done for my true love.

In a manger laid and wrapped I was,
So very poor, this was my chance,
Betwixt an ox and a silly poor ass,
To call my true love to my dance.
Sing O my love, O my love, my love, my love;
This have I done for my true love.

This text, in which the Dancer goes on to point to the major events of his life, death, and resurrection, is one in feeling with the Christmas Martyrology, the illuminated manuscripts, the stained glass, and the mystery plays. In such boldly unsubtle celebrations, one is seldom stumped by precious ambiguities or disoriented by educated profundities beyond the grasp of an illiterate commoner. The angels are always known by their wings, the saints by their halos. Christ always wears his bloodred robe; Mary is always cloaked in bright blue.[i] The God-Man finds his home on earth among the poor, the outcast, the forgotten—whether shepherds, prostitutes, or "an ox and a silly poor ass." He and his parents are just a mite uncomfortable when three exotic kings arrive to pay homage. There is no shallow cleverness; what profundity there is rests only in the depths of humane meaning that the images can conjure up.

In the last verse of "My Dancing Day," the Dancer takes his largest leap:

---

[i] Earth tones were not popular in the Middle Ages. People preferred primary colors and failed to see the point even of diamonds, inevitably choosing (if they could) large carbuncular gems of intense color. Tastefulness had yet to make its *début*.

Then up to heaven I did ascend,
Where now I dwell in sure substance
On the right hand of God, that man
May come unto the general dance.
Sing O my love, O my love, my love, my love;
This have I done for my true love.

This is a love story in which Christ the Lover seeks out Mankind his Beloved in order to welcome human beings back into "the general dance," the fantastic, if hidden, harmony of creation. In a searching theological exposition, such a thought might not appear simple, but here it is presented as if in a child's picture book.

It is impossible to date the text of "My Dancing Day." We find it printed on many extant broadsides, one-page handouts from the early age of printing. There is, however, every reason to believe that the text originated in the later Middle Ages, perhaps in the fourteenth century. For one thing, the phrase "the legend of my play" appears to be an allusion to a mystery play; and it is likely that the song was written to be performed at the beginning or end of one of those plain people's dramas. Its chorus has also suggested to many scholars that it was once a secular love song to a lady—one of the type that became popular throughout Western Europe in the twelfth century—later conjoined to the story of Jesus.

It is no easier to date the Christmas Martyrology, except to say that its literary quality seems to place it in the very early Middle Ages, perhaps in the sixth century, when Latin texts still retained echoes of classical style. Taken together, this early Christmas proclamation and the late Christmas carol, however different from each other their use of language and flights of imagination, provide a frame for us. In each of the chapters to come, as we journey through the centuries that separate carol from proclamation, we shall encounter—in prayer and piety, architecture and art, legend and social ritual, theology and alchemy, science and poetry—the all-compassionate God-Man, the tenderhearted One-for-others.

The fathers of the Eastern church would surely have found "My Dancing Day" heresy and hurled anthemas at it. Why, the cheek of pretending to get inside the unknowable mind of God, to characterize the psychology of the divine Logos! They themselves stuck unpoetically to far more abstract assertions, even if they did ask themselves why God was prompted to become man. Their answer assumed a Platonic-Plotinian scheme: our world is a world of corruption and decay, so corrupt and so very mortal that, despite the aspirations of the great philosophers, we could never reach incorruptible immortality unaided. The Logos came to our aid.

Early Western theologians found this schematically arid. Sure, Jesus's advent had saved us from eternal corruption; more important, he had saved us from our sins, our hopeless sins. Thus was introduced into theology—in large measure by the guilt-obsessed Augustine of Hippo, the greatest of the Western fathers[j]—the guilt we have never since been able to shed. Of course, it is possible to feel too guilty. We all know anxious souls whose upbringing impels them to second-guess their every action. But when we consider the actions that continue to render our world dysfunctional—whether the actions of the current Caesar or of the malicious family member—we know without question that if only these sinners were to heed their guilt, the world would be a far better place. And when we consider the rendings and regrets of our own life, we know in sadness that our sense of guilt is warranted. Guilt, as the psychotherapist Willard Gaylin has said, "is the guardian of our goodness." Without it, we would lose "the sense of anguish that we have fallen short of our own best standards." We would fall to the inhuman level of the sociopath. Guilt, in its articulation as the necessary concomitant to sin—as the "still, small voice" of conscience that forces even so monstrous a villain as Lady Macbeth to walk in her sleep and wash her hands—is one of the supreme gifts of the Judeo-Christian tradition to the Western world.

It is meaningful to bear in mind that this

[j]   You will find my presentation of Augustine's life and thought, as well as my quarrel with him, in Chapter II of *How the Irish Saved Civilization*. Here I wish only to touch lightly on one positive aspect of his immense, if ambiguous, contribution.

"Western world," which will one day be divided into "Catholic" and "Protestant," was for many centuries a cultural unity that came—and this exceedingly slowly and by infinitesimal degrees—to exclude Eastern (or "Greek") Christians, known to us as "Orthodox." The "Catholic" Middle Ages belong as much to Protestants as to Catholics. Looking backwards now from a vantage point more than five hundred years beyond the first stirrings of reformation, our eyes can see more starkly the continuity of medieval and reformation sensibilities. Martin Luther, no less than any medieval saint, understood the tenderhearted drama and poured-out love of the Incarnation. He sang in notes that summon up both Christmas Martyrology and Christmas carol. "You are to look at this little baby in the crib," said he, "and this poor man on the cross and say: This is God." And he understood as well as the anonymous lyricist of "My Dancing Day" that this Incarnation implied the impoverishment of God for the sake of our enrichment.

The great tragedy of Christian history is not the conversion of Constantine, followed by the corrupting union of church with state. From a religious point of view, there have surely been three greater tragedies: the alienation of Judaism from Christianity (and the subsequent and more horrendously consequential alienation of Christianity from Judaism); the gradual fracture of Christendom into warring "churches"; and the division of Christians into professionals and amateurs, clergy and "faithful." To the last of these we now turn.

Affirmations of Incarnation, with their mixture of many flavors—Greek intellectual distinctions, stripped-down instructions by plainspoken Roman catechists, warmly florid responses from ordinary believers—were hardly the only things happening in papal Italy in the early Middle Ages. Once the all-powerful emperor withdrew his saving presence to the Asian shore, the Italian peninsula experienced an unprecedented power vacuum. Would Italians continue to wait on the word of the faraway emperor, remaining his obedient if abandoned subjects? And what, by Christ, was to be done about the noxious barbarians, attempting to sneak over the Rhine in ever larger numbers, a looming and smelly threat to Pax Romana?

The pope and his brother bishops, all public men in the classical mode, moved quickly and deftly to secure the peace of their increasingly fractured realms (and, in the process, to aggrandize themselves). By the early fifth century, the barbarian hordes were pouring into Italy from the north and east, attracted mightily by settled farmlands and sweet vineyards. By mid-century, one massive influx—the Huns under Attila—looked to march on Rome, now a defenseless former capital. Pope Leo the Great, a bishop of massive dignity, intelligence, and purpose, traveled north to Mantua and met with Attila. The pope used every trick he had—from eloquent words to elegant panoply to a tangible aura of spiritual authority—and so impressed the Hun that he agreed to desist. It was an encounter of mythological proportions and would bolster the reputation of Rome's bishop for centuries to come. The pope could not be withstood, not even by an unbaptized savage.

A century and a half after Leo, the battle against the barbarians was long lost. Ostrogoths, Visigoths, Huns, Vandals, Alans, and Sueves had overwhelmed the old order and were settling down everywhere in Italy, Spain, and north Africa—in all the old Latin-speaking territories. Gaul and Britain, once fiercely Celtic domains—and later Roman provinces—were being subdued by yet other Germanic insurgents, Gaul by Franks, Britain by Angles, Saxons, and Jutes.[k] Rome itself had been reduced to a depressed and defeated backwater, its ancient Senate gone, its enormous population shrunk to a tenth (and by the late sixth century a twentieth) of its former size, its marvelous water delivery system of ancient aqueducts in ruins from which water leaked into the plain, creating stagnant pools of disease. Even easy communication with the outside world was blocked—by Lombard barbarians, who had come in droves to inhabit the northern half of the Italian peninsula.

[k] The end of the classical world under the impact of the barbarian "invasions" is the story with which *How the Irish Saved Civilization,* Volume I in this series, begins.

Gregory the Great, scion of a noble Roman family, served as pope at the end of the sixth century and into the seventh. He lived in a monastery of his own foundation, built on his property, the Coelian Hill, most southerly of the seven hills of Rome. He was a serious monk and would have preferred to remain in monastic solitude, but he accepted his election and made the most of it. His fasts had left him with a weak constitution and a delicate stomach, for which the obvious remedy was typically Italian: his mother Sylvia's specially prepared vegetarian dishes, which she sent him daily on a silver salver from her own home atop the Aventine Hill, a much better address than his.

Such a familial detail gives us only a fraction of Gregory and his time. By his day, the sense of aristocratic entitlement was almost the only surviving remnant of classical tradition. Science and philosophy were lost beyond recovery, buried beneath legends of saints and miracles. Beyond the confines of a few monasteries and bishops' palaces, literacy itself was in danger of extinction, so radically had the barbarian onslaught altered the Latin world. Gregory, himself a constant scribbler, yet knew no language but Latin, though he'd spent many years at the Greek-speaking imperial court in Constantinople as the previous pope's *apocrisius* (ambassador). His was an age not of academic accomplishment but of illiterate fear and fantasy. Will the barbarians attack today or tomorrow? Will the remaining urban population be wiped out entirely in the next wave of plague? Will Christ and his holy mother take pity on us? Let us fast for seven days and visit seven churches and pray before her seven images till our two knees are scraped raw.

Gregory, whose imagination was credulously medieval, not skeptically classical, was still enough of a Roman to take with consummate seriousness his role as a public man and his duty to the commonweal. He was a champion letter writer, reminding the stewards of the far-flung papal estates that they must be vigilant over their charges, keep accurate accounts, and administer the bounty to God's poor. "Promote not so much the worldly interests of the Church," scratched one of his secretaries at his dictation, "as the relief of the needy in their distress." He made certain that no resident of his city was starving; and anyone in need received abundant weekly gifts from the fruits of the episcopal farms. At his own table, still to be seen in a chapel on the Coelian Hill (as pretty and secluded today as it was in his time), he broke bread each afternoon with a dozen poor people, making sure they ate abundantly while he consumed a few spoonfuls of his mother's broth of boiled vegetables.

He sent a mission of his monks almost to the end of the earth—to the English compound of Canterbury—for the purpose of spreading the gospel among the Anglo-Saxons. The leader of the expedition was a monk named Augustine (*not* Augustine of Hippo but a timid librarian), who tried repeatedly to get out of his commission, since he had every expectation that the savages would eat him when he arrived. Once he landed and was accepted by the English, however, he found himself raised to the office of bishop and soon began to administer his diocese of Canterbury with rigid Romanitas. Gregory wrote one letter after an-other,[1] admonishing Augustine not to prefer Roman customs to English ones. "My brother, customs are not to be cherished for the sake of a place, but places are to be cherished for the sake of what is good about them." There was no need, advised Gregory, the practical Roman, to tear down the pagan temples—just remove the idols and replace them with decent Christian images. Nor was there any need to outlaw the old festivals or the customs that accompanied them. Just baptize them a bit.

By such encouragement were the customs of the northern barbarians allowed to enter the European mainstream. The masks and ghosts of Hallowe'en, the vernal and venereal tomfool-eries of May Day, as well as the lustral bathings and lantern-hung forests of Midsummer Night, taken from the Celts; the toasted cheese, toasts of warm ale, and rich desserts of northern winters and the ritual of sweetening with pine branches the claustral air in houses sealed against the cold, taken from the Germanic tribes; the word *Easter,* originally the goddess of spring accompanied by

[1]   Gregory's enormous output of letters remains with us, one of the many priceless treasures of the papal (now Vatican) library, which Gregory founded. In an age of constant crisis, the number of his accomplishments is astonishing. It is his name, for instance, that is attached to "Gregorian" chant, for he managed in his spare time to collect and document the musical traditions of the Roman church. He died of exhaustion on March 12, 604, still in his early sixties.

her fertility symbols of rabbits and decorated eggs, taken from the Saxons; the word *Yule* and the burning Yule log, taken from the Vikings—these and a thousand other customs of the savage heathens (which men like Clement of Alexandria would only have looked down their noses at) rolled into the former empire and were christened and absorbed. For this we have Gregory and many of his now nameless brother bishops to thank. Of course, they were not especially attracted to these outlandish customs, but they were too sensible to attempt to remake human beings from the ground up. They knew we all need our Christmas cookies or mug of grog or whatever we learned from childhood to associate with happiness if we are to be contented human beings.

In that time and place, zealotry was no longer in fashion among Christians. But there were certainly zealots among the barbarians. They burned things down, used books as kindling, left chaos in their wake. Christians, led by their clergy, saw their task as preservation of whatever remained intact, renovation of whatever could be salvaged, transformation of even barbarian things so long as these were not explicitly diabolical and contained even a smidgen of goodness.

All things considered, Gregory was the greatest and most humane pope in history (at least till the appearance of John XXIII in 1958). But his openness to the barbarians is characteristic of the openness of the entire Western episcopate in this period, which went a long way toward the weaving of a variegated European tapestry of characteristic personalities, specialized localities, and delightfully idiosyncratic customs and even products. (Where would we be today without French wines and cheeses, Belgian fried potatoes, Neapolitan pizza, Irish whiskey, German sausage, Hungarian goulash, and Czech beer?)

The times were against these bishops. Depredations or disease might overwhelm them at any moment. Gregory, like many other readers of the Book of Revelation, believed most sincerely that the world was nearing its final conflagration. They had neither time nor mind to waste on subtle points of doctrine or church order. They hoped only to keep themselves and others afloat as long as God allowed.

Meanwhile, in the Greek East, the barbarians remained an unreal threat. In "Waiting for the Barbarians," a droll poem in modern Greek, Constantine Cavafy presents us with the daydream of a Byzantine of this period, who imagines with mounting excitement that the barbarians will descend upon his city and save it from boredom. But nothing happens, and the Byzantines are left in their changeless immobility and cultural stasis:

> *So now what will become of us, without barbarians?*
> *Those men were one sort of resolution.*

Well, there was plenty of exciting upheaval and catastrophic resolution in Western lands, more than anyone among the surviving Old Romans like Gregory ever wished to experience. In the East, there was consternation that the Western lands of the great Roman Empire were slipping away, sometimes it seemed with the connivance of Western bishops! In the East, not a peep was heard in objection to the absolute lordship of the emperor. In the West, however, bishops, left to fend for themselves, usually came to terms with barbarian chieftains, offered them titles and even clerical help (since the chieftains, who could neither read nor write, were incapable of long-distance communication and diplomacy). Eventually, the bishops found themselves assisting their chieftains' hegemony. What else were they to do? In this new world, nominally the emperor's realm, little principalities were growing into what would become in time medieval kingdoms. Why should the helpless emperor continue to be acknowledged overlord of these startlingly novel, but unopposable, political entities?

A new political theory came gradually into being. There are two swords, the sword temporal and the sword spiritual, the first wielded by the emperor and, in their fashion, by local monarchs, the second wielded by the church, its power vested especially in the pope and (one must add under one's breath) his brother bishops. In the end, the temporal sword must yield to the spiritual. For the East, it was a shocking development.

It would trigger in time the pope's claim to be master of Christendom and king of kings. More shocking, however, than such a claim was a presumption almost hidden within it: one could challenge the Thirteenth Apostle, the emperor, the king, the state supreme, in the name of a higher good. "You have no business issuing dogmatic constitutions," Gregory the Great's successor Gregory II scolded the emperor in the early eighth century. "When it comes to dogmas, you haven't the brains; yours are too crude and militaristic."

This train of thought will lead at last to the concept of the separation of church and state and to practical challenges against law and against lawfully constituted authority by figures as diverse as the reformers of the fifteenth century, the Protestants of the sixteenth and seventeenth centuries, the *philosophes* and other Enlightenment thinkers and revolutionaries of the eighteenth century, the abolitionists of the nineteenth century, and the civil rights leaders of the twentieth century. In his "Letter from Birmingham Jail," Martin Luther King Jr. addressed the "fellow clergymen" who had criticized him for breaking the law:

> I would agree with St. Augustine that "an unjust law is no law at all." Now, what is the difference between the two? How does one determine whether a law is just or unjust? A just law is a man-made code that squares with the moral law or the law of God. An unjust law is a code that is out of harmony with the moral law. To put it in the terms of St. Thomas Aquinas: An unjust law is a human law that is not rooted in eternal law and natural law. Any law that uplifts human personality is just. Any law that degrades human personality is unjust.

In this way, a man of the twentieth century, fighting against an evil unknown to (or at least unrecognized by) people of the distant past, joined hands across a millennium and more with Augustine of Hippo and Thomas Aquinas, the most profound and lucid thinkers of the Middle Ages.

The episcopal and papal claim to a separate realm—against the emperor's claim to absolute authority—and the subsequent papal claim to absolute authority over absolute authority will grow more shrill as century follows century, eventually undermining all absolute authority (and much relative authority), as we shall discover by book's end. Leaders and rulers, whether classical, medieval, or modern, can be good or bad, their leadership and authority humane or destructive, uplifting or degrading. Only their followers and subjects—we, the laymen and laywomen, the foot soldiers and amateurs, the dissenters and protesters, the free and imprisoned, the tortured and condemned, the anathematized and damned—can finally judge.

DATING THE MIDDLE AGES

THE PERIODS GIVEN HERE REFER PRINCIPALLY TO EUROPE. THEY ARE ELASTIC, AND MANY SCHOLARS CALCULATE THEM SOMEWHAT DIFFERENTLY. THE SUBJECT OF THIS BOOK IS THE HIGH MIDDLE AGES.

THE EARLY MIDDLE AGES (ALSO CALLED THE DARK AGES)

FOURTH THROUGH ELEVENTH CENTURIES:

FROM THE ACCESSION OF THE ROMAN EMPEROR CONSTANTINE IN A.D. 312 TO THE GRADUAL INCREASE THROUGHOUT EUROPE OF SCHOLARSHIP, COMMERCE, AND THE SIZE OF CITIES TOWARD THE END OF THE ELEVENTH CENTURY

THE HIGH MIDDLE AGES

TWELFTH AND THIRTEENTH CENTURIES; FIRST HALF OF FOURTEENTH CENTURY:

FROM THE BEGINNINGS OF THE TWELFTH-CENTURY RENAISSANCE TO THE COMING OF THE BLACK DEATH IN 1347

THE LATE MIDDLE AGES

SECOND HALF OF FOURTEENTH CENTURY; FIFTEENTH CENTURY:

FROM THE BLACK DEATH TO COLUMBUS'S FIRST VOYAGE IN 1492

As early as the ninth century, a maxim was making the rounds among Western Europeans, who now spoke a simplified Latin that was already on its way to forking out into the modern Romance languages. It was a maxim that slyly subverted the worst excesses of duly (and unduly) constituted authority. We can trace it to a letter of advice that the English monk Alcuin sent his Frankish master Charlemagne, who had been awarded the newly minted title Roman Emperor of the West and crowned as such in Rome on Christmas Day 800 by Pope Leo III. Even though it is a maxim unthinkable in classical Greek, it owns deep roots in earliest Christian history: in the primitive church's universal practice of submitting all candidates for bishop (as well as lesser ministers) to popular election, since it was then assumed that this was the best way to assure that the winner was also Heaven's candidate. "*Vox populi, vox Dei,*" Alcuin reminded Charlemagne. "The voice of the people is the voice of God."

RELEVANT ROMANS

MARCUS TULLIUS CICERO, ORATOR AND CONSUL OF THE REPUBLIC	106–43 B.C.
CAESAR AUGUSTUS, FIRST EMPEROR, WIELDING ABSOLUTE POWER FROM 30 B.C.	63 B.C.–A.D. 14
CONSTANTINE I, FIRST CHRISTIAN EMPEROR, FOUNDER OF CONSTANTINOPLE	A.D. 285–337
LEO THE GREAT, POPE WHO DISSUADED ATTILA THE HUN FROM INVADING ROME	d. 461
GREGORY THE GREAT, POPE WHO WELCOMED THE BARBARIANS INTO CHRISTIANITY	d. 604
AUGUSTINE, ROMAN MONK, MISSIONARY TO THE ENGLISH, FIRST BISHOP OF CANTERBURY	d. c. 605
GREGORY II, POPE WHO REBUKED THE EMPEROR FOR INTERFERING IN RELIGIOUS MATTERS	d. 731
LEO III, POPE WHO CROWNED THE FRANKISH KING CHARLEMAGNE AS ROMAN EMPEROR	d. 816

bingen and chartres, gardens enclosed

the cult of the virgin and its consequences

I have freed my soul.

—BERNARD OF CLAIRVAUX

IN THE FIRST DECADE OF THE twelfth century, a little girl from the Rhineland town of Bermersheim, near Mainz, was offered by her parents as a sacrifice to God. Her name was Hildegard; her parents were Hildebert and Mechthild, a pious knight and his pious, well-born wife. Hildegard was eight years old when she was left for life with an anchorite named Jutta von Sponheim, who lived alone in a cell attached to the abbey church of Saint Disibod. (Disibod was a whimsical Irish monk-bishop of the seventh century who, disappointed at the lack of response to his preaching by his own countrymen, traveled to the Rhineland, became a protégé of the English Saint Boniface, evangelist to the Germans, and founded Disibodenberg, where he seems to have been rather more successful than he'd been in his native land.) Not only does Hildegard's story embody many of the cultural currents that reached their ebb in her time or soon after; this outwardly obedient daughter, her childhood cut so cruelly short, was destined to become one of the most important women of her age.

Using a living child as a religious oblation was no Christian invention. Greeks and Romans had ancient traditions of chaste priestesses and Vestal Virgins; and in the oldest records of both pagans and Jews we find evidence of "set-asides," human offerings devoted to a divinity. In the earliest archeological records, these offerings are literal human sacrifices, such as the bog burials of Scandinavia. Jewish tradition yields such offerings in surprising numbers, starting with Abraham's willingness to sacrifice his only son and continuing through Joshua's command to his troops to "devote" the people of Canaan to God under "the curse of destruction"—that is, to execute them. In later times, prisoners of war were no longer slain outright, but firstborn males still had to be "consecrated to the Lord" and then "redeemed" by an animal sacrifice that was substituted for them, as happens to the newborn Jesus in the second chapter of Luke's Gospel. There is even a further echo of Jewish tradition in the offering of Hildebert and Mechthild, for Hildegard was their tenth child—and a tenth of one's wealth, the tithe of the Hebrews, was consecrated to God.

But none of these grand historical precedents would have impressed an eight-year-old, who must have spent many a lonely, creepy night tucked away in Jutta's sparsely appointed little hut. Anchorites are no longer an everyday occurrence—I have met only one in my life, and she was nutty as a fruitcake—but in the twelfth century they could be encountered in the neighborhood of many a monastery and even within the close of an urban cathedral. The word *anchorite* derives from a Greek verb meaning "to withdraw"; and we may best think of them as hermits who lived not in obscure caves but in association with a religious community. Your typical anchorite, though not necessarily a formal member of such a community, was nonetheless part and parcel of its sacred landscape, so much so that she (or he) would normally reside in a small room built into the wall of an abbey church or cathedral, a room with a view, so to speak—a slit or screened window that allowed the anchorite to attend church services but not so large as to make her visible to the merely curious.

The liturgy for the consecration of an anchorite was actually a funeral liturgy, for it was deemed that she was dying to the world and to herself. She was spoken of as already dead and with God in Heaven. Her cell was called frankly her "burial chamber," and, dressed in her shroud, she was directed to sing a verse from Psalm 132: "This is my resting place forever, here shall I dwell for I have chosen it." The ceremony, attended gregariously by family, friends, and monastic benefactors, must strike us as a ghoulish sort of celebration, often ending with the ritual interment of the anchorite in her cell, from which it was expected that she would never again emerge. Brick was cemented on brick till the doorway to the cell was blocked and only the slit was left, enough for food and other necessities to be passed to her. If the ceremony did not conclude with an immuring, it concluded with a permanently locked door. But because this period is characterized by such variation in custom from one locality to another, we cannot be certain what was done in Hildegard's case, nor whether the growing girl was permanently locked away in the customary single room. We do possess one odd detail that may bespeak a certain mitigation: at least one servant was locked in along with the anchorites. Jutta and Hildegard were, after all, noblewomen and so could not be expected to manage even their much-reduced needs by themselves.

The idea was to serve God by permanent prayerful retreat from the world. However bizarre this may sound to modern ears, we probably all know a few people whose apartness (or even madness) might be better served if such a socially approved role were still available. Though often represented as a period of repression, heavy with superstition, the Middle Ages offered—at least in religious roles—more options than are now allowed. I doubt that a frail suppliant, plainly dressed and with a distracted air, approaching a bishop today to say that God had instructed her to build a cell into the wall of his cathedral and to carve in that wall a small window from which she could hear mass, as well as the canonical hours, would receive a warm response. But in the Middle Ages such social oddities were welcomed and assigned a place of honor. While the rest of us went about our worried lives, they prayed for us continually, speaking always to God on our behalf.

The masters of the Middle Ages had, of course, another, less public motive for honoring anchorites. The batlike monks of the Prologue who terrorized the citizens of Alexandria might have been politically useful to the patriarch, but as time went on such mobs, vociferous, usually illiterate, became a religious plague. They could not be appeased by compromise; they were rabble-rousing extremists, unswervingly certain of their rectitude. Their implacable attitudes gave bishops, as well as other public men in charge of social order, terrible headaches. How were they to be quieted? By being brought under the bishop's control, by being made subject to his rules and approval.

Every monkish mob was incited by a leader, often a desert hermit cherished for his holy ability to live apart from society, eating locusts, whipping his body, gifted with extravagant visions. The word *monk* derives, in fact, from the Greek word *monos,* meaning "alone, lonely, solitary." In the rudimentary beginnings of monastic life, all monks were hermits, and only gradually did they unite in loose association with one another. Bishops began to invite the most influential solitaries to take up more conventional habitats, closer to human society and more readily subject to episcopal pressure. Monks and nuns, *monachi* and *monachae,* were made to write constitutions by which their communities were to be governed. In time, such constitutions came to be submitted to a bishop for his approval.

In the West, Saint Benedict, Italian founder of the Benedictines, became in the early sixth century the great constitutionalist, his Rule the
standard by which all subsequent monasticism was judged. The monk's
life was utterly subject to his dictum *Ora et labora* (Pray and work). No
rabble-rousing, please. Let anarchy be not so much as mentioned among
us. In time, obedience, tranquility, and constructive employment—
building, farming, herbal medicine, relief for the poor, succor for the
sick, hospitality to wayfarers, manuscript copy-
ing, and (in the case of a gifted few) original
writing—not vision, came to rule the Christian
West. The Benedictines, in addition to vows of
obedience, chastity, and community of goods,
took a vow of stability, which meant they
could not leave the monastery grounds without
their abbot's permission. Even prayer was measured out at appointed hours. No moment of
the monk's day or night belonged exclusively
to him. The bishops, who—thanks to the
barbarians—had quite enough on their plates,
required such a church, where everyone, even a
visionary hermit, could be counted on to play an
assigned role and to stay within prescribed limits.

No one had done so much to spread the
fame of Saint Benedict as Gregory the Great,
who was himself a Benedictine monk and had
written Benedict's *Life*. By Hildegard's day,
even an abbey like Disibodenberg, originally a
foundation of Celtic spontaneity, had submitted to the Rule of Saint Benedict. In the abbey
church, the monks sang the canonical hours[a]—
as did all Benedictines from Britain to
Bohemia—and from a lancet opening in the
choir wall a single female voice united with

a   The canonical hours—
or Divine Office(s), as they
are collectively called—are
a series of public prayers,
sung by monks in
common at appointed
hours, every third hour or
so during the day and once
or twice in the course of
the night. The number
and sequence of these
"hours" (more like half
hours) have changed over
history and cultures but are
according to traditional
Benedictine usage Matins
and Lauds (during the
night), Prime (on rising at
6 A.M.), Terce (at 9 A.M.),
Sext (at noon), None
(at 3 P.M.), Vespers
(at 6 P.M.), Compline
(before retiring). The
backbone of each office
is a recitation of Old
Testament psalms and
New Testament canticles
that can be sung verse by
verse antiphonally—i.e.,
by half the choir, answered
in the next verse by the
other half. The idea is
to make prayer so much
a part of one's day as to
fulfill the injunction
of Saint Paul to
"pray always."

theirs in chant. One day, a pure child's voice joined in, inflecting the Latin words precisely, ascending gloriously and certainly to the subtle rhythm of the music. In their choir stalls the monks shivered with emotion: it was the voice of the child anchorite, the noble Hildegard.

We know little of what went on in Jutta's cell, but we know the results. Under the older woman's tutelage, the child learned to read the Book of Psalms in Latin and to sing the psalms of the monastic hours, the church's Divine Office, while accompanying herself on the expressive ten-string psaltery, a sort of dulcimer plucked by hand. Throughout her life Hildegard's Latin remained odd, at moments an almost private language. But her grasp of the principles of musicology was remarkable, eventually impelling her to compose her own chants, unusual in sound and singular in subject matter.

Beyond the Book of Psalms, Hildegard's adult writings—a substantial survival—show evidence of reading so wide as to rival and even surpass that of the most accomplished scholars of her time. She makes reference to the other books of the Bible, especially the Prophets, to the usual biblical commentaries, to liturgical texts, to the Benedictine Rule, and to the Western fathers—Jerome, Augustine, Gregory, and Bede. Her Plotinian Platonism probably came to her by way of the ninth-century Irish philosopher John Scotus Eriugena, whose sermons and ruminations were standard texts, and she seems to have read reforming contemporaries, such as Hugh of Saint Victor and Bernard of Clairvaux, as well as earlier Christian classics, such as the *Shepherd of Hermas* and Adso's *On the Antichrist*. Some have speculated that there are hints in her writings of such Carolingian[b] authors as Isidore of Seville, Rabanus Maurus, Paschasius Radbertus, and Notker of Saint Gall; and there are strong suggestions that she had access to Greek (and perhaps to Arabic) medical works and even to arcane rabbinical treatises. This, for an age in

b *Carolingian* refers to the reign and times of the Frankish dynasty established by Charlemagne (Carolus Magnus in Latin) in the mid-eighth century and which continued to rule in Germany through the first decade of the tenth century and in France till 987. Charlemagne's reign encouraged a cultural flowering, the first among the barbarian kingdoms, a small-scale renaissance such as would not be experienced again in Western Europe till Hildegard's century.

which books were scarce and precious, is an astounding catalogue, a library available to few men and to (so far as we can tell) no other woman. The library must have belonged not to Jutta, who could hardly have accommodated it in her hut, but to the liberally lending monks of Disibodenberg. What went on in Jutta's cell was a lifetime reading program.

But what of the eight-year-old who was made to live in such unnatural confinement and who survived the rigorous reading program—and even flourished because of it? Does anything of her—anything personal, peculiar, intimate—remain in the historical record? To answer these questions we must step back a bit and consider more widely the currents of twelfth-century life, not nearly as open as ours to personal preference and psychological insight.

Life spans had not increased since the classical centuries; indeed, they had dipped dramatically during the terrifying uncertainties of the barbarian influx and were only now—in the new economic and cultural stability of twelfth-century Europe—beginning to approach the best Greco-Roman levels. An eight-year-old, even a child of privilege such as Hildegard, was not as young in the eyes of her parents as she would be in ours. At the same age, her lesser-born male contemporaries were preparing for apprenticeships in the homes of strangers—millers, bakers, chandlers, glaziers, fullers, coopers, wainwrights, and such—and many of her female contemporaries, already betrothed, were beginning to contemplate their coming roles as matrons of households. Hildegard was thought quite old enough to make a lifetime commitment.

But should we assume that Hildebert and Mechthild forced their daughter into an anchorite's life? In *Scivias,* the book by which she is best known, Hildegard would counsel parents on the utter necessity of obtaining their child's consent before offering him as an oblation. "If you offer a child to Me," says the voice of Jesus,

and that offering is against his will because you have not sought his consent to it, you have not acted rightly; you have offered a ram. How? If someone offers a ram at My altar without binding

its horns strongly with ropes, the ram will certainly run away. So also if a father or mother offer their child, who is the ram, to My service, but do not honor his will, which is his horns, by assiduous care or supplication or entreaty or diligent exhortation, which are the ropes that bind him, since by all these the child should be brought to consent in good will; not having been proved by these tests, he will certainly run away, physically or mentally, unless God guards him by miracle.

And if you, O human, confine that child with such great strictness of bodily discipline that he cannot free himself from the pressure of his will's repugnance, he will come before Me [at the Last Judgment] arid and fruitless in body and soul because of the captivity unjustly inflicted on him without his consent. Then I will say to you, O human who has bound him:

I had a green field in My power. Did I give it to you, O human, that you might make it put forth whatever fruit you wished? And if you sow sand in it, can you make it grow into fruit? No. For you do not give the dew, or send forth the rain, or confer fresh moisture, or draw warmth out of the burning sun, all of which are necessary to produce good fruit. So too, you can sow a word in human ears, but into his heart, which is My field, you cannot pour the dew of compunction, or the rain of tears, or the moisture of devotion, or the warmth of the Holy Spirit, through all of which the fruit of holiness must grow.

And how did you dare so rashly to touch one dedicated and sanctified to Me in baptism, that without his will you handed him over to bear My yoke in strict captivity; so that he became neither dry nor green, not dying to the world or living in the world? Why have you so oppressed him that he can do neither? If I comfort him by miracle so that he may remain in the spiritual life, that is not for humans to look into; for I want his parents not to sin in his oblation, offering him to Me without his will.

This sometimes awkward-sounding translation (by Columba Hart) is no more awkward than the Latin original, preserving in English the taut, convoluted quirkiness of Hildegard's characteristic voice. In this passage, as in all of Hildegard's writings, one runs smack into the dense symbology of medieval imagination. Greek logical discourse has disappeared, replaced by pictures meant to convey the writer's meaning. These pictures are, however, as highly allegorical as the most rarefied passages of Philo the Jew: the ram is the child, the ropes his parents' express wishes for him, his horns his will. The mode of perception is an outgrowth of the "logic" of the Christian sacramental system—in which the cleansing waters of baptism clean both materially and spiritually and the bread of the Eucharist feeds both body and soul. Each earthly element embodies and gives voice to a heavenly reality.

But was Hildegard a willing oblation? Or was she one of those who required a special miracle in order to remain in the cloister without bitterness? (She certainly did not run away like the ram of her example.) Since the passage is as close as Hildegard ever comes to personal revelation, we cannot be sure.[c] What is extraordinary here, however, is Hildegard's unrelenting insistence on respecting the preference of a child—in a time when few people even entertained such a trivial consideration. There is a vein of sadness or even regret running through this passage that alerts us to something particular to Hildegard. "I had a green field" may be Jesus talking but it is also Hildegard. The plangency suggests either that Hildegard was forced into this life or that she has enormous sympathy for those who were. Or it may be that she recalls allowing her eight-year-old self to be too easily caught in the familial ties that bound her, caving in prematurely to her parents' announced wishes for her—for this strange daughter, sickly and full of fancies, for whom an appropriate marriage might prove exceedingly difficult to arrange. From other pas-

[c] Though the writers of the Middle Ages had before them the unique example of Augustine's *Confessions,* no one would again attempt such personal autobiography till the Renaissance. Margery Kempe, writing in English in the early fifteenth century, was a partial exception, but her memoir lay undiscovered and unpublished till 1934.

sages and from surviving anecdotal evidence we know that Hildegard gloried in her cloistered virginity. But here a note is sounded and sustained that lets us know that in her secret mind and heart she also lived other possibilities.

She tells us repeatedly that she had been a sickly child, and often in letters written throughout her adult life she complains of pain, but there is scant description of symptoms. (Like not a few chronically ill persons, she managed to live a long life, surviving to the age of eighty-one, a remarkable feat for her time.) The famous neurologist Oliver Sacks has made a case for Hildegard as a victim of migraines, her visionary experiences symptoms of her pathology; others have posited epilepsy. But no theory can be accepted as conclusive because our evidence is so slight.

What we do know about Hildegard, however, is considerable. Others who wished to dedicate their lives to God attached themselves to Jutta, forming in time a lively and famously successful community of nuns who, like their brothers the Disibodenberg monks, committed themselves to the Benedictine Rule. In later, more knowing eras, monks and nuns inhabiting the same property would provoke scandal or satire. But to twelfth-century eyes, the nuns were all consecrated virgins, the monks, if not virginal, chaste—and no one (at least no one on record) thought anything more about it.

In her teens, Hildegard made her formal profession, a ceremony parallel to the Christian marriage ceremony, in which the candidate publicly committed herself for life to her monastic vows. By this point, with perhaps a dozen women and girls taking up residence at Disibodenberg, the anchorite's severe cell had become the abbess's attractive office, and its door must often have swung open to allow Jutta's spiritual daughters to receive instruction and encouragement. In particular, several child-oblates, left by parents in imitation of what Hildegard's parents had done, must have required significant attention.

In 1136, the year Hildegard turned thirty-eight, the old abbess breathed her last. Her nuns, in strictly democratic ballot, elected Hildegard as the obvious choice to succeed the foundress. In her new position, which gave her immediate regional importance and would soon bring her pan-European fame, the young abbess began a correspondence so wide-ranging as to become one of the most important sources of our information on the twelfth century. The collection—nearly four hundred of Hildegard's letters, along with many of the letters of her correspondents—is a unique medieval survival. Given her duties as abbess and the demands made on her as a result of her growing reputation, Hildegard could never have accomplished such a feat without the help of a devoted secretary. In the monk Volmar, who had served earlier as librarian and tutor to the child Hildegard, she was blessed with the perfect assistant, hardworking, detail-oriented, self-effacing, intelligent, discerning, loyal as a dog, someone who could anticipate her needs before she articulated them—what every abbess needs.

Near the middle of the century, Hildegard was inspired to leave Disibodenberg with Volmar and her nuns to establish a new foundation. Though it was true that her increasing fame had attracted more female postulants than Disibodenberg could appropriately house, not everyone was pleased. Kuno, the abbot of Disibodenberg, knew she had no right to leave without his blessing, which he steadfastly refused to bestow. After all, Hildegard and her nuns had attracted a steady stream of pilgrims; her departure would surely entail a drop in revenues. Quite a few of the nuns fought Hildegard's plan tooth and nail: they did not look forward to taking leave of Disibodenberg's comfortable cloisters or hazarding the some-

A biography of Jutta, likely written by Volmar at Hildegard's request, turned up in 1991, casting doubt on some of our previous assumptions about Hildegard. It would seem that Jutta was only six or so years older than Hildegard and that the two may have lived together in seclusion on the estate of Jutta's father at Sponheim before taking up residence in the anchorite's cell at Disibodenberg. But since it will take scholars some time to weigh the authenticity of the sometimes conflicting narratives—Hildegard's autobiography, previously available, and the newly discovered *Vita* of Jutta—I have stuck to the information available from Hildegard's own narrative.

times perilous crossing of a great river and the subsequent rigors of homesteading in the desolate wilds of Bingen, whither their untried abbess meant to convey them. But Hildegard saw clearly the necessity of separating her nuns—financially and spiritually but also, most important, juridically—from the monks. In their new convent the sisters would be independent of male rule, and their abbess would no longer report to anyone. (Well, maybe *technically* she would still be under obedience to Kuno, but he would be so very far away.)

Hildegard's plan was ridiculed by the local nobility, without whose patronage no monastic foundation could expect to succeed. Her favorite young nun, the beautiful Richardis von Stade—for whom Hildegard confessed she "bore a deep love"—took herself off to another convent to serve as its abbess, an embarrassment and lasting suffering to Hildegard. But her iron will to have things her way—or, rather, as the voice within her wished—showed itself nakedly for the first (but hardly for the last) time. She lay on her sickbed and would not rise, claiming a "charismatic illness" sent from God, till the irritated abbot found himself trumped by womanly wiles and at last gave in. Leaving their most obdurate sisters behind to live as shadowy handmaids to the monks, the nuns crossed the river and set about establishing themselves on the hill of Rupertsberg in the ruins of a Carolingian monastery, from which Hildegard's abbatial church of Saint Rupert rose in record time—thanks in part to Hildegard's family connections—to be consecrated in 1152.

In little more than a decade, a surfeit of new followers would force Hildegard to found a satellite convent on the pleasant, vine-covered hill of Eibingen overlooking the bustling riverside settlement of Bingen-on-Rhine. It is this convent, today the Abbey of Saint Hildegard of Bingen, that has survived and prospered, now as a women's retreat house and healing center, where superhealthy cuisine, prepared to Hildegardian recipes, is served to visitors at strictly specified hours.[c] Rupertsberg was razed in the seventeenth century during the

𝕮 Contemporary pilgrims for whom spelt and lettuce do not make much of a meal will find mouthwatering dishes and superb local wines at the gracious restaurant in Bingen Castle on the opposite hill.

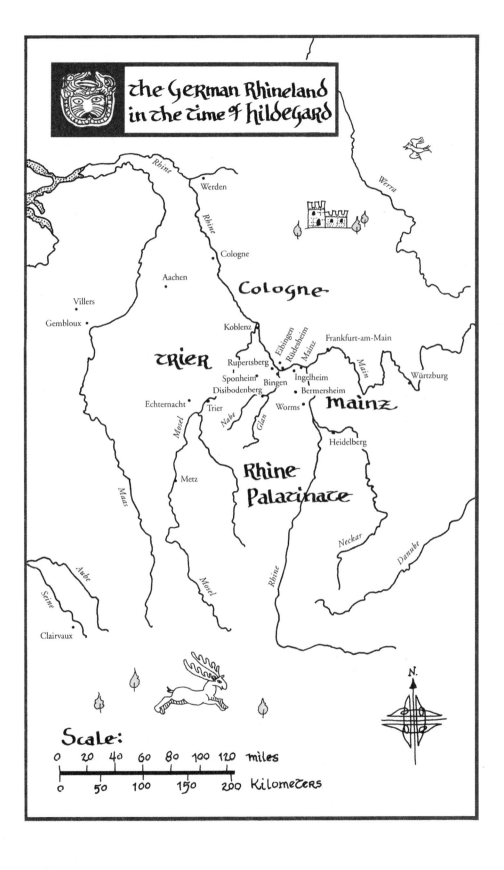

the German Rhineland in the time of hildegard

Werra

Rhine

Werden

Rhine

Cologne

Cologne

Aachen

Villers

Gembloux

Koblenz

Eibingen
Rüdesheim
Mainz

Frankfurt-am-Main

trier

Rupertsberg

Sponheim

Bingen

Ingelheim

Würtzburg

Disibodenberg

Bermersheim

Echternacht

Trier

Nahe

Glan

Worms

mainz

Main

Mosel

Heidelberg

Metz

Rhine Palatinate

Maas

Neckar

Danube

Mosel

Aube

Rhine

Seine

Clairvaux

N.

Scale:

0 20 40 60 80 100 120 miles

0 50 100 150 200 Kilometers

religious hatreds of the Thirty Years' War; and Disibodenberg was long ago reduced to just another Celtic ruin.

In her falling out with Richardis, Hildegard appears at her least likable. She refused to accept the reality of Richardis's election to the abbacy of Bassum, which lay many miles north in the neighborhood of Bremen. As Richardis set off Bassumward to take up her new duties, Hildegard wasted no time in imploring male ecclesiastical authority to declare the election invalid. Though bishops had, by the twelfth century, managed to trim back the loopier, more lawless aspects of monasticism, it could hardly be said that they had achieved firm control over the communities of monks and nuns established within their bounds. A bishop could of course find a particular community abuzz with heresy and shut it down, but his power hardly extended to the monastery's internal discipline—which was by ancient custom the monastery's, not the bishop's, business.

Relentless Hildegard pushed her losing suit through local episcopal courts, working her way through various levels of ecclesiastical machinery till her case reached the pope, who routinely returned the petition to the archbishop of Mainz for judgment. The archbishop ruled in Richardis's favor and received in consequence a scorching letter from Hildegard. What Hildegard planned to do next no one knows, but she had no intention of giving up and was stopped only by the untimely death of Richardis (though it is nearly anachronistic to term any medieval death "untimely"). In her last moments, Richardis wept to be reunited with Hildegard and her old community. That, even Hildegard had to concede, was that.

In 1141, more than ten years before the erection of the Rupertsberg abbey, Hildegard had received at Disibodenberg a call that would shape the rest of her life and the lives of countless others, a call to "cry out and write" what she saw. From earliest childhood, she tells us, she saw things that others did not see: human and animal forms, sometimes those of angels or demons, enclosed within symbolic landcapes or within elaborate, if schematic, architectonics. All these figures—and in fact the whole of

Hildegard's constant vision—were bathed in uncanny light, a luminosity that she came to call "the reflection of the living Light." At the same time, she seems to have had no difficulty separating these visions, which superimposed themselves on everyday scenes, from the ordinary realities that everyone else could see. For her, the visions were of the deeper truths within and beyond everyday experience.

In childhood she had not immediately grasped that others did not see what she saw. At five, for instance, as she and her nursemaid observed a cow, she could see the fetus inside the cow's belly and predicted—accurately, to the nurse's subsequent astonishment—the color of the calf-to-be. She soon learned to keep her visions to herself, confiding them only to Jutta, who confided them to Volmar. She felt no impulse to share them further till she was called to do so in her early forties, when she'd already been abbess for six years. The form her revelations took was characteristic of Hildegard—not the sloppy, spontaneous babblings of the typical illiterate seer but a lengthy convoluted text, *Scivias,* composed by Hildegard with excruciating exactitude over ten years and copyedited with bulldog tenacity by Volmar, whose Latin was better than hers. It's not so surprising that the result resembles at times a tightly wound cord.

Scivias is a medieval elision of *Scito vias,* which is itself an abbreviation of *Scito vias Domini* (Know the Ways of the Lord). The idea of papal infallibility would not gain currency for many centuries, but in Hildegard we already have a presumption of personal infallibility: she cannot be mistaken; she knows, she *sees* the ways of the Lord, for he has shown them to her, and she will expound them to us. To treat her ideas fairly and with any hope of completeness would take volumes, for after completing *Scivias,* Hildegard went on to write at least eight more books, none of them brief, on subjects as diverse as theology and science, medicine and music, pharmacology and biblical commentary. Besides these, we own a large collection of her poems and liturgical songs, a series of more than thirty illuminations (which

The Abbess Hildegard, inspired by fire from above,
as her amanuensis Volmar waits attentively in the
wings. From an illuminated manuscript overseen
(and perhaps illustrated) by Hildegard.

may not have been painted by her but were surely made at her bidding),
and her musical play, *Ordo Virtutum* (literally The Order of Virtues, but
more appositely The Hierarchy of Courage), which could qualify as the
West's first opera. Once she started, there was no stopping her. All that
can be done here is to point out a few of her main themes, especially as
they relate to her life and times.

Hildegard's method of writing is certainly unusual. She gives us word-pictures, a long succession of tableau-like images, described in taut, sometimes prickly phrases, often accompanied (in the original manuscripts) by illustrative illuminations. The images are static and could almost be intended for a series of elaborate stained-glass windows, but in their visual complexity and dense symbolism they cry out for an artist of the prowess of a Hieronymus Bosch to give them life and movement. Here is the First Vision of *Scivias:*

> I saw a great mountain the color of iron, and enthroned on it One of such great glory that it blinded my sight. On each side of him there extended a soft shadow, like a wing of wondrous breadth and length. Before him, at the foot of the mountain, stood an image full of eyes on all sides, in which, because of those eyes, I could discern no human form. In front of this image stood another, a child wearing a tunic of subdued color but white shoes, upon whose head such glory descended from the One enthroned upon that mountain that I could not look at its face. But from the One who sat enthroned upon that mountain many living sparks sprang forth, which flew very sweetly around the images. Also, I perceived in this mountain many little windows, in which appeared human heads, some of subdued colors and some white.

It is obvious that "the One" is God, but the further meanings of this tableau (and of all her subsequent visions) would be forever obscure did Hildegard not unlock them for us. The mountain, she tells us, "symbolizes the strength and stability of the eternal Kingdom of God." The shadow-wings show "that both in admonition and in punishment ineffable justice displays sweet and gentle protection and perseveres in true equity." The image full of eyes is Fear of the Lord, which "stands in God's presence with humility and gazes on the Kingdom of God." The child represents the Poor in Spirit who are always to be found in proximity to Fear of the Lord. The tunic of subdued color may be taken to indicate the figure's poverty, the white shoes its admirable spiritual direction. The scenes in the windows embody the idea that in "the most high and profound and perspicuous knowledge of God the aims of human acts cannot be concealed or hidden"—God's own *Rear Window.* Those in subdued colors are lukewarm Christians, those in white are pure. Hildegard concludes the First Vision by quoting from the Book of Proverbs—by Solomon, she says—on human acts: "The slothful hand has brought about poverty, but the hand of the industrious man prepares riches."

Despite the contemporary celebrity of Hildegard, it must be admitted that there is not so very much here of either theological or

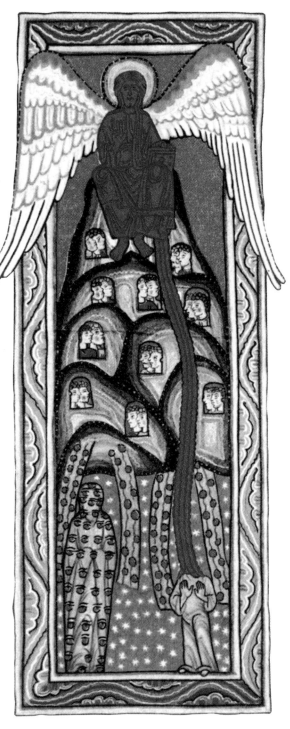

Illustration of Hildegard's First Vision in *Scivias.*

spiritual sustenance. The visions run on, chapter by chapter, book by book, seldom offering anything more arresting than stultifying orthodoxy and, as in the Solomon reference, something not far distant from pious drivel. Without the intensely colorful illustrations—the supposedly "mystical mandalas" that have lured so many in our day—I doubt that Hildegard would ever have become the toast of spiritual seekers. But we must do a little spadework to search out the secret of her celebrity even in her own day.

There is a clue at the very outset of her commentary on her First Vision:

> And behold, He Who was enthroned upon that mountain cried out in a strong, loud voice saying, "O human, who are fragile dust of the earth and ashes of ashes! Cry out and speak of the origin of pure salvation until those people are instructed, who, though they see the inmost contents of the Scriptures, do not wish to tell them or preach them, because they are lukewarm and sluggish in serving God's justice. Unlock for them the enclosure of mysteries that they, timid as they are, conceal in a hidden and fruitless field. Burst forth into a fountain of abundance and overflow with mystical knowledge, until they who now think you contemptible because of Eve's transgression are stirred up by the flood of your irrigation.

It is only in passages like this, where Hildegard evidences her—or, rather, God's—withering contempt for lukewarm and timid churchmen, however learned, and exalts her own female fecundity, that the reader is zapped into full wakefulness.

Between the time of Gregory the Great and that of Hildegard, the church had gone from apocalyptic terror to settled prosperity. The barbarians had morphed into knights and their ladies, monks and nuns, artisans and burghers. Europe had become Christian, its bishops no longer endangered but in charge. The temptation—at least among clergy—was

Man at the center of the cosmos with Hildegard as observer
(in the lower left corner): a Hildegardian mandala. Leonardo da Vinci's
later nude figure, the so-called Vitruvian Man, his arms extended within
a circle, is in the same tradition, but Hildegard's figure, lacking
visible genitals, is the nonsexist *homo* of her writings.

not to despair, as might have been the case in Gregory's day, but to lax-ity, self-indulgence, aggrandizement. The twelfth-century renaissance in thought and the arts was built on the new prosperity—and prosperity al-ways brings new temptations in its wake. In the very first page of *Scivias,* Hildegard demonstrates that she is both numbingly orthodox and on the side of the reformers who want to toughen up their slack, temptation-prone church. She is also happy to admit the weakness of her sex (always a plus with self-adoring males who lack self-knowledge), even to glory in it; and at the same time she folds a frisson of suggestiveness into her rhetoric—all that abundance, overflow, and irrigation.

Throughout Hildegard's writings, the good people are always burst-ing with *viriditas*—greenness or greening or springtime ("The force that through the green fuse drives the flower")—the bad people cracked and desertlike in their aridity. There can be no question that from childhood *viriditas* had poured from the forested ridges and clear waterways of the wild Rhineland, impressing itself on the sensorium of a lonely child. Her scientific works are replete with what can only be personal observa-tions of local animals, fish, and plants. For the local rivers—the Glan, the Nahe, and the Rhine—she catalogues thirty-seven species of fish, giving us evidence that, if she didn't do a lot of fishing herself, this nominally cloistered nun must have talked at length to an awful lot of fishermen. *Viriditas,* a Latin feminine noun, is in Hildegard's fertile imagination es-pecially associated with women, in particular with her virgin sisters. "The enclosure of mysteries" is Christian revelation, but it is also the cloister with its healing herb gardens and nourishing orchards, tended by flowering virgins, each of whom is in human form what the cloister is in architectural terms, an enclosed garden. "She is a garden enclosed, my sister, my promised bride; a garden enclosed, a sealed fountain," sings the author of the Song of Songs, one of Hildegard's favorite books of the Bible (also believed in her day to have been written by Solomon). Dryness, brittleness, inability to reproduce—these are qualities associated in Hildegard's works with sinners in general but especially with the lax, unreformed churchmen of her day.

There is no reason to doubt Hildegard's sincerity, her belief in her visions. But no human motives are unmixed, and it is not difficult to identify the many passages in which she so sides with the reform party as to call out for their recognition of her as a prominent ally. And recognition is what she got.

In 1147, prior to her move across the river, she sent her incomplete *Scivias* to Bernard of Clairvaux, a Frenchman[f] of the Cistercians, a monastic order of strictly observant Benedictines who were spearheading ecclesiastical reform. He was the most famous religious figure of his day, and Hildegard was looking for confirmation. In her covering letter she abases herself in the approved manner ("Wretched, and indeed more than wretched in my womanly condition") and hallows Bernard ("Steadfast and gentle father"); she even recounts her vision of Bernard as "a man looking into the sun, bold and unafraid." Bernard was, in fact, one of the most aggressive players of his time, always on the hunt for heretics, allowing no quarter to anyone who disagreed with him, preacher of the disastrous Second Crusade. No admirer of women, he was famous for his bons mots: "It is more difficult to live with a woman without [moral] danger than to raise the dead to life."

Bernard was also mentor to the current pope, Eugene III, who (as luck would have it) was himself in receipt of a copy of the incomplete *Scivias*. Kuno, abbot of Disibodenberg, had sent this copy to his own archbishop, Heinrich of Mainz, humbly begging Heinrich to judge its orthodoxy. Heinrich handed the work to Eugene, who was just then presiding over a synod at nearby Trier, the old Romano-Germanic hub, still graced with impressive Roman stoneworks as well as elegant new medieval buildings, bankrolled by the synod's hosts, the increasingly prosperous merchants of Trier.

Eugene read out passages from the lionized local abbess's work to the assembled bishops. (Theirs was an age for reading aloud to others, not alone in silence.) One can only imagine the supercilious expressions on the well-fed faces of the costumed hierophants—till a gaunt, starkly

[f] "Frenchman" is proleptic; Bernard was Champenois. France would not acquire the region of Champagne for more than a century after Bernard's time.

Viriditas, or the abundance of nature,
both cultivated and wild: a Hildegardian mandala.

Town houses of wealthy merchants in the main square of medieval Trier.

robed monk, Bernard, attending the synod as papal theologian, stepped forward meekly to one-up them all, explaining that he had already been sent his copy, had read it diligently, and approved of every word the woman wrote. Hildegard, approaching fifty, became instantly famous, receiving papal approbation as a genuinely orthodox but prophetic seer. Suddenly, no one could praise her highly enough, one attendee, Abbot Bertolf, writing her a breathless fan letter: "Indeed, you have far exceeded your sex by having surpassed with manly spirit that which we were afraid even to approach!"

9 The full text is "Let a woman learn in silence and in full submission. I permit no woman to teach or to have authority over a man; she must keep silent" (1 Timothy 2:11–12). The medievals, lacking a science of textual history, had no way of knowing that this letter was written not by Paul but by someone taking his name—and with a highly selective agenda—decades after his death. See *Desire of the Everlasting Hills,* pp. 155ff.

Hildegard was launched on a new career as preacher to the people of her time, the only woman allowed to break the supposedly absolute New Testament proscription, contained in the First Letter to Timothy, that "no woman [is] to teach or to have authority over a man."**9** The exception made for Hildegard is evidence not only of her universal celebrity but of the quirky singularities of medieval life. It is seldom possible to say of the medievals that they *always* did one thing and *never* another; they were marvelously inconsistent. Not only does a

Fifteenth-century depiction of Bernard of Clairvaux with the Devil at his heels. By the Belgian artist Dirk Bouts.

woman preach; a cloistered nun, once offered to God as a solitary, travels from town to town—by boat, by horse, on foot, probably by litter—talking to everyone.

In the last two decades of her life, she made sensational preaching tours of the Rhineland and beyond, wherever she went attracting overflow crowds to the unique spectacle of herself. Though the reports of her sermons are in Latin, we may guess that she spoke German to Germans, saving her halting Latin for Lorraine and similar French-speaking districts. She is full of scorn for heretics such as the Cathars, a Manichean sect that had gained purchase amid the newly literate populations of eastern France, western Germany, and northern Italy. The Cathars, like their successors the Albigensians, were purists who hated human bodies, the Christian sacramental system, and the entire material world. They were the twelfth-century manifestation of an antiphysical bias that resurfaces continually through Christian history. They would have made common cause with the Encratites; had they known of him, Plato would have been to their taste; and they would have adored Plotinus. They disapproved of marriage and normal sexual intercourse—though they were rumored to approve the anal variety, like their predecessors the Bogomils, who had hailed from Bulgaria (and thus were also called Bulgars or Buggers). For the apocalyptic, survivalist Cathars, both church and state were absolute evils to be shunned. In 1163, not long after Hildegard preached at Cologne, the local authorities rounded up their Cathar neighbors and burned them at the stake.

Hildegard is mindful that Heaven is the final goal of everyman and presses ordinary people to live a life that will make them welcome there. But above all she attacks the clergy for their enervated presentations of Christian truth and the scandal of their compromised lives. The sermon she delivered at Trier on Pentecost 1160 is typical. She begins by denigrating herself as "a poor little female figure"—"*paupercula feminea forma*" in the Latin report—lacking health, strength, courage, and learning. And yet she is the bearer of God's words to the bishops and their clergy. Because these men have failed to "sound the trumpet of justice," the four corners of the earth have grown dark and cold. We see no longer in the east the dawn of good works; in the south the warmth of virtue grows chill; in the west the twilight of mercy has given way to the blackness of midnight; and from the north Satan blows his noisy wind of pride, faithlessness, and indifference to God. In her day, the courage of "poor little" Hildegard's attack would have been thrilling enough to make the hairs on a listener's neck stand up.[b]

b In the ancient world, women never addressed large crowds, not only because their opinions were unsought but because there were no public address systems, and the unaided casting of the voice to a large crowd, especially in the open air, presented insurmountable difficulties to most women. Even men who were to assume public

The bishops, she says, are sleeping, "while justice is abandoned. Thus did I hear this Voice from heaven saying: O Daughter of Sion [that is, the church], the crown will fall from your head, the far-flung mantle of your riches will be collapsed to a narrow confine, and you will be banished from place to place. Many cities and monasteries will be scattered by the powerful. And princes will say: Let us deprive them of the iniquity that turns the whole world upside down."

What nerve this woman had. No wonder that in later times these sermons will be read as prophecies of the Reformation. But Hildegard is thinking of the twelfth, not the sixteenth, century; and we need go no further than her own time to find confirmation of her majestic references. As early as 1153, she had fired her first verbal missile at a pope, Anastasius IV, an octogenarian who lasted but a year and a half: "You, O Man, who are too tired . . . to rein in the pomposity of arrogance among those placed in your bosom . . . why do you put up with depraved people who are blinded by foolishness and who delight in harmful things, like a hen that cackles in the night and terrifies herself? Such people are completely useless."

Her advice and her prayers were sought by the kings and queens of her day—the list of her correspondents in the last decades of her life reads like a roll of the royal houses of Europe—and to all she gave what succor she could, as well as frank counsel. No one, in the end, was beyond the reach of her criticism, not even the emperor himself. Early in his imperial reign, the young, vigorous, widely admired Frederick Barbarossa (or Redbeard) had sought an alliance with the nun, confirming her status and asking her sweetly what prophecies God might have for him. When he held court at Ingelheim, she came into his presence by his invitation, promising him privately that certain gifts from Heaven were to come his way—which, he wrote her subsequently, they had:

roles had to be specially trained to project their voices. The late Romanesque and Gothic cathedrals of the Middle Ages, because they were echoing sound boxes, gave women their first opportunity to address large meetings. Such a happening would not have been possible much before Hildegard's time. She gave her sermon in Trier Cathedral, a lofty late Romanesque structure. Right next door is the Liebfrauenkirche (Church of the Virgin), one of Germany's first (and most exquisite) Gothic churches. Together, these two constitute a textbook account of the transition from Romanesque to Gothic, as well as of spatial sensibility, in the age of Hildegard.

> *Frederick, by the grace of God Emperor of the Romans and always august, sends his grace and every good to the Lady Hildegard of Bingen.*

We inform you, holy lady, that we have now in hand those things you predicted to us. . . . We will continue to strive with all our efforts for the honor of this our kingdom. Therefore, beloved lady, we sincerely beseech you, and the sisters entrusted to your care, to pour out your prayers to almighty God for us so that He may turn us to Himself as we labor on our earthly business and so that we may merit to obtain His grace.

Please be assured that with regard to that matter you directed to our attention we will be swayed by neither the friendship nor the hatred of any person, but we intend to judge with perfect equity.

We cannot guess what the secret "matter" may have been, but Hildegard was always one to seize an opening that might further her own pet projects. Her replies, in any case, were no less sweet, no less courtly than his, till Frederick interfered repeatedly in church elections, even backing antipopes (irregularly designated candidates who he knew would prove more malleable than the validly elected popes). At the appointment of a second antipope, Hildegard was moved to a withering reappraisal. "You juvenile fool," she scolded the emperor. In 1168 Frederick, now well into his campaign to reunite Germany and lift his reduced Western Roman Empire to the kind of greatness it had achieved under Charlemagne, appointed a third antipope upon the death of the second. Hildegard's (probably final) communication to the emperor was terse: "He-Who-Is says: 'I destroy disobedience and the rebellion of those who scorn me. Woe, woe to the malice of evil men who turn from me! Hear this, O king, if you wish to live; otherwise, my sword shall run you through.' " The emperor, who could easily have silenced, even executed, the little nun for such impudence, wisely left her in peace.

Like other medieval monarchs, he would learn that interference with the church was not a strategy for long-term success. By 1176, he was defeated at the Battle of Legnano—the first time in history that infantry defeated cavalry, presaging an age in which plodding bourgeoisie

Twelfth-century late Romanesque dom (or cathedral) of Trier, its foundations laid by the Emperor Constantine in the fourth century. Hildegard preached here to capacity crowds. Next door (on the right) is a graceful early Gothic church dedicated to the Virgin Mary.

would loom larger than swashbuckling nobility—and had to admit that he would never be able to reclaim the Lombard dominions of Charlemagne. The next year, two years before Hildegard's death, he knelt and begged the valid pope's forgiveness for his intrusions into papal politics—at a public ceremony in Venice.[i] Pope Alexander III graciously forgave. In 1190, a dozen years after Hildegard's death, Frederick Barbarossa, long a romantic figure to his German subjects but now in his late sixties, drowned while crossing the River Saleph (in modern-day Turkey) as he led his knights to Jerusalem on the expiatory adventure of the Third Crusade.

i In 1077, exactly one hundred years before Barbarossa's submission, his predecessor Henry IV had knelt in the snow of Canossa, begging the pope to lift his excommunication, incurred by his interference in church affairs. In 1172, just five years before the Peace of Venice, Henry II of England had endured scourging for his inadvertent role in the murder of Thomas Becket, his archbishop of Canterbury. Each of these monarchs learned in his turn that the church was not to be trifled with.

Despite her continuing publicity, Hildegard remained in important ways a very private person—and an artist of markedly individual spirit in a time when individuality was just beginning to show its face again in society after centuries of banishment. Her music is chant, largely unaccompanied, as was most church music of her time, but quite possibly polyphonic (despite the fact that the manuscripts give us only the line of melody), since polyphony, appearing as early as the ninth century, had become the musical dessert of Hildegard's day. But no one else was singing songs that sounded like what the nuns of Bingen were singing. The melody lines of Hildegard's compositions alternate between moments of rigid control and those of floridly swooping excess, as the melody threatens to abandon pattern altogether and jump the tracks. The rhythms are as far from ti-dum, ti-dum as can be imagined, full of wild irregularity, yet coming together in an intelligible whole. The words, also by Hildegard, are one with her music, obedient to no known rules, loosely metrical but unbound, the Western world's first free verse. As one follows her kaleidoscopic patterns, melting into chaos, melting into new patterns, one cannot but think of the abandoned sensuality of jazz. Her songs would have made sense to Bessie Smith. This was one loose sister; and nothing is more arresting than the bald passion of her subject matter:

O dulcissime amator, o dulcissime amplexator:
adiuva nos custodire virginitatem nostram.
Nos sumus orti in pulvere—
heu, heu, et in crimine Adam;
valde durum est contradicere
quod habet gustus Pomi;
tu erige nos, salvator Christe.
Nos desideramus ardenter te sequi.
O quam grave nobis miseris est
te immaculatum et innocentem
regem angelorum imitari.
Tamen confidimus in te—
quod desideres gemmam requirere in putredine.

Nunc advocamus te, sponsum et consolatorem,
qui nos redemisti in cruce.
In tuo sanguine copulate sumus tibi
cum desponsatione, repudiantes virum
et eligentes te, Filium Dei.
O pulcherrima forma,
o suavissimus odor residerabilium deliciarum,
semper suspiramus post te in lacrimabili exilio.
Quando te videamus
et tecum maneamus?
Nos sumus in mundo
et tu in mente nostra,
et amplectimur te in corde
quasi habeamus te presentem.
Tu fortissimus leo rupisti celum
descendens in aulam Virginis,
et destruxisti mortem
edificans vitam in aurea civitate.
Da nobis societatem cum illa
et permanere in te,
o dulcissime sponse,
qui abstraxisti nos de faucibus diaboli
primum parentem nostrum seducentis.

O sweetest lover, sweetest hugger,
help us keep our virginity.
We rise from dust—
alas, alas, from Adam's guilt.
How very hard to hold out against
whatever tastes of the Apple;
thou, savior Christ, set us aright.
Ardently we long to follow thee.
O what a struggle it is for us, the wretched ones,
to imitate the king of angels,

spotless, innocent.
Still, we trust in thee—
that thou wouldst find again the jewel in the filth.
Now do we call upon thee, spouse and comforter,
who redeemed us on the cross.
In thy blood we couple with thee
in betrothal, refusing a husband
and choosing thee, Son of God.
O most beautiful figure,
O sweetest smell of longed-for delights,
always do we sigh for thee in tearful exile.
When shall we see thee
and stay with thee?
We are in the world,
and thou in our mind,
and we hug thee to our heart
as thou wert here with us.
Thou, mightiest lion, tore open the sky,
descending to the Virgin's vestibule,
and destroyed death,
building life in the Golden City.
Give us fellowship in that city
and rest with thee,
O sweetest spouse,
who dragged us from the jaws of the devil,
our ancient ancestor's debaucher.

She's a virgin but no prude, and she makes no attempt to mask or excuse the sex and violence that inhabit her. ("If I go to church on Sunday / Then just shimmy down on Monday / 'Taint nobody's business if I do," sings Bessie Smith in a not entirely dissimilar vein, big Bessie of the assertive, unafraid voice, who was orphaned early, mentored by the bisexual Ma Rainey, and worked so hard to achieve her fleeting fame.) Virginity is Hildegard's torment, as she salivates over the lingering taste of the Apple that tempted Adam and Eve—which was seen by medievals as a sexual temptation. Like a debased creature from *The Story of O,* she is a jewel defiled by rottenness. Her only defense is the presence of Christ in her heart, a sensation she heightens by reminding herself of his arms around her and the very smell of him, as they couple in his blood. She sees her mighty lion-lover rending the sky itself to come *"in aulam virginis"* (to the Virgin's vestibule), her empty entry space. This is the moment of Incarnation: just as the Word of God entered the Virgin Mary, he may enter Hildegard.

Her medical writing, as useless to us as the rest of medieval medicine, is notable for its uncompromising descriptions of human sexual organs and activities. Hildegard was a woman who made the best of the situation in which she found herself, a believer but a realist. She never doubted the reality of Christ, nor did she disguise the fierce strength of her own temptations. This is, after all, an age of unabashed public confession, not of shamed defensiveness, for the judgmental repressions of Calvinism will not infect Europe for many centuries.

As I see her, she is a small woman, wrinkled in old age—"Schrumpilgard" (Wrinklepus), she was called derisively by a demon who possessed a young woman named Sigewize. Only Schrumpilgard, screeched the demon, could bring the possession to an end, which she did. But she is a know-it-all, always right about everything. Her sisters could find her unendurable because of her "insufferable hammering way" and they would glower at her and, in her words, "tear me to pieces behind my back."

The lonely child became a lonely grown-up, one still full of fantasies. She dressed her sisters like princesses for special feast days. As they processed into the abbey church, singing one of Hildegard's remarkably personal compositions, they presented a sight seen nowhere else. Unlike other nuns, who sheared their hair and covered what was left, Hildegard's virgins wore their hair long and unbound, scarcely concealed by the flowing silk veils, pure white—Hildegard's favorite color—that trailed in their wake, attached to their heads by elaborate crowns as golden as the many rings that adorned their fingers and the bangles that clinked down their arms. When the superior of another congregation, one Tengswich, wrote to Hildegard, inquiring how she justified such practices—in a letter as full of catty innuendo as the dialogue from an episode of *Desperate Housewives*—Hildegard's response was serene:

> A woman, once married, ought not to indulge herself in prideful adornment of hair or person, nor ought she to lift herself up to vanity, wearing a crown and other golden ornaments, except at her husband's pleasure, and even then with moderation. But these strictures do not apply to a virgin, for she stands in the unsullied purity of paradise, lovely and unwithering, and she always remains in the full vitality of the budding rod.

Take that, bitch. And as for Mistress Tengswich's other objection to Hildegard's m.o.—"that you admit into your community only those women from noble, well-established families"—the great abbess gave this unblushing reply:

> God keeps a watchful eye on every person, so that a lower order will not gain ascendency over a higher one, as Satan and the first man did, who wanted to fly higher than they had been placed. And who would gather all his livestock into one barn—the cattle, the asses, the sheep, the kids? Thus it is clear that differentiation must be maintained in these matters, lest people of varying status, herded all together, be dispersed through the pride of their elevation, on the one hand, or the disgrace of their decline, on the other, and especially lest the nobility of their character be torn asunder when they slaughter one another out of hatred. Such destruction naturally results when the higher order falls upon the lower, and the lower rises above the higher. For God establishes ranks on earth, just as in heaven with angels, archangels, thrones, dominions, cherubim, and seraphim. And they are all loved by God, although they are not equal in rank.

In the twelfth century, virginity had its pleasures. So did noble birth. Without both these ancient social institutions, we would never have heard of Hildegard. Thank God her parents didn't marry her off and keep her mute for the ages.

I n our Age of the Common Man, nobility has fled the field, which makes it difficult for us to come to terms with the temper of an age in which class structures were taken for granted and everyone was duly expected to fulfill his or her divinely assigned role, an age in which shoe-makers remained forever shoemakers, and duchesses duchesses and fish-wives fishwives, and no one entertained even a whisper of hope for an improvement in status. The disadvantages of such a society are so evident to us that its contentments may remain hidden from view. We fail to ac-knowledge, on the one hand, how full of anxiety our own society is, how its lack of assigned roles leaves so many individuals woefully iso-lated, permanently nervous about the random fluctuations of their for-tunes. If, on the other hand, one could say, "I am the shoemaker of Trier, as was my father before me, as will be my son after me; I am an integral part of my community, even necessary to it; my neighbors respect me and depend on my skill," one could own an abiding peace that eludes all but a very few children of the twenty-first century.

Even more confounding to us *Sex and the City* devotees is the honor awarded virginity within the medieval world. Why did they privilege a life without sex? What on earth were they thinking? What were they feeling?

Each society makes assumptions that it regards as effectively ax-iomatic—as so obvious that no explanatory defense is needed. In the world in which I came to adulthood, the value of unending progress was just such an unassailable assumption. Each generation was an improve-ment on the one before, each new invention a leap forward in the bet-terment of human life; and sinking backwards was unthinkable. It is possible that the vast majority still hold similar assumptions, even though the limitations of the globe itself—a round, finite sphere with strictly finite resources—are becoming all too obvious; nor will struggles between haves and have-nots be put off forever.

In the medieval world, the value of virginity was an unassailable assumption; or, more precisely, the unassailable assumption was the centrality of Jesus Christ who, because he took flesh in the womb of a virgin and remained himself virginal through the course of his brief life, had sanctified virginity, exalting it above all ancient precedents, and had given virgins a role that rendered them integral and necessary to society. The sacrificial virginity of exceptional religious figures, which made them more Christ-like than the rest of us, was offered to God on our behalf. Their renunciation of ordinary pleasures and expectable satisfactions gave them an aura of perfection: they were, in a sense, already living in the world beyond the veil, companions of angels and saints, standing, as Hildegard boldly put it, "in the unsullied purity of paradise, lovely and unwithering." Such extraordinary connection to Heaven turned them into mediating intercessors on our behalf, human like us but not so distracted by earthly concerns, living consciously in the presence of God. The medieval cult of virginity may have been wrapped in the severe shadows of Platonic antimaterialism, but there was also something quite new about it.

The ancient Greek-speaking world had been, for one thing, a world of argument and abstraction; the medieval Latin-speaking world became a world of image and imagination. As early as the late second century, images of the Virgin Mother with the Divine Child on her lap appeared in the Roman catacombs on rough arches high above the tombs of early Christians. In these quickly daubed, fading frescoes Mary may still be discerned, surrounded by other biblical figures, some in shallow relief:

She turned up first in Rome,
impressed upon a catacomb,
a hieroglyph relief
conceived by a martyred primitif.

Madonna and Child of the late second century from
the Roman Catacomb of Santa Priscilla. The figure to the
left is a prophet, either Balaam or Isaiah, each of whom
was thought to have prophesied that Christ would appear
as a star or light. Above the Madonna's head is a star to
which the prophet is pointing. Despite the poor state
of preservation, we can discern that the Madonna is seated,
wears a short-sleeved tunic, and is tenderly bent
toward the baby, offering her breast.

Apse of Santa Maria in Trastevere. The mosaic of Christ and the Virgin, enthroned beneath the hand of God and flanked by saints, was made about 1140. The mosaics lower down between the windows illustrate the life of the Virgin Mary. They were made in the late thirteenth century by the extraordinary medieval artist Pietro Cavallini.

For all we know, these are not the first Christian images of Mother and Child, only the first to survive. It is even possible that the worship of the Virgin Mary is as old as apostolic times. In any case, here, close to the very beginning of her Roman cult, the Virgin is shown as the Virgin of Christmas—as Mother, affectionate and nurturing. Her connection to the divine is a connection so ordinary, so quotidian, so human as to be almost bathetic. Like all mothers, she comforted the child in her arms, offered her breasts to his sucking lips, and wiped his little bum—actions repeated so often that they constituted the most visible and unremarkable work performed in the ancient world (or in ours, for that matter).

This early exaltation of Mother and Child already demonstrates the innovative Christian sense of grace, no longer something reserved for the fortunate few—the emperors and their retinues—but broadcast everywhere, bestowed on everyone, "heaped up, pressed down, and overflowing," even on one as lowly and negligible as a nursing mother. In the words of a famous Latin hymn, "God . . . is born from the guts of a girl."[j] For even the most ordinary people in their most ordinary actions can serve as vessels of God's grace. Though awarding them equal political status with society's leaders would have been unthinkable, their value as persons was newly absolute, for, as even haughty Hildegard understands, "they are all loved by God."

The worship of this Virgin of Virgins culminates in Rome in the magnificent Basilica of Santa Maria in Trastevere, the earliest church dedicated exclusively to Mary (soon after Christianity's legalization in the fourth century), on the site of a remembered miracle, the sudden eruption of a healing fountain of oil at the very moment—or so legend had it—that Jesus was born in Bethlehem. The shimmering twelfth-century mosaic apse of Santa Maria, ornamented with prophets, apostles, saints, and symbolic sheep, gives us at its very center the Throne of Mercy, on which are seated Christ and Mary, welcomed into Heaven after her death by her son, who had preceded her.

Up to this moment, Western art had imitated all the staid solemnities of the Greeks, and it is often impossible for a layman to tell a Roman image from an Eastern ikon. Mary of Trastevere is adorned as a Byzantine empress, elaborately crowned, decked out in golden, bejeweled garments. The gravity of her expression is tempered somewhat by the rounded oval of her face, shown to us not starkly straight-on but in a three-quarters view, turning toward her son. But Jesus is patently Italian, not Greek. The set of his figure, though dignified, is easy, informal, radiating affection. His broad, naked feet are planted solidly on the floor in clear contrast to his mother's dainty slippers. His happy face is close to cartoonish, contented, playful, amused, *capriccioso*, almost mouthing "Mamma"; and since this is a moment of sub-

j The hymn is "Adeste Fideles," composed in the eighteenth century (in a very medieval spirit) by John F. Wade. The full text of the cited quotation is *"Deum de Deo, Lumen de Lumine / Gestant puellae viscera"* (The God of God, the Light of Light / Is born from the guts of a girl). The second line was unfortunately translated in the nineteenth century by Frederick Oakley as "Lo! he abhors not the Virgin's womb."

lime felicity, his right arm is extended across his mother's back, his right hand tenderly cupping her shoulder.

This tremendous movement—the Son of God hugging his earthly mother!—had never been seen before. Hildegard had dreamed of such a thing, calling Christ her "sweetest hugger," but now a visual artist, we don't know who, shows it spectacularly above a pontifical altar. Anatomically, kinetically, instinctively, this is an entirely novel moment in the history of sacred art and the beginning of a characteristically Italian contribution. By this single gesture, Western art is freed from its Eastern enchantment. The long tradition of representing spirit by super-serious faces and two-dimensional, stick-figure human bodies, starved, denatured, aloof, and devoid of movement, is about to give way, as Western Europeans discover a new embodiment, a new earthiness, a new bounce—a new kind of Heaven.

And if saints can hug, so can we.

Europe, a smallish place (at least when compared to the earth's other great landmasses) and hardly a continent at all (attached to great Asia and all but touching sun-baked Africa), has been washed by successive waves of migrants—Celts, Germans, Slavs, Vikings, Arabs, Turks, north Africans—each fresh migration contributing to its intricately interlocking puzzle pieces of small countries and peculiar customs. In the early tenth century, a band of Norwegian Vikings, led by a Dane called Hrolf the Ganger ("Rollo" in subsequent French literature), settled around Rouen in the lower Seine valley. In short order they carved out for themselves a sizable province, henceforth called Normandy—home of the Northmen, or Normans. These tall, straw-haired, cold-eyed, calculating warriors, more adept at battle than any of their neighbors, would soon extend their reach far beyond Normandy.

The Normans would also do something few conquerors had done before them: wholeheartedly adopt the language and customs of their conquered territories. In France they became quintessentially French, in England English (though changing the language of the court from Anglo-Saxon to French and thus lending modern English its rich Franco-Latin vocabulary), in Ireland "more Irish than the Irish themselves." Even before they'd firmly established their dominance over Atlantic Europe—under their talented champion Duke William the Bastard, known after the Norman invasion of England in 1066 as King William I the Conqueror—some Normans were turning their attention eastward. Robert Guiscard (the Crafty) gradually conquered much of Italy and based himself in Sicily, where he adopted the style of a Byzantine emperor. His son Bohemund, a leader of the First Crusade, subdued Antioch in 1098 and there their descendant, Roger II of Sicily, was crowned king in 1130. The Norman genius for organization forged unions from the most unlikely expressions of ethnic diversity—Anglo-Norman, Sicilo-Norman, Normano-Syrian—and everywhere, from the Holy Land to the British Isles, the turreted stone castles of the Normans

still stand as their lasting memorials and the lofty towers of their petitioning cathedrals still reach toward the sky.[k]

If their castles were functional fortresses, in their cathedrals they permitted their imaginations to run riot, for these great churches, the seats
of their bishops, were wild experiments in balance, very nearly the art of
juggling reconceived as architecture. No buildings before or since have
ever defied gravity so bravely and so lastingly. Before the twelfth century,
European ecclesiastical architecture was Romanesque, squat and solid,
dark and gloomy. Despite its many discrete and innocent charms (such as
the apse of Santa Maria in Trastevere), the Romanesque does not tend to
lift one's spirits on a rainy day. The new Norman building, however,
partly inspired by the rediscovery of the amazing texts of Euclid, embod-
ied aspiration—pointed arches and soaring spires, caught in the act of
leaping to Heaven, their movement complemented by immense windows stretching upward, admitting dazzling pools of colored light that
drifted through the church as the sun moved across the sky. Structural
details, such as the ribbed vaulting, conveyed an inner delicacy or, in
the case of the flying buttresses, an inner balletic exuberance, almost an
interior merriment. The sculptural details were orchestral, with elongated saints and angels grouped like massed choristers and instrumentalists on ascending platforms. From various high crooks and corners,
half-hidden demons, hilariously indecent, sniffed the air like beasts or
drooled downward toward their human prey. It was a total rethinking of
human-inhabited space, which was now to be shared with supernatural
reality. In contrast to the multiple cosmic dimensions that flew above
them, the worshipers at ground level (and even
the hierophants who occupied the immense
raised chancel) were barely three-dimensional.

One day this astonishing architecture will be
called "Gothic" (that is, barbaric)—a name that
still sticks to it—by neoclassicists who in their
exclusive love of Palladian building will look
down on everything medieval. It will then take
the medievalists of the nineteenth and early

---

[k] In truth, the
Norman style never quite
caught on in Italy, which
went from Romanesque to
Palladian almost without
the intervening "Gothic"
connection. Famous
exceptions, however,
include Florence's gemlike
Santa Croce and the
splendidly extravagant
Duomo of Milan.

twentieth centuries to restore the reputation of the Norman cathedrals. Of the many scholars, architects, and amateurs who set about this task, none was more eloquent or influential than Henry Adams, grandson of President John Quincy Adams and great-grandson of President John Adams, one of the founders of the American Republic. Henry, who taught at Harvard and can still lay claim to being our most distinguished practitioner of American history, found himself late in life drawn as by a

Cathedral of Notre-Dame, rising above the town of Chartres and called by the art historian Emile Male "the mind of the Middle Ages manifest." The nearer spire, in late Romanesque style, is a restored survival from an earlier cathedral begun in the early eleventh century, whereas the taller spire, in Flamboyant Gothic style, dates to the beginning of the sixteenth century. But the body of the cathedral was built in the late twelfth and early thirteenth centuries and contains the Virgin's Veil, a celebrated relic.

mysterious force to the twelfth and thirteenth centuries, especially to the Norman churches of France and most especially to Notre-Dame de Chartres, the most extraordinarily beautiful of dozens of beautiful French cathedrals of this period dedicated to Jesus's mother. "Most persons of a deeply religious nature," insisted Adams, "would tell you emphatically that nine churches out of ten actually were dead-born, after the thirteenth century."

For Adams, the force behind the art was the Virgin Mary herself—

> the highest energy ever known to man, the creator of four-fifths of his noblest art, exercising vastly more attraction over the human mind than all the steam-engines and dynamos ever dreamed of . . . All the steam in the world could not, like the Virgin, build Chartres. . . . Symbol or energy, the Virgin had acted as the greatest force the Western world ever felt, and had drawn man's activities to herself more strongly than any other power, natural or supernatural, had ever done; the historian's business was to follow the track of the energy. . . .

Which is what we propose to do in this book. In following "the track of the energy," we shall bear in mind at least some of Adams's exclusions: that, for instance, "this energy [is] unknown to the American mind" and that the Virgin "was popularly supposed to have no very marked fancy for priests as such; she was a queen, a woman, and a mother, functions, all, which priests could not perform. Accordingly, she seems to have had little taste for mysteries of any sort, and even the symbols that seem most mysterious [those emblematic of Mary's femininity and motherhood] were clear to every old peasant-woman in her church." A mystery accessible to the humblest.

Nor shall we be unmindful of the vivid descriptions of the construction of Chartres Cathedral as related in a contemporary document, a letter of Archbishop Hugo of Rouen quoted by Adams. "The faithful of our diocese," wrote Hugo, have joined with others much farther afield to transport all necessary materials to the plain of Chartres, where the cathedral will be built. Before participating, each person must have

> been to confession, renounced enmities and revenges, and rec-
> onciled himself with his enemies . . . Powerful princes of the
> world, men brought up in honor and in wealth, nobles, men and
> women, have bent their proud and haughty necks to the harness
> of carts, and, like beasts of burden, they have dragged to the
> abode of Christ these wagons, loaded with wines, grains, oil,
> stone, wood, and all that is necessary for the wants of life or for
> the construction of the church.

All this they—"often a thousand persons and more"—accomplish "in such silence that not a murmur is heard, and truly if one did not see the thing with one's eyes, one might believe that among such a multitude there was hardly a person present." This prayerful, anonymous work— for we lack the name of a single artist or architect who contributed to the enterprise—went on for years, for generations, and involved, as Hugo tells us, "old people, young people, little children," all of whom thought themselves well rewarded by the grand edifice rising in their midst.

We shall especially bear in mind Adams's instruction that Chartres was built as "a child's fancy; a toy-house to please the Queen of Heaven,—to please her so much that she would be happy in it,—to charm her till she smiled." Nor shall we fail to notice that here at Chartres Hildegard's "garden enclosed," her exclusive retreat for virgins, has become—in its aisles and arches, its chapels and crannies, its floating islands of color and pastry-like sculptures, its scores of separate (but con- nected) spaces of theatrical encounter—the playground not only of the popular Virgin Queen of Heaven but of all humanity, nobles and com- mons, "men and women . . . old people, young people, little children," a secret yet universal garden. *"Regina coeli laetare, alleluia!"* goes the an- cient Easter hymn, now given new life in the numberless Norman cathe-

God, affectionately and with great care, fashioning Adam from clay. A twelfth-century sculpture from the north portal of Notre-Dame de Chartres.

Gently elongated prophetic figures—from the left, Isaiah, Jeremiah, Simeon, John the Baptist, and Simon Peter—from the north portal of Chartres Cathedral. The first four are shown as prophets of the Incarnation. Peter, as the first priest of the new order, is dressed as a medieval pope.

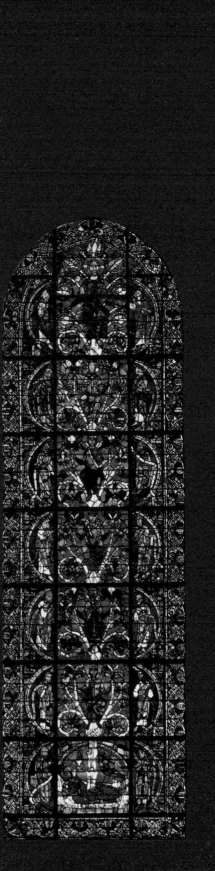

Triptych of stained-glass
lancet windows from the
Royal Portal of Chartres
Cathedral. The window
on the right shows the
ancestors of Jesus, sprung
from the root of Jesse.
The middle window is
a celebration of the
Incarnation, showing
scenes associated with
Jesus's conception, birth,
and early life. The window
on the left depicts the
Passion, Death, and
Resurrection. Needless
to say, the visual stress is
on the Incarnation; and
once again Mary is
centrally honored.

Noah's Ark, symbol of the church surviving through time despite calamities and guided by the dove (or Spirit of God). Scenes below the Ark are of people lost in the Flood, meant to remind the viewer of the consequences of the Last Judgment. Chartres Cathedral.

Twelfth-century masterpiece, Notre-Dame de la Belle-Verrière (Our Lady of the Beautiful Stained Glass), Chartres Cathedral.

drals—Notre-Dame de Chartres, Notre-Dame de Paris, Notre-Dame de Laon, Notre-Dame de Noyon, Notre-Dame de Rheims, Notre-Dame d'Amiens, Notre-Dame de Rouen, Notre-Dame de Bayeux, Notre-Dame de Coutances . . . *presque sans fin*—set aside just for her. "Queen of Heaven, rejoice, alleluia!" In fact, whoop it up like a child set free—through your chancels, choirs, transepts, and naves.

Chartres is replete with images of Mary in sculpture and stained glass, in hidden nooks and wide bays. One in particular has held the attention of millions of pilgrims down the centuries, Notre-Dame de la Belle-Verrière (Our Lady of the Beautiful Stained Glass), a late-twelfth-century window in the choir next to the south transept. "A strange and uncanny feeling seems to haunt this window," wrote Adams. The lines of the face have little in common with the residual severities of the Virgin in the apse of Santa Maria in Trastevere. Instead of light glistening on mosaic tiles, here light shines through colored glass. The self-dramatizing Greco-Italian faces of Trastevere have been replaced by the faces of a sweetly sensible Frenchwoman and her placidly solemn child. But there is continuity in the merriment. Like the Christ of Trastevere, the Virgin Mary smiles, if more broadly. As he was happy to be reunited with his mother, she, a royal but very earthly woman, is even happier to be the mother of her son.

And that is how the vision of a few became the devotion of the many.

TWO

aquitaine and assisi, courts of love

the pursuit of love and its consequences

*Be free in bed, infrequent
in business.*

—ADVICE OF THE EMPRESS MATILDA
TO KING HENRY II, HER SON

S EX HAS NEVER BEEN ABSENT from any age. It rises in heat even if the age views passion as hardly more remarkable than eating and elimination (as did the Greeks), even if the age exalts chastity (as did the medievals), even if the age considers sexual matters beyond polite discussion (as did the Victorians). I would venture that the level of private sexual activity is a constant in the human chronicle and that only our public attitudes toward it change from one era to another. But as we all know, sex and romance are not identical, since sex is available with or without the latter. Romance as a sexual attitude was, in fact, almost unknown before the age of Hildegard.

This may seem, at first, incredible because we have so conjoined the two that it is impossible for our minds to unhook them, but also because we may recall snatches of ancient poetry that have left us with the impression that poets have always been romantics. Weren't Sappho, Ovid, and Catullus of this persuasion? Didn't they write all-consumingly of their love objects as might a modern poet or novelist? Didn't they hurl themselves into the path of their beloved, promising all manner of service, hoping to be permitted to spend an eternity with her? Didn't they mope and despair when rejected?

Yes and no. People have always had sex with one another, whether inside marriage or outside. Since before modern times all marriages were arranged and the betrothed seldom had contact with each other prior to the wedding night, romantic pursuit ending in marriage was impossible. What we may think of as romance in ancient poetry is strictly confined to the occasional extramarital affair, either homosexual, as in Greek Sappho's case, or heterosexual, as in the cases of Ovid and Catullus. But both Roman poets are writing about sexual obsession for a particular woman—which, as we all know, is anything but everlasting. Catullus's passion is for "Lesbia," a pseudonymous married aristocrat, whom he comes to hate; and women in general fare badly in his poems, which are often obscenely degrading. For Ovid, passion is something of a joke; and if we read his *Ars Amatoria* (The Art of Loving) seriously, we miss his meaning. For Ovid's famous work is actually a kind of send-up of self-help books, giving heaps of bad advice to the would-be lover, who is seen to be in the throes of a ridiculous appetite. Ovid's irony becomes undeniable in passages where he lets us in on the joke:

Magna superstitio tibi sit natalis amicae:
    Quaque aliquid dandum est, illa sit atra dies.
Cum bene vitaris, tamen auferet; invenit artem
    Femina, qua cupidi carpat amantis opes.

On her birthday, just be far away—
    no gifts, but fine excuses of all sorts.
She knows the art of taking all she may
    And leaving you with nothing but your shorts.

The love object is a demanding, even a devouring, female, her suitor a temporarily infatuated fool. In the more earnest age of Hildegard, however, *Ars Amatoria* was cherished as a straightforward how-to manual for knightly lovers of lovely women.

The cultural transformations that were coming to bud about the time of Hildegard's birth—in the late eleventh century—and that reached full flower in her lifetime were several and extraordinary. We have already seen examples of two of these: the growing power of women in religious life and the rise of the cult of the Virgin Mary. Like Hildegard, afterwards known as "the Sybil of the Rhine," many other abbesses and female visionaries began to occupy the public imagination in a way they'd never done during the long, hard Dark Ages that had preceded the lighter, more luminous twelfth century. One virgin lady in particular, Mary, formerly peasant girl of Nazareth, now Queen of Heaven, was given so much publicity that she came to overshadow her divine son in popular devotion and ecclesiastical art. It is not so surprising that the cults of such women, whether of flesh and blood or of stone and stained glass, should be especially vibrant in Germanic and Celtic realms, where women in pagan times had held more power than they ever exercised in the Greco-Roman world.

Beyond these transformations, feudalism, the basic medieval socioeconomic system, was evolving rapidly. Feudalism was a complex set of relationships to military service and land ownership. In theory, all land was owned by the sovereign, who bestowed it in "feud" (or "fee," or "fief") on those who had fought (or were pledged to fight) for him in war.[a] The recipient of the king's (or duke's or count's) land was

a Though *feud* and *fief* are medieval words, *feudalism* is a modern term, which has in recent years come to be seen as a conceptual over-simplification of the actual medieval situation—it was, for instance, possible to own freehold property not deeded by the sovereign—but it serves us well enough here.

called a "knight," a word of Germanic origin that meant "boy" but came to accrue the meaning of "servant of the lord" or "vassal." Throughout the Middle Ages it was used to translate the Latin words *miles* (soldier) and *eques* (cavalryman). Only someone at the level of a knight could be properly addressed as "sire" (or "sir") by those beneath him, who were termed "villeins," "churls," or, if female, "wenches."

By the twelfth century, however, many knights were (more or less) landless retainers of the local lord, kept in readiness just in case; and between wars they were left to idle at his court, where women were in short supply. There were, of course, the lord's wife, the well-guarded female members of his family, and their female attendants. But the exceeding number of young, lively, unattached males hanging out in the castle precincts presented something of a challenge. Goneril's description in *King Lear* of her father's retinue, though doubtless exaggerated, paints a vivid picture of the challenge confronting the well-protected courtly family:

> *Here do you keep a hundred knights and squires [attendants to the knights],*
> *Men so disorder'd, so debosh'd and bold,*
> *That this our court, infected with their manners,*
> *Shows like a riotous inn. Epicurism and lust*
> *Makes it more like a tavern or a brothel*
> *Than a grac'd palace.*

The true knight was, of course, far from such scenes. He was imagined in the courtly literature of the Middle Ages as a valiant, questing soul, modest, full of quiet strength, incapable of bragging, though known to be deadly in warfare. Like the "verray parfit gentil knight" of Chaucer's *Canterbury Tales,* he was always one who "loved chivalrye, / Trouthe and honour, fredom and curteisye," the ideal male. It is most relevant, however, that Chaucer, immediately following this portrait, gives us another—of the knight's son the squire, not a lover of chivalry, truth, honor, etc., just "a lovyere, and a lusty bacheler," his clothing em-

broidered as if he were a meadow "Al ful of
fresshe floures, whyte and rede," "Singinge he
was, or floytinge [fluting] all the day; / He was
as fresh as is the month of May." If Chaucer's
knight is shown as the ideal, his son the squire
is portrayed as the more common reality, the
idle frat boy. A well-stocked castle might easily

host a hundred dancing layabouts like this one, "wonderly deliver, and
greet of strengthe," as Chaucer tells us, and "So hote he lovede, that by
nightertale / He sleep namore than dooth a nightingale."

Whether the lord or his lady felt more challenged by this situation
we cannot say for certain, for we have little historical evidence as to how
the next step in social evolution took place. We can say, however, that
what resulted was a culture of adultery—the most mannerly adultery in
history, but adultery nonetheless.

"Any idealization of sexual love," wrote the great medievalist C. S.
Lewis, "in a society where marriage is purely utilitarian, must begin by
being an idealization of adultery." If, as Henry Adams believed, the
Virgin of Virgins was the mysterious dynamo at the heart of the Middle
Ages, extramarital sex was the ordinary electricity. How the two were
connected is by no means obvious; and the attempt by historians to make
a connection has precipitated a dozen theories, revisions, and counter-
theories. What we can claim without cavil is that both the pious worship of the Virgin and the adulterous worship of the lady of the manor
were connected to the general rise in the status of women during this
period. If it is not, on the face of it, evident how widespread adultery
can be connected to the social advancement of

women, it will be, once we have examined the
special rules for adultery invented in the courts
of the twelfth century.

The queen of the castle (or duchess or
countess or dame or lady-in-waiting) was a
prize to be won. Since there were few women

of stature resident at each court, many worthy knights contended for the fair hands and full hearts of the few, all women in arranged marriages with time on their hands and daydreams in their heads. To debauch a virgin was a risky maneuver, one that could lose you life or organ, especially if the fruit of your love became the all-too-visible fruit of her womb. But a married lady, with obscure chambers at her personal disposal and guarded at evening only by female confidantes, could manage even an adulterous pregnancy rather nicely. ("Why, of course, it's yours, my lord!" she replied indignantly. "Haven't you noticed? It looks just like your mother.")

Idle men in barracks (or even in barricaded castles) inevitably invent games for themselves. The twelfth-century game: who is knight enough to win the lady? Athletic talents useful to the soldier were recalibrated for displays of peacetime jousting, tilting, melees, and similar diversions at organized tournaments—bloody, often deadly, affairs that are the origin of our field sports. A knight might enter the lists wearing a delicate flower or bright swatch of cloth, a secret (or not-so-secret) pledge of his vassalage to a certain lady. Furtive strategies of the battlefield were retooled for wooing in gardens by means of stolen glances and in passageways by means of whispered words and clandestine tokens.

It seems most likely that women set the rules of this new game, perhaps after many hours spent poring over vernacular translations of Ovid:

Siquis in hoc artem non novit amandi,
>Hoc legat et lecto carmine doctus amet.
Arte citae veloque rates remoque moventur,
>Arte leves currus: arte regendus amor.

If there is anyone who needs to know
>*The Art of Loving, come along with me.*
It's but a skill—like sailing, riding—so
>*It can be learned in lessons one, two, three.*

It's simple, really—and Ovid, who claimed that Venus had dubbed him *"artifex tenero Amori"* (artist of tender Love), will instruct us all.

We should not think that these courts of love, as they came to be called, were confined to individual strongholds. They were as itinerant as Benedictine monasteries were stable, settling into one castle for a few months or even weeks, moving on to a hunting lodge perhaps, then on to another of the lord's castles, then crashing at the fortress of some lesser lord who was duty-bound to put up the greater lord's whole household, which could number a hundred or more—the lord and his knights, the lord's spouse and her ladies, his councillors and other officials, the steward, the butler, the cooks and kitchen staff, the chamberlain, the treasurer, the bodyguards and others designated to keep order, the clerks, servants, and grooms, a chaplain or two, the packhorses and oxen, carts and wagons. For a king's entourage there would be much additional paraphernalia to be stored (dramatic changes of clothing and jewelry, supplies of parchment and coin) and many additional figures to be housed: a high-ranking constable or marshall, a keeper of the king's seals, and "ushers, huntsmen, horn-blowers, watchmen, guards, archers, men-at-arms, cat-hunters, wolf-catchers, keepers of the hounds, keepers of the royal mews [stables for horses and hawks], keepers of the tents, the chamberlain of the candles, the bearer of the King's bed, the King's tailor, laundresses, including the King's personal washerwoman, and a ewerer, who dried his clothes and prepared the royal bath," in the words of Alison Weir, a biographer of medieval royalty.

Mention of "the royal bath" gives us a clue as to why this large assembly had to keep journeying on. The insoluble medieval problem in the face of such a company was sanitation. Plumbing was unknown; and the tradition of public bathing, though as much a part of the Greco-Roman heritage as plumbing had been, had perished beyond Byzantium. Because individual bathing in a copper basin in a drafty castle could lead so easily to chill, then to fever and death, kings and queens seldom bathed more than once a month, those with neither washerwoman nor ewerer at their command scarcely more than once or twice a year. Despite their silks and linens, their frequent changes of costume, their liberal burning of Arabian incense, the royals stank, as did their retinues. More than this, the chamber pot was the sole device for receiving human waste.[b] A small castle—or even a large one—might become downright uninhabitable after many weeks of residence by such a throng.

When Duncan, an eleventh-century king of Scotland, arrives at the castle of the treacherous Macbeths, he remarks:

> *This castle hath a pleasant seat, the air*
> *Nimbly and sweetly recommends itself*
> *Unto our gentle senses.*

Ah, yes, but after some months of habitation by the king's enormous retinue, "sweet" would not be the adjective that would come nimbly to mind. The clammy castle would need to be vacated for some time so as to be adequately aired. The chaos occasioned by all this to-ing and fro-ing served as an additional aid to the privy assignations of gay ladies with their adoring knights.

The language by which the knight addressed his prey was so reverent that it could be easily mistaken for prayer, even prompting one jolly North-country mistress to set her poetical suitor straight:

> *I'm no the Queen o' Heaven, Thomas,*
> *I never carried my head sae hee,*
> *For I am but a lady gay*
> *Come out to hunt in my follee.*

[b] Some later Norman keeps did have a closet off the lord's bedchamber containing a holed seat atop a descending shaft— accessible at ground level to those whose honor it was to muck out and bury the lord's donations. But I have found no evidence of this improvement prior to the fifteenth century.

This quatrain expertly reverses the dramatis personae of the hunt: it is the lady, not her knight, who does the hunting. The idea of the knight as pursuer was a convenient social construct. He writes the romantic poetry, gives the gifts, and mopes mournfully about, but it is the down-to-

earth lady, smarter and more strategic than he (and even more intent on her "follee"), who secretly controls the pace of the chase, having determined well in advance whether or not the poor devil will get his reward in the end.

As in fact the abundant literature flowing from the courts of love makes clear, the lady is to render conquest as difficult as possible:

> *An easy conquest sells love on the cheap;*
> *a hard one shows the cost of love runs deep,*

instructs Andreas Capellanus, a somewhat plodding late twelfth-century imitator of Ovid, in his best-selling Latin treatise *De Amore* (On Love). Among Andreas's many "rules of love": "It is genuine jealousy that makes the feeling of love grow." So go ahead, torture him.

No one knew the rules better than Eleanor, duchess of Aquitaine, afterwards queen of France, then of England, a courtly lady who played a singular role in the history of her time. She was born in 1122 to a family that reigned not only over Aquitaine but over Gascony, which gave access to the kingdoms of Castile, Navarre, and Aragon (and thence to the delicacies of the Spanish-Muslim south), and over Poitou and its *très riche* capital of Poitiers. The affluent vineyards of Bordeaux lay within the family's domains, as did the lucrative salt flats of Saintonge. At the time, France was still a tiny kingdom, an island of property squeezed between Champagne and Blois, while the dukes of Aquitaine ruled a swath of territories ten times as large. Aquitaine itself was a sunny and fertile land of waters ("Aquitania," as the Romans had named it), dotted with charming red-tiled villages, whitewashed walls, yellow gates, rolling hills, fields of deep green, yellow-green, and velvet brown, prosperous monasteries, and gloriously welcoming castles. Its people, aware of their happy fortune, were easy, attractive southerners known for their good manners. Men, eschewing the usual bowl-top haircut, wore their hair long and

Eleanor's palace at Poitiers. The Maubergeonne Tower to the right,
built by Eleanor's grandfather, housed his mistress Dangerosa.

commonly shaved their faces—a most uncommon sight in the rest of
Europe—and both sexes delighted in fine fabrics and elegant costuming.
A mixture of Basque natives and Roman colonists, they were viewed by
the sterner Franks of the Germanic north as trivial pleasure-seekers.

She was christened Alienore, an elision of the Latin *Alia Aenor*—for
her mother was Aenor and the baby was to be "Another Aenor." She
seems to have set herself the task of becoming anything but a copy of her
unfortunate mother; she would not be another anyone but the world's
first (and for some time only) Eleanor. Granddaughter of William IX,
the world's first romantic poet and a "vehement lover of women,"
Eleanor grew up in a household of extraordinary refinement, where poetry and music were honored and sex and power were prized above all.

The dukes of Aquitaine were distinguished by their violent willful-
ness. Finding himself attracted to the wife of one of his vassals, a woman
aptly named Dangerosa, William IX stole her from her castle at
Châtelleraud and bore her to his palace at Poitiers, installing her during

his wife's absence in his newly built Maubergeonne Tower. When the shocked duchess returned from her charitable enterprises, she engaged the papal legate to do battle on her behalf. William was perennially on the outs with churchmen: he had once drawn his sword in the Cathedral of Saint-Pierre and threatened to behead a bishop in the act of excommunicating him. So the legate's warning of a second such sentence fell on deaf ears; and William swore at the bald man that hair would grow on the legate's head before the duke would return Dangerosa to her meekly silent husband. After his second excommunication, the defiant duke had his paramour's portrait painted on his shield, announcing that "it was his will to bear her in battle as she had borne him in bed," according to a contemporary account by the lively monastic historian William of Malmsbury. The duchess ceded the field and hid herself in Fontevraud Abbey, her favorite nunnery, where she soon died.

Before long, Dangerosa proposed that William's son, William, should be married to her daughter, Aenor. And so it happened—though young William had little love for the woman who had displaced his mother or for her daughter. As heir to his father's ducal lands, however, he had no choice but to bow to the dominatrix's wishes if he did not want to be disinherited. Eleanor was born a year after the wedding, and five years after that William IX was dead, duly succeeded by Eleanor's father, now William X. Three years further on, Aenor died, as did Eleanor's only brother, William Aigret. Eleanor at eight was heiress of Aquitaine.

Her father, a perspicacious man less violent than his father, saw to it that Eleanor was taught the unwomanly art of reading both her own language, the *langue d'oc*[c] (or Provençal, or Old French of the south), and Latin. "Brought up in delicacy and reared with abundance of all delights, living in the bosom of wealth," in the words of a contemporary chronicler, Eleanor loved musical performances, especially the newly harmonized *chansons* and *gai saber* (gay knowledge) of the troubadours—of whom her grandfather had been the first, a sort of knightly Chuck Berry to a younger generation of Beatles and Rolling

[c]   *Langue d'oc* may be contrasted with *langue d'oïl*, the Old French of the north, which became normative. *Oc* and *oïl* are "yes" in each of the two dialects. *Oïl* would eventually be compressed to *oui*.

Stones. Throughout her life she was a patron to singers and instrumentalists, especially those who sang of love and *les chagrins d'amour.*

These performers, still a novelty in Eleanor's girlhood, had exactly the same revolutionary effect on the sensibility of her time that rock music would have on Westerners in the mid-twentieth century. As their elders recoiled in disgust, young people everywhere loosened up and rocked their bodies and their lives to a new beat. In the courts of the south, the new music encouraged the delightfully novel practice of mixed dancing. Whereas dancing had formerly been exclusively homosexual, men performing only with men and women with women, now a knight was taught the art of bowing to a lady, gracefully offering his hand, and gliding forth with her in a series of complicated steps that mimicked the art of courtly wooing.

Before undertaking a pilgrimage for his sins and the sins of his fathers to the shrine of Saint James the Apostle—Santiago de Compostela in northwestern Spain—William summoned all his vassals and commanded them to swear public homage to Eleanor. They came from every corner of the duke's domains and found themselves kneeling before a tall young woman of surpassing beauty—"*perpulchra,*" they described her—a blue-eyed, reddish blonde who carried herself with regal assurance. At thirty-eight, the duke had every intention of returning from pilgrimage, marrying again, and engendering a male heir to carry his legacy. But just to be safe, he made Eleanor a ward of King Louis VI of France, who was nominal overlord to the more powerful William. As part of their agreement, Eleanor was affianced to Louis's son Louis. William's foresight paid off: he never returned from Compostela, dying in the cathedral there after drinking polluted water on his journey. At fifteen, Eleanor was duchess of Aquitaine and Gascony, countess of Poitou, soon to marry the crown prince of France.

Alas for royal marriages, always arranged, seldom satisfying. Louis the Fat—for such was the nickname of Louis VI—became so adipose in his later years that he could no longer rise from his bed. His chief adviser, the brilliant Suger, child of peasants and abbot of Saint-Denis, knew that he would not last much longer. Unfortunately, Louis's heir, Philip, had broken his neck when his horse threw him; the younger son, Louis, who had been meant for the church, was therefore brought out of mothballs and crowned as his father's successor—during his father's lifetime in accordance with French custom. Little Louis would have made a fine monk, but he would make a less impressive king and a husband of dubious value. Less than four months after her father's death, a scarlet-gowned Eleanor and her Louis—he at sixteen just a year older than his wife—were married amid great pomp on a Sunday in late July of 1137 in the cathedral of Saint-André in Bordeaux. Afterwards, as they journeyed north to Paris, they received the news: Louis the Fat had expired; they were king and queen of France.

Eleanor did not admire the Cité, Louis's old Parisian palace, which she found drafty and grim. Very soon her apartments were modernized in the southern manner and redecorated with colorful tapestries from the workshops of Bruges. She introduced tablecloths and napkins and even insisted that her pages wash their hands before serving her dinner. She invited troubadours, *jongleurs,* and theatrical troupes to entertain the court. The courtiers were not amused; they found the emotions expressed in the words of the south to be downright scandalous. It would take another generation before these northerners would succumb to the sensual delights of this *nouvelle vague.* Though Louis seems to have been unimpressed by all her innovations, he loved his wife "almost beyond reason," in the words of John of Salisbury, later bishop of Chartres and an astute commentator.

Someone in whom the troubadours found a responsive listener was Eleanor's younger sister, Petronilla, who soon commenced a steamy affair with Count Raoul of Vermandois, a married man thirty-five years her senior. In an unrelated move, Louis refused to allow the pope's candidate to take his seat as archbishop of Bourges, which impelled the pope to impose an interdict on Louis's household, which meant that no member of the household could receive the sacraments of the church till the interdict was lifted. Not only could no masses be offered for the benefit of the living and the dead, but no marriages could be celebrated, no confessions heard, and neither communion nor anointing could be given to those in danger of death. They must face their deaths unshriven, unreconciled, most likely damned, nor could their bodies be buried with funeral rites in consecrated ground; and babies who perished without baptism must face the same unceremonious damnation.ꝺ This was rough justice, to say the least, and for the pious Louis a tragic reversal.

ꝺ The doctrine of Limbo, the happy yet sad "borderland" of Heaven (*limbo* being early Italian for "hem" or "border") where the souls of unbaptized infants must stay forever, never having been washed clean enough to enjoy the sight of God himself, will not be introduced as a possible alternative to the Augustinian damnation of unbaptized infants till the teaching of Thomas Aquinas in the thirteenth century, when eternity in Limbo will be grasped at as a vast improvement over going to Hell. The modern Catholic Church, embarrassed by its own teaching, has been mum about Limbo since 1951, when Pius XII, perhaps already a bit dotty, referred to it in an inane address to midwives. The doctrine (which presupposes a cruel God, though not one as cruel as the pre-Thomistic model) has become quietly inoperative. It was lately referred by the current pope to a committee, where it is no doubt meant to suffer the final theological indignity—death by committee.

As if this were not misfortune enough, Raoul succeeded in having his marriage annulled by three suborned bishops, who then proceeded to solemnize his marriage to Petronilla. But Raoul's castoff wife was not without defenders, especially her powerful brother, Count Theobald of Champagne, who brought her case to the pope. The pope suspended the three offending bishops, excommunicated the lovers, and laid their lands under interdict. Louis, who felt his manhood threatened, marched an army into Champagne and surrounded the town of Vitry-sur-Marne, which lay in the shadow of one of Theobald's castles. The town was burned to the ground by the flaming arrows of Louis's army, and more than a thousand innocents— children, women, the elderly and infirm—who had taken refuge in the cathedral died by fire. Louis could never afterwards forget the smell of burning flesh and the screams of the hopeless victims.

None of Louis's aggressive initiatives, whether against church or Champagne, were sanctioned by Abbot Suger, canny adviser to the elder Louis, who suddenly found his sage advice unheeded and unwelcome. Weir suggests that Eleanor had become young Louis's chief adviser and was urging him to cut a more dashing figure on the international scene. This is certainly what Bernard of Clairvaux surmised. The intimidating ascetic, who would in this same decade of the 1140s champion the writings of Hildegard, was nonetheless no friend to women, especially to women of the world beyond the reach of the cloister's severities. For Eleanor, whom he met, he had nothing but scorn and suspicion. Carefully noting her regal bearing, her high chin, her stately (or, as Bernard said, "mincing") step, and all the particulars of the fashion in which she was dressed—the lined silk, the flowing sleeves, the bright colors, the fur, the bracelets, the earrings, the headdress, the diadem—he reached the conclusion that she was "one of those daughters of Belial," a biblical name for Satan. "Fie on a beauty that is put on in the morning and laid aside at night! The ornaments of a queen have no beauty like the blushes of natural modesty that color the cheeks of a virgin." Virgins good; queens bad; women who make themselves sexually desirable, certainly one of a queen's chief duties, daughters of the Devil. Bernard's approach may be said to have the stark virtue of simplicity, but the truth is he was terrified of real women, especially one like Eleanor who, perfumed and painted, dared look him straight in the eye and speak as if addressing any other subject.

Though he continued to love his wife, Louis, full of guilt over the atrocities committed by his army in Champagne, fell more and more under the influence of monks like Bernard, even dressing like a monk himself, fasting, wearing a torturous hairshirt against his skin, and spending many hours on his knees in prayer. Eleanor, widely described as the most beautiful woman of her time, dressed ever more splendidly and, now in her twenties, grew restless with her role as queen of France and childless wife to Louis. She had had more engagement (and more fun) in the short time she had ruled alone as duchess of Aquitaine.

Bernard and Suger managed to patch up the quarrel between Louis and Theobald and prevailed upon Louis to set aside his opposition to the pope's choice for archbishop of Bourges, so that the interdict could be lifted. In time, as part of a shrouded quid pro quo, the pope recognized Petronilla's irregular marriage, awarding Raoul the same annulment that the three suspended bishops had once given: Raoul and his first wife were third cousins, which was considered by the church to be a consanguinous relationship too close for marriage. Marriage law is one of the most notorious arcana of the medieval church. Since so many European nobles and royals were related, it was relatively easy to discover after the fact some sort of "consanguinous relationship," however attenuated, that could nullify a marriage and leave the partners free. This Divorce Medieval–Style, though useless to ordinary people (who hadn't the financial resources or the influence to pursue their cases in church courts), was a great help to the leading families of Europe in their ever-shifting alliances.[e]

In the course of the extended melodrama of the Petronilla affair, Bernard raised an issue no one had voiced before: Louis and Eleanor were third cousins. Why was Louis so contemptuous of Raoul's first marriage when the same standard could be applied against his own? Louis paid no heed, but Eleanor was transfixed.

In 1145, some eight years after their Bordeaux nuptials, Eleanor gave birth to their first child, a daughter named Marie. Marie could not inherit the throne of France as her mother had inherited Aquitaine, Gascony, and Poitou, for the Salic law of Charlemagne and his successors, still in force in France, excluded females from dynastic succession;[f] but she would one day become Marie de Champagne, "the joyous and gay countess, the light of Champagne," and a famous patron of poets. On Christmas Day in the year of Marie's birth, Louis revealed to his assembled vassals that he

[e] This was why Henry VIII of England in the sixteenth century felt so put upon when a pope refused to annul his marriage to Catherine of Aragon on the grounds of incest-by-marriage (Catherine having been previously married to Henry's since-deceased brother). After all, he wasn't even demanding special treatment.

[f] The "Salic law" may have been only a latter-day concoction by jurists, determined to keep a woman from ruling them, but it was widely believed to be inviolable.

would, at the urging of the new pope, Eugene III, and of the pope's mentor Bernard of Clairvaux, "take the Cross," that is, lead the Second Crusade to further the "liberation" of the Holy Land from "the Crescent"—the Muslims. The initial announcement met with few cheers, since the vassals viewed Louis as something less than a leader of men and rightly suspected that the king's new undertaking was for him a further form of penance rather than an adventure of conquest.

The First Crusade, preached by the wily Pope Urban II in 1095, had proved a roaring success, capturing Edessa, Antioch, and Jerusalem for Western forces and shedding the blood of countless combatants and not a few noncombatants, including communities of Jews the crusaders encountered along their way. The surviving crusaders (as well as the ones who did not survive, for that matter) were buoyed in their conviction that the pope had promised Christian participants a plenary indulgence, erasing all their sins and rendering them Heaven-ready. Pope Eugene now promised no less; and Bernard's eloquence lent an aura of sacred destiny to the mustering of troops across the ancient realms of Charlemagne. In a departure from previous tradition, Eleanor enthusiastically announced that she too would take the Cross, which brought many of her vassals, personally loyal to Eleanor, to her side, increasing considerably the army's muscle. As, impelled by Bernard's tireless voice, the coming crusade began to sound its drumroll of historical inevitability, enormous numbers of men and not a few women in French- and German-speaking lands joined up, red and black crosses pinned to their clothing, shouting *"Deus vult!"* (God wills it!) and "To Jerusalem!" as they set out southeastward across Europe.

Louis's vassals, however, had had the right reaction in the first place. For all its fiery rhetoric and holy panoply, the Second Crusade turned quickly into an anarchic mess and, finally, an unmitigated disaster. It is an axiom of history—which it would reward contemporary politicians to consider—that few human endeavors prove as pointless as projects of religiously inspired military idealism unaccompanied by worldly understanding, strategic thoughtfulness, and common sense.

The German army was under the command of the reluctant emperor Conrad III, who had been shamed by Bernard into participating. On their way to the Holy Land, the Germans made permanent enemies of the Orthodox Greeks—for whom all Catholic Europeans were (and still are) "Franks"—by senselessly pillaging, burning, raping, and murdering as they marched. In battles against the Turks, however, nine-tenths of them were slaughtered. The remaining Germans straggled home, their emperor sliced by head wounds—which caused Louis to weep when he saw them.

The French, constantly harrassed by Turks over rough, unfamiliar terrain, made it to Antioch, then to Jerusalem, both cities still under the Western dominion imposed by the First Crusade. Louis, fasting in preparation for his entry into the Holy City, burst into tears of joy on first glimpsing the turreted walls of Jerusalem. He never came near achieving his main objective, to restore crusader dominion to Edessa, which had been overrun by Turks. He never even came near Edessa. The French did attack Damascus, till then a Muslim city friendly to the crusader states, and were ignominiously routed. In their many quixotic maneuvers, led by their oft-fasting, oft-weeping king, they were hardly helped by the need to protect the large numbers of noncombatant women and clergy who accompanied them, along with the many chests of costly robes, precious jewelry, and sacred vessels the noncombatants deemed necessary to their progress. By the end of the crusade, however, few gowns remained to the ladies, and even some bishops were forced to go barefoot. The French battlefield losses, though not as immense as the German, were great, the losses from hunger, plague, and accidental death even greater. More than three thousand French troops, lured by the first wholesome meal they'd had in months, remained behind and converted to Islam.

By crusade's end something had gone badly wrong between the royal couple. They were no longer speaking to each other and were seldom seen together. It was said that Eleanor had spent far too much time in the agreeable company of her uncle Raymond of Poitiers, the athletic ruler of Antioch. Prince Raymond had wanted the French to attack

Aleppo before going on to Edessa—which would have been a better plan and would also have greatly shored up Antioch's defenses. Eleanor pressed Raymond's plan on Louis, who was already hot under the collar about his wife's endless meetings with her uncle, "taller, better built, and more handsome than any man of his time," according to a contemporary witness. When Louis voiced his pilgrim desire to visit Jerusalem before heading for Edessa, Eleanor said that in that case she would remain as Raymond's guest at Antioch, along with her vassals—which would have crippled any further military effort on Louis's part. Wounded in spirit, Louis threatened to remove Eleanor by force, at which point "she mentioned their kinship, saying it was not lawful for them to remain together as man and wife," in the account of John of Salisbury.

Louis did remove Eleanor by force and drag her to Jerusalem; and from that time forward she seems to have had as little as possible to do with her husband. As far as hard facts go, we have almost no more information. We can, as everyone did at the time and everyone has done since, speculate about what was going on between them. There can be little doubt that Eleanor had tired of Louis and that she had for some time played with the idea of the "consanguinous relationship" as a convenient excuse for ending their marriage. Whether or not she had an affair with her uncle—who was but ten years her senior—his manly vigor must have made a vivid contrast to Louis's weepy pieties and may have clinched her determination to have done with the king. If she did have an affair with Raymond, it is unlikely to have been her first.

The sexual carryings-on of European royalty were as fascinating to the chronicling clerk-clerics of the twelfth century as are the similar carryings-on of today's celebrities to our own clerisy, whom we call journalists. We have a story from Giraldus Cambrensis (Gerald the Welshman), which he claims to have had from the sainted lips of Bishop Hugh of Lincoln, that Eleanor, even before the Second Crusade was launched, had managed a discreet pas de deux with the ambitious, overreaching Count Geoffrey of Anjou. Giraldus, a waspish gossip and first-class suck-up, is nonetheless generally accurate when it comes to royal peccadilloes. We know from John of Salisbury that Louis, in despair over Eleanor's cold stubbornness, consulted his court eunuch, Thierry Galan (bad choice, Louis!), whom Eleanor loathed, and that it was the eunuch who urged Louis to use force on his wife to avert "lasting shame to the kingdom of the Franks."

Eleanor's life would prove a long one, far too full of adventure and incident for us to follow adequately in one chapter. Here I would wish only to give some essential information on what happened to her next and then take a look at how she exemplifies certain trends of her time. What, finally, was the role of this unusual woman in an age of virginal saints?

Eleanor dumped Louis, though not immediately. A smart cookie, she knew to bide her time and give the appearance of growing anxiety over the possible moral (and therefore eternal) consequences of their "incestuous" union. If their marriage was no marriage in the eyes of God, it could—horrid thought!—result in their damnation, could it not?

Both Louis and Eleanor, crossing the Mediterranean on different ships of the same fleet, had much trouble reaching safe harbors, Louis somewhere in Calabria, Eleanor—after months of being blown about— at Palermo. The royal couple, then reunited after their long separation, journeyed north to visit the pope at Frascati, south of Rome, where he kept a palace. There Eugene acted as marriage counselor, hearing each side's complaints and even personally setting up a sort of marriage bower—an alluringly decorated bedchamber, hung with precious silks— where he ordered the pair to resume relations. If from the perspective of the twenty-first century this fussing about with bed linens seems an odd activity for a pope, it may be said that Eugene was no disinterested third party. Urged on no doubt by the Abbot Suger's dynastic preoccupations, he was also acting as the Catholic Church has always acted, preferring large political units to small, intending in this case to prevent the dissolution of the union of Eleanor's vast inheritance with the kingdom of France. Eleanor, realizing she had been outflanked, kept her own counsel and gave in to the pope's coaxing, becoming pregnant in the process.

The issue was a second daughter, Alix, a crushing disappointment to the king, who needed a male heir. After nearly a decade and a half of marriage, his hope of a son was fading. He began to find the idea of an annulment more attractive.

Eleanor, meanwhile, had met the man she intended to have as her second husband: Henry of Anjou, eleven years her junior, who would inherit Anjou, Le Maine, and Normandy from his father and had good reason to believe he might claim England as an inheritance from his mother, the *très formidable* Matilda, formerly empress of Germany. The red-haired Henry had the face of a lion, the body of a bull, and the voice of a crow. A natural leader, he possessed, according to the Anglo-Norman Walter Map, a favorite clerk of Henry's, a countenance "upon which a man might gaze a thousand times, yet still feel drawn to." A great horseman and huntsman, a man of gargantuan squalls of temper, who was never quiet and "shunned regular hours like poison," he had all the energy and passion that Louis lacked. His much-feared anger could sometimes be averted by wit, for Henry himself had an impish sense of humor and loved a good joke. Yet he was also an educated man who enjoyed reading, especially the stories of King Arthur and Camelot, then coming into vogue. That he was rumored to be Satan's spawn—as a scion of the house of Anjou, which according to legend was descended from the Devil's daughter—may only have increased his attraction in Eleanor's eyes.

In late summer of 1151, they met in Paris, whither Henry had come, after threatening Louis with war, to pay grudging ceremonial homage to the French king and formally receive back his inheritance of Normandy, over which Louis reigned as nominal overlord. Bernard of Clairvaux, now old and ill, had stepped in to arrange a truce. In their first meeting, Eleanor, at the acme of her grace, and Henry, pulsing with adolescent energy, fixed each other with "unchaste eyes," according to Map. Henry's father, Geoffrey the Fair, forbade his son to have anything to do with the queen because she was, after all, the wife of his overlord and, well . . . "because he had known her himself"—according to the gossipy Giraldus, who turns up his nose at "these copulations."

Suger's death earlier that year had deprived Louis of his most devoted adviser, one skilled in all the chess moves of power and a wise interpreter of every intrigue. More in the dark than ever, Louis at last gave way to Eleanor's insistent requests and agreed to seek the annulment she so desired in the same month that Henry's father, Geoffrey, died suddenly, making Henry duke of Anjou, Le Maine, and Normandy. A synod of archbishops, duly constituted, dissolved the royal marriage the Friday before Holy Week in 1152. The sole ground was consanguinity. With holy Bernard as go-between, even Pope Eugene gave his consent. The two princesses—Marie then six or seven, Alix not yet two—were found to be legitimate (because their parents had entered into marriage in good faith) and were made wards of their father. Both king and queen were present at the synod. After taking their leave, they would never see each other again, nor is there any record of a further meeting between Eleanor and either of her daughters, not that she had ever seen much of them before this parting of the ways.

Eleanor, having escaped the gray-stone north and now at her capital of polychrome Poitiers to celebrate Easter, happily recommenced single rule of all her dower territories, given back to her under the stipulations of the annulment. Straightaway, she sent a message to Henry informing him of the annulment and praying him to ride out immediately and marry her. On Pentecost Sunday, less than two months after receiving her annulment, Eleanor, the wealthiest woman in Europe, was wed to Henry, count of Anjou, Le Maine, and Normandy, who was already planning his invasion of England. The ceremony, though celebrated in the Cathedral of Saint-Pierre at Poitiers, was a hastily arranged affair, having "neither the pomp nor the circumstance befitting their rank," according to the tut-tutting authors of the *Chronicle of Touraine*. By uniting their continental possessions, this medieval power couple now held sway over nearly half of today's France, dwarfing and fairly engulfing Louis's Lilliputian kingdom.

When Louis recovered from his extreme shock at hearing the news, he realized he had been blindsided by Eleanor. Since both she and Henry were Louis's vassals and had no business marrying without his permission (and since they were related just as closely as he and Eleanor), Louis summoned the offending pair to his presence to explain themselves. When he received no reply, Louis marched into Normandy at the head of a small army that included noblemen who had quarrelled with Henry. In little more than a month, Henry defeated the king's forces and, having made himself undisputed strongman of Europe, turned his attention once more to the matter of England, which, after a small war and some negotiations, was settled to his satisfaction.

On December 19, 1154, in Westminster Abbey, Henry and Eleanor were crowned king and queen of England by the archbishop of Canterbury amid the general rejoicing of their subjects, who rightly saw in Henry an unswerving leader who would bring them peace and prosperity. In less than a score of years, Eleanor would bear Henry eight children, five of them male—seeming to ensure the succession of Henry's line, which would become known as the Plantagenets.[9] Eleanor's relationship to her children by Henry, especially to the boys, was much closer than had been her relationship to her daughters by Louis. The Plantagenets' first child, however, was dead within three years of his birth, and two other males, Young Henry and Geoffrey, would die while still in their twenties. Henry would take care that his daughters made good marital alliances, Matilda with the powerful duke of Saxony and Bavaria, Eleanor with the king of Castile, and Joanna with the king of Sicily. (After her first husband's death and Henry's, Joanna would marry the count of Toulouse, a man of harrowing violence.) Only two of the male children would survive long enough to occupy the English throne after Henry, Richard Coeur de

[9] It was Henry's father, Geoffrey the Fair, son of Fulk the Quarrelsome, who was responsible for giving the name Plantagenet to his line on account of a broom flower (*planta genista* in Latin), that he wore jauntily in his hatband.

Lion (or Lionheart), who would die in 1199, and John Softsword, the youngest of the children, who would succeed Richard and reign till 1216. Despite the early deaths, the children of Eleanor and Henry would produce thirty-four legitimate grandchildren.

But the Plantagenets were no Brady Bunch. As many observers noted, there was palpable electricity between the young king and his queen. They had, after all, chosen each other, the first married couple in recorded history to have managed to do so; and though Henry remained pleased with Eleanor for many years, it took him little time to resume his bits on the side. By the time Eleanor was done with childbearing, Henry had entered into his most buzzed-about adultery—with "Fair" Rosamund de Clifford, the barely pubescent daughter of one of his most loyal Norman knights. As years sped by, the poets of England, France, and Germany wrote ever more extravagant praise of Eleanor's beauty:

> *If all the world were mine*
> *From the seashore to the Rhine,*
> *That price were not too high*
> *To have England's queen lie*
> *Close in my arms,*

goes the anonymous Latin of *Carmina Burana,* a celebrated collection of student songs composed in Germany in this period. But the only arms Eleanor had wanted round her were Henry's; and the love of this peculiar man, not the predictable praise of poets, was what she had hoped for. Despite her disappointment, there is no evidence she was ever unfaithful to Henry. After many years of inevitably cooling relations, however, she did turn against him.

From 1168 onward, Eleanor lived apart from her husband. The separation served Henry's administrative requirements well, Eleanor watching over his continental realms while he continued to put his governing impress on England, which had been badly administered before his accession, though it was also true that Henry never stayed anywhere for long and was constantly, or so it seemed, flying back and forth across the Channel. As their sons reached manhood, Henry bestowed titles and inheritances on them but kept changing the terms and retained all real power for himself, leaving the sons resentful and in the dark as to his ultimate dynastic intentions. In 1173, at Eleanor's urging, the three eldest living sons (John alone being too young to participate) rode to Paris, where they sought alliance with Louis for the purpose of bringing their father's reign to an end. Their intention was to use the armies of France and of their mother's vassals to carve up England, Normandy, and their mother's dower territories among the three of them. Louis, who began to refer to Henry as "the former King of the English," was delighted to sign on.

The ensuing war was hard fought on both sides, the sons "laying waste their father's [continental] lands on every side with fire, sword, and rapine," in the words of Ralph of Diceto, dean of Saint Paul's Cathedral, London, and a most conscientious historian. But Louis, who took command of his side, was no better at war than he'd ever been; and as Henry bore down upon him, "like a bear whose cubs have been stolen," according to Ralph, Louis found it wise to sue for peace. "Thus the mighty learned that it was no easy task to wrest Hercules's club from his hand," commented Richard FitzNigel, bishop of London and Henry's treasurer. The peace was a wobbly one, however, and would remain so for the rest of Henry's life. Though Henry forgave with fatherly magnanimity "his sons whom he loved so much" (Ralph's phrase), he could never again trust them; and they continued to smolder with resentment.

Eleanor's fate was unique. In the course of the familial hostilities, she fled her headquarters at Poitiers and, disguised as a man and brazenly riding astride her horse, was intercepted on her way to Paris. She was turned over to Henry and made his prisoner—and so she would remain for sixteen years, till Henry's death in 1189. For a long time, no one even knew where she was; and it was hardly in the king's interest to announce the site of her captivity. At any rate, public opinion now turned decisively against Eleanor. From time immemorial royal sons had rebelled against their fathers. In the Bible itself one reads of the uprising of the beloved ingrate Absalom against David, the greatest of Israel's kings. But never in any chronicle had a royal wife turned on her husband. Eleanor's betrayal was as unique as would be her punishment.

She was kept under lock and key in various bleak fortresses, usually at Sarum or Winchester, where she was closely watched by men the king knew to be completely trustworthy. Allowed but one personal servant, she was assigned a tiny allowance for her few needs. Though never abused, there was no doubt she was the king's prisoner. He hated her, in the account of Giraldus the gossipy celibate, and imprisoned her "as a punishment for the destruction of their marriage," while he "returned incorrigibly to his usual abyss of vice." More likely, he feared her indomitable will and felt far more capable of limiting his young sons than of confining Eleanor's activities, were he to set her free.

We know little of her life during these years. She was permitted few correspondents and almost no visitors, not even her sons, and the chroniclers fall silent about her, having no news to chew on. Eleanor had become a nonperson. Henry did toy with the possibility of seeking an annulment and proposed that the queen be vowed as a nun at Fontevraud Abbey in Poitou, her favorite monastic foundation, the very place her grandmother had sought refuge when displaced by Dangerosa. Henry even offered to have Eleanor made abbess. She declined him frostily and smuggled a message to the archbishop of Rouen, in whose diocese Fontevraud was situated, that she required his help, for Henry was attempting to force her into the convent. She would rather be Henry's prisoner than God's. And so she stayed.

Four years into her imprisonment, Louis, her first husband, died, leaving his personal wealth to the poor. He was succeeded on the French throne by Philip II, his son by Adela of Champagne, his second wife; and Louis's body, dressed in his monk's habit, was exhibited to the people of Paris in the old nave of Notre-Dame. Six years later, Eleanor's oldest surviving son, Young Henry, died in the midst of a war in Aquitaine against his brother Richard, who now became King Henry's heir apparent.

Before his death, Young Henry with deep emotion confessed his sins against his father and his brother and, like Louis, gave his wealth to the poor. His last request was to his father that he show mercy to Eleanor and set her free.

The queen received the news of the death with tranquility, telling her messenger that she already knew that her son was dead, having seen him in a dream. She described her dead son with two crowns above his head, one the crown he had worn in life, the other a crown "so pure and resplendent" that it could signify only "the wonder of everlasting joy. This second crown was more beautiful than anything which can manifest itself to our senses here on earth. As the Gospel says, 'Eye hath not seen, nor ear heard, neither have entered into the heart of Man, the things which God hath prepared for them that love Him.' "

It is actually Paul's First Letter to the Corinthians, not the gospel, that Eleanor is quoting. And though Paul, adopting phrases from the prophets Isaiah and Jeremiah, is speaking of the revelation entrusted to the first Christians, medieval Christendom took his words as reference to the unearthly joys that will come to the faithful Christian after death. But it must be admitted that the queen's words, composed, reflective, even visionary in a Hildegardian manner, suggest a new Eleanor.

And now, because of the unsettled political situation on the continent, Henry needed her once more—to assert her right of ownership over certain properties the new French king was claiming and to quiet the continuing tension between their remaining sons and between the sons and their father. So Eleanor, still closely guarded, was allowed a trip to the continent. From this time forward, Henry would permit Eleanor more freedom of movement, though she was still in custody and would never again reside with him. "What he and Eleanor now achieved," remarks Weir, "was a working, mutually beneficial relationship designed to preempt any resentment against the king on the part of their sons for the way in which he had treated her."

Eleanor, more practical than ever and casting aside whatever resentment she may have harbored, was happy to serve as mediatrix of familial

peace. But it may not be too much to say that during her ten-year imprisonment she had, like so many long-term prisoners for whom the
press of daily events is no longer meaningful, reached an inner peace that
could not be taken from her. Certainly, there was no longer any hint of
scheming on her part. She did refuse to be part of Henry's plan to deprive Richard, her favorite, of her inheritance, which had been previously settled on him. But Henry was always reorganizing the territories
to be awarded his sons according to whatever humor was on him—
which made them all nervous as cats. For daring to gainsay her lord once
more (though more circumspectly than she had ever done before), she
was imprisoned again. But soon she would be given a role that only she
could play and that no one could have foreseen.

The sons continued to scheme, however, their ranks reduced in the
summer of 1186 by the death of Geoffrey, trampled at a melee in Paris,
where he had gone to plot with King Philip. For a while, Philip and
Richard became extremely chummy, sleeping together in the same bed
and dining from the same plate; and Richard was betrothed to Philip's
sister Alys. In the autumn of 1187, the Turks captured Jerusalem. By
January, Henry, Philip, and Richard had all taken the Cross and committed themselves to regaining the Holy City in what would become the
Third Crusade. But no one left for the East, as the intermittent, low-
level war between England and France proceeded apace, the French king
now assisted by Richard. Henry's once-secure territories of Anjou,
Le Maine, and Touraine began to desert to the French banner; and
Philip's forces even captured Le Mans, where Henry had been born.

"Oh, God," cried the ailing monarch, now old, fat, gray, and no
longer invincible. "Thou hast vilely taken away the city I loved best on
Earth! I will pay Thee back as best I can. I will rob Thee of the thing
Thou lovest best in me, my soul!" Forced to accept terms and even to
bestow the kiss of peace on Richard's cheeks, Henry continued to ful-
minate, croaking at his son, "God grant that I may not die till I have had
a fitting revenge on you."

"Why should I worship Christ?" Henry, no longer able to walk or ride and carried by litter, croaked hoarsely to the sky as he departed the peace parley. "Why should I deign to honor him who takes my earthly honor and allows me to be ignominiously confounded by a mere boy?" But that night, at the urging of the archbishop of Canterbury, he confessed his sins and received absolution. The next morning, he attended mass, as he had every day of his life, and received communion. But that day, he also received a fatal blow: he was informed that John, his youngest and favorite son, whom he had always counted as his ally, had been with Richard all along. As he descended into delirium, Henry muttered repeatedly, "Shame, shame on a conquered king." On July 6, 1189, Henry II, surely one of the best monarchs the English ever had, died, attended only by the faithful Geoffrey, one of his bastards.

The difficult Richard was now king—and Eleanor at sixty-seven was free, free as she had never been before. From the continent, Richard sent the trusted Plantagenet servant William Earl Marshal to England to end the queen's captivity and ask her to act as monarch in his absence. She reigned with such sagacity that when in September Richard arrived for his coronation and barred all women from the event, Ralph of Diceto tells us that "the earls, barons, and sheriffs" of England demanded that Eleanor be present. Her rehabilitation was complete.

After bleeding England dry to finance his crusade, Richard embarked for the Holy Land, leaving his mother in charge of all his European territories. She had much work on her hands, for John was not idle in stirring the pot and attempting to take away lands from his absent brother. But according to one chronicler, the old queen was "determined, with every fibre of her being, to ensure that faith would be kept between her younger sons, so that their mother might die more happily than had their father." With tenacity she kept John in England when all he wished to do was sail to the continent where he could more easily claim territory with the aid of Philip, who was now willing to move against his old friend Richard because Richard, discovering that his father had slept for years with Philip's sister Alys, was dragging his feet about marrying her.

The Third Crusade was blighted by the death by drowning of Frederick Barbarossa, whose participation might have greatly improved the outcome. Returning from the Holy Land after a series of disappointing engagements—in which he captured a couple of cities but could not get near Jerusalem—Richard was taken prisoner outside Vienna by Duke Leopold of Austria, a man of mountainous pride whom Richard had mortally insulted in the course of the crusade. Triumphantly, Leopold refused to free Richard or even to divulge his whereabouts. It took more than a year for Eleanor to win Richard his liberty, as she badgered emperor, pope, and anyone who might be able to bring pressure on Leopold. Her letters to the new pope, the aged and spineless Celestine III, are masterpieces of canoodling, threat, and innuendo:

> For the Prince of the Apostles still rules and reigns in the Apostolic See, and his judicial rigor is set up as a means of resort. It rests with you, Father, to draw the sword of Peter against these evildoers, which for this purpose is set above peoples and kingdoms. The Cross of Christ excels the eagles of Caesar, the sword of Peter is a higher authority than the sword of Constantine, and the Apostolic See higher than the imperial power.

Eleanor adopts this wheedling tone because she is trying to get Celestine to excommunicate the emperor, Leopold's overlord. Celestine had a clear right to do so, for Leopold, with the emperor's connivance, had broken the so-called Truce of God by which no European monarch was allowed to take advantage of a crusader during his absence from his realm. He was not permitted, for instance, either to invade another sovereign's territory or to imprison him. Without this papal mechanism, no sovereign would have been willing to go on crusade in the first place. But Celestine, palsied with anxiety, could not bring himself to make a move.

Besides having the full-time task of negotiating Richard's release, Eleanor was regent of England, which she contrived to rule "with great wisdom and popularity," becoming in the process "exceedingly re-spected and beloved" by her subjects, in the words of the fine thirteenth-century historian Matthew Paris.[b] Among her less agreeable tasks was keeping in line her sneaky son John, who saw a great opportunity in Richard's imprisonment and even put out the rumor that his brother had died in captivity.

On March 12, 1194, after submitting to a humiliating and extor-tionate settlement in Austria with the treacherous Leopold, Eleanor and Richard landed in England, Richard for the first time in five years. In two months' time, however, they would depart their well-run country for the continent, in order to counter Philip, who had occupied Richard's lands in Normandy. Neither the king nor the queen mother would ever return to the island kingdom.

Eleanor ended her days as a nun at Fontevraud Abbey, having taken the veil she once refused. But her religious vows were made eight years after she and Richard sailed from Portsmouth to Barfleur on their last voyage across the Channel, two years before her own death at eighty-two. The eight years before she cloistered herself were among the most active of her life, getting Richard out of trouble with an uncompromis-ing new pope—the fearless Innocent III—rescuing her daughter Joanna from the clutches of Joanna's second husband, arranging retribution against rebellious vassals, fielding armies against Philip (and her own up-start grandson Arthur of Brittany), gladly granting charters to the freshly independent cities of her realms, crossing the Pyrenees to arrange a marriage between her granddaughter Blanche of Castile and Philip's son and heir as part of a new pact of peace between Philip and the Plantagenets.

Her worst ordeal during these years had little to do with travel, war, or policy. It was to mourn the deaths of two more of her chil-dren. Her first child by Henry had died long ago in 1156, Young Henry in 1183, Geoffrey in

[b] Matthew Paris, though generally reliable, is hardly inerrant. His *Chronica Majora* contains the harrowing narrative of the murder of Little Hugh of Lincoln by his Jewish neighbors, one of the first literary instances of the medieval "blood libel" against the Jews.

1186, Matilda in 1189, Eleanor's daughters by Louis, Alix and Marie, in 1198. The abused Joanna died in childbirth in 1199, and Richard Lionheart died in the same year of a suppurating arrow wound received in a minor skirmish. (He asked to be buried in Fontevraud at his father's feet in reparation for having risen against him.) Only two of her ten children, Eleanor, queen of Castile and mother of Blanche, and John, Henry's favorite but certainly not Eleanor's, would survive their mother. Though she had long ago given up all rights to her daughters by Louis, she seems to have tried mightily to be a proper mother to her children by Henry and even to Berengaria, the sweet-tempered, abandoned wife of her son Richard, whom he had wed after decisively rejecting Alys of France. Her service to the desperate Joanna, who took the veil at Fontevraud just before dying, and her admiration for Joanna's courage and spiritual intensity in her last hours may have been what prompted Eleanor's own belated vocation.

There can be no question, however, that Richard's death was a blow from which Eleanor never recovered. He was as much of a mixed bag as his father, full of explosions, a cunning strategist, a fearless warrior, but cruel, willful, faithless (and possibly homosexual, which would have left the humble Berengaria up a tree). Eleanor may have been attracted to the same qualities in Richard that had once attracted her to Henry. Certainly, Richard, despite his gouging taxations and arbitrary judgments, was loved by the English people—which could never be said of his successor, the slimy John. Richard, a tower of a man nearly six and a half feet tall in a time when most men stood scarcely more than five feet, became a legend—the heroic, lionhearted crusader who befriended Robin Hood (though Robin Hood, if he actually existed, belongs to a later century)—whereas John became a historical lesson in how not to be king.

John gained the nicknames "Softsword" and "Lackland" because he lost most of his continental fiefs to Philip, who, annexing Anjou, Le Maine, Normandy, Touraine, and most of Poitou, began to build what would become modern France. Having quarreled with Pope Innocent, John found England under interdict and himself excommunicated, which subsequently pushed him into the humiliating posture of becoming the pope's vassal. Finally, he was forced by his barons to seal Magna Carta, the first time in European history that the power of a king was limited by law.

What strikes me most forcibly about Eleanor at the end of her long life is her generosity—toward kin and in-law but also toward servants, toward the poor, and toward God. She became in her last years an almsgiver of marked largesse: to those living who had helped her or her children (cooks, governesses, even her jailers, all of whom received properties of consequence) and to many religious foundations that cared for the poor (and that received everything from chantries to enlarged kitchens "for the weal of her soul and of her worshipful husband of sacred memory, King Henry, of her son King Henry, of goodly memory, and of that mighty man King Richard, and of her other sons and daughters"). She freed many people from "all accustomed services" that had previously bound them, just as she had earlier freed cities by charter from their former feudal obligations. Among her descendants are the expectable kings, queens, and even an emperor, but also two royal saints: Louis IX of France, son of Blanche of Castile, a truly good king whose inveterate peacemaking serves as a prophecy of the peace of Europe in our time,[i] and Ferdinand III of Castile, a more conflicted figure than Louis IX but nonetheless rebuilder of the cathedral of Burgos and founder of the University of Salamanca. It may be said of Eleanor that she made more than one erratic start in life but she made a good end.

To make a good end was indeed the chief goal of all medieval lives. One recalls the exceedingly incarnational Marian prayer, *Ave*

[i] Louis also sent deputies touring throughout his realm to investigate complaints of injustice, their bias always being in favor of the poor over the rich, women (widows in particular) over men, and children (orphans in particular) over adults. At the judgment of these investigators, substantial amounts of money and property were returned to the defrauded. Harassed Jews, however, and, more especially, heretics had little reason to be grateful to Louis. Moreover, Louis had a brother, Charles of Anjou, who cut a frightening figure through Spain, Italy, and the Middle East, plotting with popes to limit the reach of the German emperor and effecting large-scale slaughters in many regions. Though Louis, always preferring a political settlement to war, didn't care for his brother's incursions, he never stopped him (and probably couldn't have, because of Charles's considerable independent resources).

Detail of Eleanor's tomb. The face appears to be a late likeness of Eleanor, who kept her beauty despite her great age.

Maria, which came into existence in its present Latin form only in the twelfth century: *"Ave, Maria, gratia plena, Dominus tecum; benedicta tu in mulieribus et benedictus fructus ventris tui, Jesus. Sancta Maria, Mater Dei, ora pro nobis peccatoribus nunc et in hora mortis nostrae. Amen"* (Hail, Mary, full of grace, the Lord is with thee; blessed art thou among women and blessed is the fruit of thy womb, Jesus. Holy Mary, Mother of God, pray for us sinners now and at the hour of our death. Amen).[j] The hour of one's death is the decisive hour.

The Middle Ages were, at least for the leading families of Europe, a combustible combina-

j   In its first half the prayer combines the salutation of the Angel Gabriel to Mary in Luke 1:28 with the salutation of her cousin Elizabeth in Luke 1:42 and is taken from Jerome's Vulgate. Though medieval theologians thought that *gratia plena* ("full of grace") meant that Mary was awarded the "fullness of grace" by God, the Greek original means simply "well-favored one." The second half of the prayer ("Holy Mary . . . ") is not directly scriptural but arises out of medieval piety.

Eleanor's tomb in Fontevraud Abbey, next to that of her second husband, King Henry II. Taller than Henry, Eleanor was the genetic source of their son Richard's great height.

england and france in the time of henry II

north sea

wales

england

London
Canterbury
Portsmouth

flanders

holy Roman empire

english channel

Cherbourg
Barfleur
Bayeux
Rouen
Coutances
Caen
normandy

Vexin
St. Denis
Paris
Fontainbleau
France
Rheims
champagne

'Mont St. Michel'

Blois

Sens
Troyes

brittany

maine
Le Mans

Orléans

Vézelay

Nantes

anjou
Fontevraud
Loudun

Tours
Chinon

Blois
Loches

Bourges

Burgundy

touraine
berry

Burgundy

atlantic ocean

N.

Poitou
La Rochelle
Saintes

Poitiers

angoulême
Limoges
Châlus
la marche
limousin

aquitaine

Burgundy

saintonge

périgord
Bordeaux

quercy

Cahors

languedoc

gascony

agenais
Toulouse

toulouse

castile

Bayonne

béarn

navarre

aragon

Barcelona

mediterranean sea

☐ plantagenet empire
☐ french Royal Demesne

tion of sex, violence, and religion. The powerful have always had license to fulfill their sexual whims in ways unavailable to simple folk. But till the Age of Eleanor such fulfillment was almost entirely limited to males. Likewise, statecraft, political power, and armed combat were instruments for alpha males that no woman was invited to handle. Eleanor, despite the discretion and equilibrium her imprisonment would teach her, was the first woman in the history of civilized Europe to have the experience of choosing her husband, leading an army, going to war, and ruling over countries for considerable periods of time—all without the need to defer to husband, father, brother, or son.

If her beauty and grace were legendary, her competence and decisiveness became more so. If Hildegard proved that a woman could be as profound a mystic and as orthodox a theologian as any man of her time, Eleanor proved that a queen could be as free a sexual being, as wise a ruler, as strategic a general as any king. But though Hildegard remains in important aspects forever medieval, Eleanor is an entirely modern woman. One feels that one meets her in the pages of history as one might meet any woman of consequence in the world we now inhabit. Her desires are ours, her objectives our own. And just as certain noble ladies throughout Europe held her up as a model, many ordinary women too came to find in Eleanor a standard by which they might measure their own actions and rehearse the roles they could win for themselves. For as King Henry V of England would remind the royal Katherine of France in Shakespeare's history play, "We are the makers of manners, Kate."

Besides the living models of abbesses like Hildegard and queens like Eleanor, besides the omnipresent liturgical and artistic model of the Virgin Mary, there is the literary and musical model, the courtly love that provided constant subject matter for writers and composers of the twelfth century and later. In this endeavor, the poets and musicians repeatedly took inspiration from primitive Welsh and Breton stories, told and retold, of an early British king, Arthur, whose Knights of the Round Table were models of chivalry for all time, whose queen,

Guinevere, was the most beautiful of all, and whose court of Camelot would have enjoyed eternal life, had it not been for the queen's adultery with the king's good friend Lancelot, the perfect knight. Did the life of Eleanor feed the legend of Guinevere or did early versions of Guinevere's story, now lost in the mists of time, give Eleanor the courage to act as she did?[k]

It is unlikely that we shall ever know for sure. An educated guess would be that the expanding cult of the Virgin Mary in the language of prayer and in the images of art served as the inspiration for all subsequent exaltations of women in religious life, in the worshipful literature of the troubadours, and in the courts of Europe, which soon devised a more secular form of devotion— courtly love—which in turn influenced women like Eleanor to seize control of their destinies. Though this feminism is certainly not the result that churchmen would have wished when they reluctantly blessed the growing popular enthusiasm for devotions to the Virgin, it is also true that all cultural revolutions tend sooner or later to press beyond whatever initial limits were set for them.

In one aspect only does the singular Eleanor agree with the figures that surround her, the others whom we have met in the course of her story: her religious attitudes are the same as theirs. She was dismissive of churchmen—this is what Bernard of Clairvaux sensed in her—and her exasperation and irreverence toward the pretensions of the official church are unmistakable in her correspondence with the doddering Pope Celestine. But she is nonetheless a believer, who takes seriously the presence of an immortal soul in

[k] Merlin, King Arthur's court wizard, was believed to have left a series of prophecies, some of which were interpreted as referring to Henry II and his family. In Merlin's language, Henry was "King of the North Wind" and Eleanor "the Eagle of the Broken Alliance" who "shall rejoice in her third nesting," the birth of Richard, her third child by Henry. There was also a prophecy of the rise of Henry's bellicose sons: "The cubs shall awake and shall roar loud, and, leaving the woods, shall seek their prey within the walls of the cities. Among those who shall be in their way they shall make great carnage, and shall tear out the tongues of bulls." At Henry's direction, the Isle of Avalon, where Arthur was said to have died—Glastonbury in southwest England—was searched for Arthur's

every person, a soul that will outlast the body and that is destined for eternal happiness with God or, because of a final refusal to seek God's mercy and forgiveness, eternal damnation. Every medieval life, including Eleanor's, was lived against this horizon of apocalypse, for life was a great drama ending awesomely in Four Last Things: death, God's judgment, Heaven, and Hell.

grave, which was duly found by the local monks beside the grave of a blond-haired queen, obviously Guinevere. With Arthur's bones was a leaden cross inscribed in rhyming Latin: *"Hic jacet Arturus / Rex quondam rexque futurus"* (Here lies Arthur, / Once and future king). The graves, in all likelihood a monkish ploy to raise the status of Glastonbury Abbey, were destroyed at the Reformation.

The record survives of many of Eleanor's grants to individuals, often made in the name of Richard, "our son of blessed memory; may his soul be at peace forever." There can be no doubting the anguished sincerity of Eleanor's hope. She was no saint and would likely have ridiculed the notion of a Saint Eleanor (and, perhaps because of her realistic view of human activity, of a Saint Anyone). She was, rather, a smart, spirited, incautious young woman, who developed into a wise, effective, generous old woman.

One is hard pressed to find examples of unbelievers anywhere in medieval Europe. Henry and Eleanor's youngest child, John, could be named as such. He was famous in his day for chatting and giggling his way through mass, refusing communion, and hooting at the preacher to hurry up and finish so he could eat. When Bishop Hugh showed John a new depiction of the Last Judgment, a favorite medieval subject, and pointed out the happy souls ascending to Heaven, John scandalized all present by pointing to the damned, pulled down to Hell by demons, and shouting, "Show me rather these, whose good example I mean to follow!" But even this was more likely braggadocio than an expression of atheism.

What is discernible, however, in John's taunts, as in his mass-frequenting father's threats against God, is a disjunction between their undoubted beliefs and their daily lives. The biographies of medieval royals are reminiscent of the formula for a Cecil B. DeMille film—lots of sex and violence followed by a pious ending—which does not, however, discredit the authenticity of their piety. They did use the church and its doctrines to their advantage—twisting the arms of clerics as needed, confessing their sins and receiving absolution and then returning to their sins, leaving grants to monasteries so that masses would be offered in perpetuity for their imperiled immortal souls—but they didn't trust churchmen any more than they trusted other princes, and the lives they led were nearly as pagan as those of their barbaric forebears.

Throughout Europe two languages were used: Latin, the high-minded language of the church, and one's vernacular, Anglo-Saxon or Anglo-French or Langue d'Oc or High German or whatever. In the emerging vernaculars, there was plenty of room for practical matters, for concerns of fleshly existence, and even for sensuous delight and erotic need, but there was little room for God and the things of the spirit. There was still a fissure in European consciousness between flesh and spirit that needed to be healed, a fissure symbolized by the two languages of life, Latin and vernacular, language high and language low.

As local languages slowly gained ascendency, fewer and fewer people understood Latin, which was on its way to becoming the language of power, of priests and lawyers, of deeds and charters and mysterious ceremonies, no longer the language in which a mother caressed her children or a man embraced his wife or a friend gave his hand to a friend. Somehow or other, for the sake of an integrated consciousness, the Incarnation—the original, early medieval resolution of the tension between flesh and spirit—needed to penetrate the vernacular. To experience the impact of the most extraordinary experiment in vernacular spirituality since the parables of Jesus, we must make our way from Fontevraud Abbey in the lush Loire Valley and, crossing the barrier of the Alps, return to Italy.

In 1182, three years after the death of Hildegard and in the same year Eleanor turned sixty, a boy was born to Pietro di Bernardone, a worldly-wise, tyrannical cloth merchant, and his long-suffering wife,

Pica, who lived in a prosperous hill town of Umbria called Assisi, nestled in the foothills of the Apennines. The child was christened Giovanni shortly after his birth. His father, however, on returning from one of his many business trips to the larger France of Philip II,[1] where he purchased the bolts of stylish cloth he would sell to Italians, demanded his new son be renamed Francesco, "the Frenchman," Francis in English. Francis of Assisi was to become, in the course of his forty-four years, the greatest of all medieval saints, for many thoughtful commentators the greatest Christian figure since Jesus Christ.

But for the first half of Francis's life there was nothing remarkable about him. A spoiled rich man's son, he became in his teens a dissolute layabout, whose supremely practical father tried repeatedly and unsuccessfully to interest him in the particulars of the cloth trade. Though bored by the business of the business, Francis appears to have enjoyed his many trips with his father to France, picking up along the way the songs, stories, and easy morals of the early French poets. He had a good ear and a fine memory and was an excellent mimic, all of which enabled him to retain the Provençal verses he heard and to sing them back throughout his life whenever a situation seemed to require entertainment or a crisis needed to be defused by a moment's jollity.

The poems young Bernardone committed to memory exhibited all the *gai saber* of the troubadours and told of brave knights and beautiful ladies, of furtive romances and whispered assignations. They provided the adolescent with a worldly, even a fashionable, education and with models of conduct that set his imagination afire. They also gave him whatever literary and historical grounding he had beyond three meager years of schooling from his parish priest, who had taught Francis to read, to write, and to parse elementary Latin—a typical education for the time. For tucked away within the *gai saber* were references to lost traditions and buried knowledge. As Chrétien de Troyes wrote in the prologue to *Cligés,* a long poem about a knight's quest:

[1]   Philip II, son of the handsome but ineffectual Louis VII, Eleanor's first husband, was most unlike his father. Hunchbacked and ugly, he was an admirable warrior and wily politician who annexed to France most of Henry II and Eleanor's continental lands, for which achievement he was hailed as Philip Augustus.

Par les livres que nos avons
Les feiz des anciiens savons
Et del siecle qui fu jadis.
Ce nos ont nostre livre apris,
Que Grece ot de chevalerie
Le premier los et de clergie.
Puis vint chevalerie a Rome
Et de la clergie la some,
Qui or est an France venue.
Deus doint qu'ele i soit retenue . . .

From books of ours we ken
The deeds of ancient men
And ken the days of old.
These books of ours have told
That Greece was first in yearning
For chivalry and learning.
Then chivalry came to Rome
And of all learning the sum,
Which came to France at last.
God grant we hold them fast . . .

Cligés, which concerns a knight's love for the married lady of the title and involves hideaways and love potions and is set in part at Camelot, runs to more than a hundred pages, even in modern editions. However extended some of these romances were, they were simple singsong affairs, rigidly bound in rhyming couplets, each line containing exactly four iambs (which, because of the terseness of English, cannot be simulated in translation). But they offered incidental learning (or *clergie* in the Old French of Chrétien, showing just how closely knowledge and learning clung to the clergy) about many things. These early lines, for instance, were intended to demonstrate how the refined manners and intellectual seriousness of Greece and Rome had found their way to contemporary France—here seen not just as the tiny realm of Louis VII but as the broad country of all Francophones. In their wide-ranging references, the troubadour poems, whether long or short, opened Francis to a changing world far beyond the bounds of his Umbrian parish. These business trips with his overbearing father provided him with his true school of learning.

But for all that, Francis could not seem to rise above the role his fellows had designated for him, *rex convivii,* master of the revels. The emerging middle class, to which the Bernardones belonged, did not exist in isolation from the rest of Assisi, a typical European town of its time, full of extremes of poverty and wealth, charity and violence. Women and girls had to be closely guarded at all times to prevent rape, while the streets clanged with strutting young male revelers, such as Francis and his friends—so much so that we could almost be in the Verona of Romeo and Juliet, of the Montagues and Capulets, as in the Assisi of the Bernardones.

Assisi was then a commune—that is, a new kind of town with elected officials—but it still owed allegiance to the German emperor, for Assisi lay within the Holy Roman Empire. After the burghers of the town decided to cut all feudal ties, they found themselves in a pitched battle with the aristocrats they had previously expelled—and who arrived at the walls of Assisi with overwhelming reinforcements from Perugia, Assisi's ancient enemy, twelve miles to the west. Francis, thinking himself a knight of the new order, answered the call to man the battlements and soon found himself imprisoned in Perugia, where he languished for a year in a dark, airless dungeon and contracted malaria. Ransomed at last, he returned home but would never be his old self again. No longer master of the revels, he had become a depressive who "began to regard himself as worthless." He did make one quixotic attempt to join the forces of a Norman nobleman in Apulia. He even assembled an expensive knight's costume in preparation for his role as vassal. "I know that I shall become a great prince!" he vowed to all who would listen. But the malaria returned and his unrealistic plans for chivalric glory had to be laid aside. He would remain sickly for the rest of his short life.

On a bright afternoon in the summer of 1205, Francis, returning from an errand for his father, took refuge from the heat in the ruined coolness of the chapel of San Damiano at the foot of the hill of Assisi. There above the cracked altar, surrounded by signs of neglect and decay, was a miraculous survival: an intact crucifix of painted linen, stretched across a wooden frame. The image on the cloth, a crucified Christ in the Byzantine style, its severity mitigated by Italian tenderness, was looking directly at Francis. Then the young man thought he heard a gentle voice saying, "Francis, don't you see my house is being destroyed? Go, then, rebuild it for me." Francis felt a mysterious change steal over him, a change he could never afterwards describe. "So," writes Thomas of Celano, Francis's first biographer, "it is better for us to remain silent about it, too."

This was the turning point of Francis's life, the moment at which a new and unexpected vocation took hold of him and sent him racing along a path he could not previously have imagined choosing. An irreligious man, he had found the love of his life—God, or more precisely, God revealed in Jesus—and this discovery made sense of everything else, putting all others, whether people or things, in their proper perspective. As one looks back over Francis's boyhood, one sees that bolts of cloth and columns of coins could never have held him. He required an overpowering vision to make him function properly; and it's no wonder that the stimulus of poetry and the ideal of knighthood had been the only previous things to capture his attention or win his homage. He was in every sense of the word an extremist.

Donald Spoto, Francis's most recent biographer, warns his readers that real saints are "not normal people." As the screenwriter Frank Cottrell Boyce put it, "Even Saint Francis—who was one of the two or three greatest human beings ever to walk the earth—could be a bit weird." I would go so far as to say that Francis was a naturally bipolar personality, a sort of less literary and more self-denying version of someone like Robert Lowell, who could never have settled down to oxlike

Crucifix of San Damiano that spoke to Francis. Like the apse of Santa Maria in Trastevere, it is an example of the new tenderness introduced by Italian artists of the twelfth century into their tradition of Byzantine-inspired art.

domesticity but required a great and continuing enterprise if he was to function at all. Once that was sorted out, however, he could function brilliantly, excessively, erratically, eccentrically—which is what Francis did for his remaining twenty-odd years.

At first, he took literally the words of Jesus and painstakingly restored San Damiano to its previous beauty. As he did so, he often prayed his now famous Prayer Before a Crucifix:

> *Most high and glorious God,*
> *enlighten the darkness of my heart*
> *and give me true faith, certain hope, and perfect charity,*
> *sense and knowledge, Lord—*
> *that I may carry out your holy and true command. Amen.*

In this, Francis's first composition, he could hardly have been more plain, more humble, less adorned, less rhetorical. This is the prayer of a man who has left the startling colors and bold materials of the fabric shop behind him, a man without ornament or pretension.

He took to wearing a hooded peasant's tunic, cinched by a wide leather belt, and sandals. He lived in a hermit's cave and carried a pilgrim's staff. When a little later he noted Jesus's instructions to his disciples in Matthew's Gospel, telling them to "take no gold or silver or copper in your belts, no bag for your journey, nor two tunics nor sandals nor a staff," he would abandon his staff, go barefoot, replace his belt with a bit of rope, and divest himself of all changes of clothes. His colorless vagrant's costume would become the uniform of the early Franciscans, the world's first hippies.

But Francis's father, the cloth merchant, mortified by the mad behavior of his son, hauled him into Assisi's central square and beat him brutally in the sight of everyone. When that failed to dissuade Francis from his bizarre behavior, Bernardone locked him in a storage room, from which he escaped with his mother's complicity. When Bernardone discovered that Francis had sold some of the family's precious bolts of cloth to get money for San Damiano's repairs, he was overcome with rage and brought his case against his son to Guido, the exceedingly wealthy, no-nonsense bishop of Assisi. Guido conducted his court in the great piazza before the cathedral in the hearing of many witnesses.

To the amazement of all, Francis emerged from nowhere, bathed, trimmed, and elegantly outfitted in one of the plumed and patterned costumes from his abandoned wardrobe. Bernardone began his complaint before the bishop: his son was a thief who had mortally dishonored his father, who had the right to compensation for the cloths the young man had stolen. Sounding no more sympathetic than Shylock demanding his pound of flesh, the father was startled by the response of his son, who agreed to return all the money forthwith, as well as anything else he had from his father. Francis then ducked into the cathedral, reappearing shortly thereafter stark naked and holding his clothes in a bundle in front of him, surmounted by a purse full of coins. All these he handed to the imperious bishop, who could not mask his astonishment.

"Listen to me, all of you," the unashamed naked man addressed the crowd, "and understand. Till now, I have called Pietro di Bernardone my father. But because I have proposed to serve God, I return to him the money on account of which he was so upset, and also the clothing that is his, and I wish from now on to say only 'Our Father, who art in Heaven' and not 'My father, Pietro di Bernardone.'" As Bernardone stumbled off with his bundle and purse, Bishop Guido descended the steps of the cathedral and covered the naked man with his enormous cloak.

There is no record of a reconciliation between Francis and his parents nor of any words he ever spoke of them again. There can be no doubt that Francis, for all his blunt simplicity and spontaneity, was capable of forethought and even guile. There was nothing unrehearsed about the episode before the cathedral, nothing Francis had left to chance. He had played it all out beforehand in his mind's eye and planned it for maximum dramatic effect. No one present could ever forget the plain force of Francis's nakedness or of his uncompromising and quite final words. As Hildegard had used the symbolic sensibility of her age to fashion allegorical word pictures, Francis used that same heightened sense to create gestures of renunciation and attachment that left such a searing impression on human imagination that they could have been firebrands.

Symbolic gesture, Francis's natural language, was the profound source he was able to call on throughout his life, though seldom as dramatically as he did that day before the cathedral. He was no good at organization or at long-range strategies, and he knew it. As men, and then women—led by the self-denying and steel-willed Clare of Assisi—began to present themselves as followers, Francis accepted them, befriended them, told them to hear the gospel and to stand beneath the Cross. But he gave them little else, certainly nothing resembling an elaborated rule of community, such as Benedict had left behind. Francis expected his brothers and sisters to live like him as the Lesser Brothers and Sisters, as laypeople rejecting any distinctions of class among themselves and lacking all honors of church or king or commune, taking the words of Jesus literally, never owning anything, married to their poverty and suffering for God's sake, befriending every outcast—heretic, highwayman, leper—that God thrust in their path. They must not remain at home, making themselves virtuous and fat like the established religious orders.[m] They must go forth on the roads to live the gospel of God's love and preach it to all—farmer, bishop, emperor, pope—yet condemn no one. Judgment was the exclusive province of the all-merciful God; it was none of a Christian's concern. "Give to others, and it shall be given to you. Forgive and you shall be forgiven" was Francis's constant preaching.

"May the Lord give you peace" was the best greeting one could give to all one met. It com-

---

[m] There was no way, in an age in which unescorted women were seen simply as candidates for rape, that the Poor Clares, as the sisterhood came to be called, could wander as freely as the Brothers. They were confined to cloister.

promised no one's dignity and embraced every good; it was a blessing to be bestowed indiscriminately. May the Lord give you peace, George and Jacques. May the Lord give you peace, Osama and Saddam. May the Lord give you peace, my annoying aunt. May the Lord give you peace, my unbearable neighbor. May the Lord give you peace, my loathsome enemy. Francis's great insight was that humanity could find its way back to the Garden of Eden, to the aboriginal innocence, but only if we blessed both the murderer and the murdered, the defrauder and his victim, the robber and the robbed. And so Francis went on his way.

Such an approach, in an age when the most visible signs of the Christian religion were the wars and atrocities of the red-crossed crusaders, was shockingly otherworldly—and slyly effective. It silenced sermonizing windbags and brought archbishops up short. It even impelled Francis himself to join the Fifth Crusade, not as a warrior but as a healer. He sailed across the Mediterranean to the Egyptian court of al-Malik al-Kamil, nephew of the great Saladin who had defeated the forces of the hapless Third Crusade. Francis was admitted to the august presence of the sultan himself and spoke to him of Christ, who was after all Francis's only subject. The attempt to proselytize a Muslim would have been cause for on-the-spot decapitation, but Kamil was a wise and moderate man who was deeply impressed by Francis's courage and sincerity and invited him to stay for a week of serious conversation. Francis, in his turn, was deeply impressed by the religious devotion of the Muslims, especially by their fivefold daily call to prayer—and it is quite possible that the thrice-daily recitation of the Angelus[n] that

n   The Angelus, a verse-and-response prayer originally said in monasteries, is a dramatic evocation of the moment of the Incarnation, the Infleshing of the Word of God in the womb of the Virgin Mary. It takes its name from its opening versicle: *"Angelus Domini nuntiavit Mariae"* (The angel of the Lord brought the news to Mary). As church bells sounded at dawn, noon, and sunset, people throughout Europe stopped in their tracks, no matter what they had been doing, crossed themselves, and recited the prayer with bowed heads. Likewise, the rosary, its invention attributed to the Spaniard Dominic de Guzmán, Francis's contemporary and founder of the Dominicans, actually came to Christian Europe from the Eastern practice of using prayer beads.

became current in medieval Europe was precipitated by the impression made on Francis by the repeated call of the muezzin. Francis was not impressed by the crusaders, nominal Christians whose sacrilegious brutality horrified him. They were entirely too fond of taunting and abusing their prisoners of war, who were often returned to their families minus nose, lips, ears, and eyes.

O There were five major crusades against Islam and the lands of the Middle East. All but the fourth of these have been mentioned so far. The Fourth Crusade was in one respect the most notorious, for it captured Constantinople, a Christian city, giving abysmal depth to the rift between Catholicism and Orthodoxy. After the Fifth Crusade, the crusading ideal, such as it was, was corrupted even further as popes began to call for "crusades" against heretics in France and Spain. As late as the fifteenth century, the belligerent and avaricious Teutonic Knights continued to mount cruel "crusades" against the Orthodox of Eastern Europe. There is no evidence that the so-called Children's Crusade ever took place. The stories of such an event are probably based on a feckless, quickly extinguished crusading movement of poor people, who were called *pueri* (boys, children).

It is a tragedy of history that Kamil and Francis were unable to talk longer, to coordinate their strengths, and to form an alliance. Had they been able to do so, "the clash of civilizations" might not even be a phrase in our world. Francis went back to the crusader camp on the Egyptian shore and desperately tried to convince Cardinal Pelagio, whom the pope had put in charge of the crusade, that he should make peace with the sultan, who, though with far greater force on his side, was all too ready to make peace. But the cardinal had dreams of military glory and would not listen. His eventual failure, amid terrible loss of life, brought the age of the crusades to its inglorious end.[o]

Francis, whom Spoto rightly calls "the first person from the West to travel to another continent with the revolutionary idea of peace-making," now saw himself as a failure. He had failed in his mission of peace; he had failed in keeping the Lesser Brothers propertyless, ruleless, and dependent only on God. Now that there were several thousand such Brothers (and smaller communities of Sisters) spread across Europe, the official church stepped in, demanding all the organizational appurtenances that

Saint Francis by Cimabue, almost certainly a
likeness. The stigmata, or wounds of Christ in his
Passion, are shown on the saint's body, but,
despite pious legend, it is unlikely that he was so
afflicted. The bald circlet on the top of his head
is his tonsure, which all clerics had to submit to.
Francis did not wish to be made a cleric, but
Innocent III insisted on it and personally
tonsured Francis.

Francis in his spontaneity had fought. He was old before his time; his fasts and his uncaring abuse of his own body left him frail, blind, and covered in sores. His malaria returned; and it is possible that he had contracted leprosy from his affectionate ministrations to the poorest of the poor. In his last days, he endured exquisite tortures at the hands of medieval physicians who applied sizzling irons to the flesh around his eyes in a crackpot attempt to restore his sight.

But even in this condition he was able to leave us some of his finest words, a poem of profound reverence in the gladsome spirit of the troubadours, "The Canticle of the Creatures," the first poem written in the emerging Italian vernacular and the founding document of Italian literature:

Altissimu, omnipotente, bonsignore,
    tue sono le laude,
    la gloria elhonore
    et omne benedictione.

Most High, all-powerful, good Lord:
    yours are the praises,
    the glory and the honor,
    and all blessing.

Ad te solo, Altissimo, se konfano
    et nullu homo enne dignu
    te mentovare.

To you alone, Most High, do they belong,
    and no human is worthy
    to speak your name.

Laudato sie, misignore, cum tucte le tue creature,
spetialmente messor lo frate sole,
loquale iorno et allumini noi par loi.

Praised be you, my Lord, with all your creatures,
especially Sir Brother Sun,
who is the day and through whom you give us light.

Et ellu ebellu eradiante cum grande splendore:
de te, Altissimo, porta significatione.

And he is beautiful and radiant in great splendor:
and carries your meaning, Most High.

Laudato si, misignore, per sora luna ele stele:
in celu lai formate clarite
et pretiose et belle.

Praised be you, my Lord, through Sister
Moon and the stars:
in Heaven you formed them, clear
and precious and beautiful.

Laudato si, misignore, per frate vento
et per aere et nubilo
et sereno et omne tempo
per loquale a le tue creature
da sustentamento.

Praised be you, my Lord, through Brother Wind,
and through the air, both cloudy
and serene, and every kind of weather,
through whom to your creatures
you give sustenance.

Laudato si, misignore, per sor aqua,
    laquale et multo utile et humile
    et pretiose et casta.

Praised be you, my Lord, through Sister Water,
    who is very useful and humble,
    precious and pure.

Laudato si, misignore, per frate focu,
    per loquale ennalumini la nocte:
    edello ebello et iocundo
    et robusto et forte.

Praised be you, my Lord, through Brother Fire,
    through whom you light the night
    and he is beautiful and playful,
    and robust and strong.

Laudato si, misignore, per sora nostra matre terra,
    laquale ne sustenta et governa,
    et produce diversi fructi
    con coloriti flori et herba.

Praised be you, my Lord, through our Sister, Mother Earth,
    who sustains and governs us
    and produces diverse fruits
    with colored flowers and herbs.

    Such a free, anarchic soul was Francis. How he went against the grain of his hierarchical, ordered, aggressive, divisive society. Even here he bursts the seams of troubadour convention: no regularly metrical

lines, no expectable pattern of rhyme. What an im-
proviser the man is. What a sexual democrat,
dividing the cosmos equally between
male and female. What a lover. His
whole life was a gesture, a gesture of renunciation and
attachment, a gesture by which the lover shows his refusal to become obsessed with single things—glittering
finery or stacks of gold—but loves the Creator in *all*
his creatures.

The man who hymned his gratitude for the sun could no longer see,
and even dim light was painful to his blind eyes. The man who called the
fire "Brother" was tortured by fire's effect in the form of sizzling irons.
"My brother Fire," said Francis on that occasion, "you are noble and
useful among all the creatures the Most High has created. Be courteous
to me in this hour. For a long time I have loved you. I pray our Creator
who made you, to temper your heat now, so that I may bear it." He bore
it and worse—the subsequent cutting of the veins in his temples—while,
as one brotherly witness admitted, "we who were with him all ran away,
and he remained alone with the doctor." If, as he thought, his life was a
failure, his was the failure of Christ, abandoned by his disciples, racked
by pain, calling out to his Father from the cross "My God, my God, why
have you forsaken me?" yet living forever as the heavenly standard by
which all our own earthly actions are judged.

Francis had two gestures yet to perform, which gave him two last
chances to add verses to his canticle of love. Assisi was beset by a fresh
wave of violence on account of a murderous dispute between Bishop
Guido and Oportulo de Bernardo, the *podestà,* or mayor. In the course
of the dispute, Guido had (what else?) excommunicated Bernardo. Now
Bernardo was threatening to clap into chains anyone who had any further dealings with the bishop. The dying saint asked to meet the two before the bishop's palace, to which he was carried on a stretcher. Neither
could refuse the saint's invitation, nor could the citizens of Assisi miss
out on such an encounter. Francis lifted himself up and sang to the
bishop, the mayor, and all of Assisi:

Laudate si, misignore, per quelli ke perdonano,
>   per lo tuo amore
>   et sostengo infirmitate et tribulatione.

Praised be you, my Lord, through those who forgive
>   *for the sake of your love*
>   *and bear up under weakness and tribulation.*

Beati quelli kel sosterranno in pace,
>   ka da te, Altissimo,
>   sirano incoronati.

Blessed are those who maintain peace,
>   *for by you, Most High,*
>   *shall they be crowned.*

The two men asked forgiveness of each other; and peace, however uneasy, was restored to Assisi. Back in his empty cell, Francis prepared for his own death by adding one last verse to his canticle:

Laudato si, misignore, per sora nostra, morte corporale,
>   da laquale nullu homo vivente poskappare.
Gai acqueli ke morrano ne le peccata mortali!
Beati quelli ke trovarane le tue sanctissime voluntati,
>   ka la morte secunda nol farra male.
Laudate et benedicite misignore,
>   et rengratiate et serviate li cum grande humilitate.

Praised be you, my Lord, through our Sister Bodily Death,
>   *from whom no one living can escape.*
Woe to those who die in mortal sin!
Blessed are those whom death will find in your most holy will,
>   *for the Second Death shall not harm them.*

Praise and bless my Lord
and thank and serve him with great humility.

At the end he asked to be stripped of everything, even the bed on which he lay, and to be laid naked on the floor. "I have done what is mine," were his last whispered words to his companions. "May Christ teach you what is yours to do." Larks sang and flew in circles above the house where he died. As Francis had always noticed, they are the birds who "are friends of the light."

And that is how romance became prayer.

Commonwealth of iceland

Kingdom of Norway

Kingdom of Sweden

...ests

Republic of Novgorod

Knights of the Sword

north sea

Kingdom of Scotland

Lithuanians

Baltic sea

Prussians

Polotsk Principate

Turov - Pi Principate

Kingdom of Denmark

Polish Principates

Principate of Volhynia

Principate of Galacia

irish

Kingdom of england

welsh

atlantic ocean

Kingdom of Bohemia

German Empire

Kingdom of hungary

Kingdom of france

Kingdom of navarre

Venice

bosnia

Kingdom of Leon

Assisi

Rome

serbian Principate

Kingdom of Portugal

Kingdom of Castile

Kingdom of aragon

Kingdom of Sicily

Bulgarian Empire

Latin Empi...

despotate of epirus

almohad caliphate

monemvasia

Mediterranean

almohad caliphate

Frontier of islam

western christendom

eastern christendom

The Religious divisions of Europe and the middle East in the time of Francis Fassisi

Great Principate of Vladimir

Principate of Smolensk

Principate of Chernigov

Volga Bulgars
to islam

Qarakhitai Khanate

Aral

Cumans

Principate of Pereyaslavl

Alans

Caspian Sea

Shirvan

Empire of the Khwarizm Shah

Black Sea

empire of Trebizno

Kingdom of Georgia

Azerbaijan

Constantinople

Empire of Nicaea

Seljuk Sultanate of Rum

Kingdom of Armenia

Principate of Antioch-Tripoli

Luristan

Abbasid Caliphate

Despotate of Rhodes

Kingdom of Cyprus

Kingdom of Acre

Sea

Ayyubid Sultanate

Red Sea

N.

entrances
to other worlds

the mediterranean,
the orient, and the atlantic

*The scourge of heaven's wrath
in the hands of the inhuman
Tartars, erupting as it were from
the secret confines of Hell,
oppresses and crushes the earth.*

—POPE ALEXANDER IV
TO ALL THE PRINCES OF CHRISTENDOM

TO MEDIEVAL MAN, THE COSMOS WAS full of "secret confines," arcana no one knew the way to and few knew anything about but which one might stumble upon without warning. As in those fables rooted in the Middle Ages and collected by the Brothers Grimm in the nineteenth century, a secret door or a hidden path might lead the unsuspecting traveler almost anywhere. Like Alice's rabbit hole or the wardrobe that leads to Narnia or Hildegard's imagined mountain perforated by windows, reality itself was permeable. Not only did Hell have secret cupboards; so did Purgatory and Heaven. And our world of ordinary reality was intersected by other worlds, both night-marish terrains of infernal cruelty and in-candescent landscapes of impossible beauty and passionate peace. When medieval peo-ple beheld the night sky, they were not terrified, as would be Blaise Pascal in the seventeenth century, by the "eternal si-lence of these infinite spaces." They believed that just above their heads there moved a harmonious universe, resound-ing with the Music of the Spheres, far too lovely for earthlings to appre-ciate, and that the sky was full of winged angels in their serried ranks, invisible to most of us most of the time.

Alfred the Great, Christian king of the West Saxons, whose success diminished the pagan Danish presence in England at the end of the ninth century and paved the way for the eventual union of England under one crown, was a practical leader of both military prowess and considerable learning. Fearful that knowledge of Latin might perish entirely, he was responsible for the translation of a whole library of standard Latin texts into Old English. But he was also a visionary, impelled onward by voices and pictures from another world. As G. K. Chesterton presents him in *The Ballad of the White Horse,* young Alfred, then in flight from the Danes, was confronted by the Virgin Mary, who spoke to him in a voice "human but high up, / Like a cottage climbed among / The clouds":

> *"The gates of heaven are lightly locked,*
> *We do not guard our gain,*
> *The heaviest hind may easily*
> *Come silently and suddenly*
> *Upon me in a lane.*

"And any little maid that walks
In good thoughts apart,
May break the guard of the Three Kings
And see the dear and dreadful things
I hid within my heart.

"The meanest man in grey fields gone
Behind the set of sun,
Heareth between star and other star,
Through the door of the darkness fallen ajar,
The council, eldest of things that are,
The talk of the Three in One."

But as for the question Alfred has posed to her—will his English forces be able to overwhelm the Danes in the end?—she offers no help, reminding the king only that predicting the future is an occupation for pagans, not Christians:

"The gates of heaven are lightly locked,
We do not guard our gold,
Men may uproot where worlds begin,
Or read the name of the nameless sin;
But if he fail or if he win
To no good man is told.

"The men of the East may spell the stars,
And times and triumphs mark,
But the men signed of the cross of Christ
Go gaily in the dark."[a]

a The belief that time is processive rather than cyclical—and that, therefore, the only thing real about the future is that it has not happened yet (and that, therefore, it is useless to consult oracles)—represents the first great step that the ancient Jews took to separate themselves from the age-old cultures that surrounded them. This was, therefore, the first great step in the creation of a distinctively Western sensibility. For an exposition of this remarkable process and its historic reverberations, see *The Gifts of the Jews,* Chapter II ("The Journey in the Dark: The Unaccountable Innovation") and passim.

No wonder that in such a universe a voice from another world could speak to Francis through a crucifix.

If a concealed latch or a shadowed staircase might beckon one suddenly to an unknown spirit world, medieval maps abounded in recommendations for more corporeal journeys. Francis's voyage across the Mediterranean brought him face to face with an exotic sultan, his strangely elegant palace hung with the same sorts of precious cloths that Francis's father imported from France. By the time of their meeting, the Mediterranean had become, in fact, a Muslim sea, its African and Asian coasts entirely dominated by the Crescent. The Islamic call to prayer still sounded on the salty air of southern Spain; and one might even imagine hearing the ghostly cry of the muezzin in Sicily and along the Amalfi coast, where the boldly abstract domes of magnificent Christian cathedrals owed their dazzle to the skill of Islam's ceramic artists. France had long ago beaten back the Muslim challenge, only to find itself importing the gorgeously elaborate cloths of Islamic Persia and north Africa, while French dyers created new versions of Islamic designs, poor imitations at first that gradually abandoned the rigidity of the originals and took on a free-form Gallic liveliness of their own.

France had turned back the Islamic armies in the early eighth century. By the late eleventh century, Franco-Normans had taken Sicily from the Muslims, though Muslims would long remain a social and artistic presence there as well as throughout the racially and religiously mixed populations of southern Italy, now ruled by Normans. Bit by bit, the Christian kingdoms of the Iberian Peninsula were gaining territory and pushing the Muslims farther south, though the expulsion would not be complete till the last decade of the fifteenth century, when (in the same year as Columbus's first voyage of discovery) the forces of Ferdinand and Isabella would overwhelm the emirate of Granada. All the same, confrontations between the Eastern forces of Islam and the Western forces of Christianity have never completely abated. Famous battles to come include Lepanto in the sixteenth century and Gallipoli in the twentieth, not to speak of wars still raging.

Though the Catholic Christianity of the West managed to stop Islam from overwhelming Europe, Greek Orthodoxy, based not in Rome but in Constantinople, was less fortunate. It was geographically inevitable that the golden city of Constantine would fall finally to Islam, which it did in May of 1453, when its legendary line of two hundred towers, unbreached for ten centuries, was turned to rubble by Turkish bombardment, the first time in history that gunpowder would claim such a victory. But long before gunpowder had come from the Far East, the ancient Near East, home to the apostolic centers of Byzantine Christianity—Alexandria and all of northern Africa, Jerusalem, Antioch and all of Asia Minor—had exchanged the Cross for the Crescent and become the Middle East that we know to this day. Were it not for Orthodoxy's missions north and northeastward—into the Balkans and Russia—it is unlikely that this ancient form of Christianity would still be a presence in our world.

The presence of Islam, however, has become impossible to ignore. This Arabian religion, which almost since its inception in the seventh century has stalked the West as a periodic threat, has now risen up against us in its most fanatical form, promising—and delivering—atrocities without warning. People living in explicitly targeted Western capitals (New York, Washington, London, Madrid, Copenhagen, Milan, Rome) and even in less likely targets can sometimes feel like characters in a horror film, waiting only for the next explosion—where and when we know not, knowing only that it will come. It is tempting, therefore, to allow fear to run riot over reason and to demonize all of Islam without exception.

I do not mean to indulge in the sort of weakly mooing rhetoric of tolerance one sometimes hears. Yes, the wealthy West has yet to face up to its responsibilities to poor nations. Yes, the Bush/Blair invasion of Iraq was an immense blunder engineered by adolescent fantasists, ignorant of cultural realities. But no one, whether Bush or bin Laden, has the right to blow up innocent civilians. And since 9/11 preceded the American invasion of Iraq by a year and a half (and since the initial attack on New York's World

Trade Center preceded that invasion by ten years), we may reasonably conclude that there is an element in Islam intent on devastating the West, quite apart from any concessions the West may be prepared to make.

Islam began as a warrior religion bent on worldly conquest. The followers of Islam, the brainchild of a (probably illiterate) camel driver named Muhammad, gained their initial prominence by raiding caravans and claiming territory. This religion was first spread by coercion, not conversion. Nonetheless, the simplicity of its demands—proclamation of monotheistic belief, five-times-daily prayer to the one God, almsgiving, daylight fasting during the month of Ramadan, once-in-a-lifetime pilgrimage to Mecca[b]—ensured its wide acceptance by simple societies like that of the Arabs, who were still in the midst of a transition from nomadic herding to settled farming and trading.

Rather quickly, Islam sprouted a body of law, subsequently called *shari'ah,* by which all Muslims were to be governed. Its regulation of women, though in its time an advance over the more degrading customs of the polytheistic Arabian tribes, was extremely confining, at least when compared with the position of women in medieval Christian societies. (Nor can there be any doubt that the relative flexibility of medieval Christian attitudes toward women served as an essential stepping-stone to their modern emancipation.) To apply these inflexible laws today— laws that so severely limit a woman's rights to property, inheritance, divorce, movement, and self-determination—is as antic and oppressive as it would be for Christians to reinstitute the ducking stool or insist that known sinners stand at the church door in sackcloth and ashes.

Muhammad, in his simplicity, thought that he would be accepted as a prophet by other monotheists, that is, by Jews and Christians. In fact, Islam contains considerable borrowings—

b Mecca, where Muhammad hailed from, contains a shrine called the Kaaba, which was venerated from time immemorial by Arabian polytheists. Islamic tradition claims that the central feature of the Kaaba, a black cube containing what is almost certainly a meteorite, was God's gift to Adam, the first man. Much of the Quran, Islam's holy book, contains such allusions to and reworkings of Old Testament stories and themes. But Muslims refuse to allow either the Kaaba or the Quran to be subjected to scientific investigation in the same way that the relics and scriptures of Judaism and Christianity have routinely been.

dietary restrictions, circumcision, the rigid separation of the sexes and exclusion of women even from such essential exercises as communal prayer, endless reformulations and interpretations of a voluminous body of religious law by experts—from rabbinical Judaism, in particular. When Muhammad failed to find acceptance among both Jews and Christians, his attitudes toward these "People of the Book," as he called them, turned harsher. At times, he actively persecuted Jews; and he declared Mecca the central earthly locus of holiness. (Jerusalem, to which he had earlier given that honor, was reduced in status, still holy but not the holiest.) His final attitude toward followers of other religions was that though idolaters, if they were unwilling to convert to Islam, were to be executed, Jews and Christians could be tolerated in Muslim society, provided they paid a special tax and refrained from proselytizing as well as from all public religious display.

Above all, it was Muhammad's military successes that brought most of Arabia to submit to Islam (which means "submission"), either through outright conquest or through admiration. If he won such victories, God must be with him. The weakened empires of Persia and Byzantium then became easy prey to Muhammad's hordes. And it would not be long before the forces of Islam stood at the gates of Western Christendom, demanding obedience. By then, *jihad* (holy war) had become a supreme duty of every Muslim male. One who died in such a war was a martyr to whom the gates of Paradise would be flung open. (The papal dispensing of plenary indulgences to soldiers participating in crusades is no more than a Christian imitation of a Muslim idea.)

All these things must be said—and they are the usual things trotted out whenever a Westerner wishes to prove that Islam and the West are engaged in inevitable conflict. On the other side, the genial Islamic toleration of (and even interaction with) Jews and Christians in Muslim Spain, the bloodthirsty cruelty of the crusades, the West's indifference to disfranchisement and economic suffering in Muslim (and especially Palestinian) lands, the West's bottomless greed for oil, America's mindless war in Iraq—just the latest "crusade," to employ the designation that escaped from Bush's own lips,[c] discolored by the blood of thousands—the capture and interminable imprisonment of innocent Muslims, and the appalling abuse of Muslim prisoners are all brought forth to bolster the justice of even moderate Islam's hatred of the West and its backing for the destabilization of Western societies.

Obscured by the clashing debating points on each side, however, lies the essential thought that a religion as old as Islam has developed a range of paths, schools, options, strategies, and interpretations. It is no longer simply the artifact, however impressive, of a seventh-century desert trader. It cannot be reduced to a handful of historical factoids and anecdotal caricatures. It is rather a vast and colorful spectrum. Each of the great religions creates finally a spectrum of voices that ranges all the way from pacifist to terrorist. But each religion, because of its metaphorical ambiguity and gradual intellectual refinement, holds within it marvelous potential for unexpected development and subtle adaptation. This development will be full of zigzags and may sometimes seem as slow as the development of the universe, but it runs—I would say, almost inevitably—from exclusivist militancy to inclusive peace.

To what point Islam has advanced in this development is a question beyond the scope of this book. But it may be said without fear of contradiction that Islamic society and Christian society have been generally bad neighbors now for nearly fourteen centuries, often eager to misunderstand each other. We stand in desperate need of contemporary figures like al-Malik al-Kamil and Francis of Assisi to create an innovative dialogue. We in the West must come to accept that a people now numbering 1.3 billion and parked at our door[d] for a millennium and a half will not

[c] In the words of the percipient Jonathan Raban, "At the time, I heard it said that Bush used the word 'crusade' by accident and was probably ignorant of its significance, particularly for Muslims. This seems unlikely, given the amount of writing and rewriting that goes into presidential speeches. Perhaps Bush himself was not entirely aware of what he was saying, but some White House scribe surely intended to put us at least loosely in mind of Richard Coeur de Lion."

[d] Not only parked at our door but inside the house. There may be, for instance, more Muslims living in the United States than Jews and Episcopalians combined.

go away. This is a force that cannot be conquered but must be reckoned with. Similarly, the Islamic East must come to terms with the immense spectrum of the Christian/post-Christian West, a variegated society twice as large as Islam. We will not go away, either.

Despite the fact that medieval Christians were normally unable to distinguish one wave of Islam from another, the Muslims who came in contact with Europeans originated in different places—Arabia, Syria, Persia, Iraq, Turkey, Egypt—and had differing relationships to Islam. The Mongols, originally nomadic horsemen who rode from the north and west of China across the endless grasslands of the steppes, had by the mid-thirteenth century conquered most of Asia—from southern Russia to northern India. Such legendary cities as Baghdad, Kiev, Samarkand, and Peking fell to their ferocity. Even parts of Eastern Europe, where they played the part of the "inhuman Tartars" of Pope Alexander IV's hyperbolical address, were absorbed into their orbit. Shamanistic animists to begin with, many Mongols became in time Buddhists, Christians (of a heretical variety), and most especially Muslims, as their conquests touched areas controlled by these more complex religious outlooks.

The Mongols' establishment of an Asian ecumene that stretched from the Black Sea to the Sea of Japan made it possible for European traders to penetrate for the first time as far as Asia's Pacific coast. The memoirs of one such trader, *The Book of Marvels* by the Venetian jewel merchant Marco Polo, became a publishing sensation throughout Europe at the beginning of the fourteenth century. Marco had spent more than twenty years in the service of Kublai Khan, Mongol conquerer of China and descendant of Genghis

Khan, the frightening founder of the Mongolian Empire. His tales of the fabulous wealth of the Mongol rulers, the incredible immensity of their cities, the exquisite refinement of their courts, dazzled his readers. They devoured his narrative as we might an account of interplanetary travel. To them, where Marco had been and what he had seen were as strange as the most fanciful fiction. If such people could exist, if such customs could thrive, surely anything was possible.^c

Though contact with the Orient hardly changed the course of European civilization, it enlivened imagination and complicated social intercourse at least as much as the earlier contacts with Muslims had done. Spices, pasta, paper, and of course gunpowder all came to us from the Far East. And such firing of the imagination helped set the scene for the amazing discovery of a previously unknown continent at the end of the fifteenth century. The medieval intellectuals whose task it was to think about such things—the cartographers and the geographers—had long surmised that since the people of the world they knew inhabited but one hemisphere, it would make sense that there was in the unknown hemisphere another series of lands—"on the opposite side of the earth, where the sun rises when it sets to us"—and that these lands might well be inhabited. They called this hypothetical territory the Antipodes.

As early as the sixth century, the Irish boatbuilder Brendan the Navigator may have visited North America. His epic saga, labeled *Navigatio Sancti Brendani Abbatis* (The Voyage of Saint Brendan the Abbot), was a staple of medieval wonder literature. In this as in many other mat-

---

c   The gradual awareness that the world beyond Europe was large and diverse may be plotted in medieval depictions of the *magi* who came to pay homage to Jesus after his birth, as related in the second chapter of Matthew's Gospel. The incident is intended to emphasize that "the kings of the earth," even those from exotic places far beyond Judea recognized Jesus as Savior. In later tradition, there were thought to have been three visiting *magi* (or kings), though Matthew gives no number and in art more are sometimes shown. Matthew tells us they all came "from the East," almost certainly from Persia (if they are historical figures). But in early artistic depictions, one of the *magi* is often shown as a black African, the others as Europeans or as men of the Middle East. After the circulation of Marco Polo's travel memoirs, however, one of the *magi* was sometimes depicted as Chinese.

ters, the intangible dreams of medieval man could become solid reality only in the next age, even if the Viking voyages to North America seemed to confirm the existence of a large island in the far Atlantic. And as the Atlantic seafaring nations of Portugal, Spain, France, and England increased their fleets, technical expertise was building to the point where the Age of Discovery would become possible. Portugal, in particular, was colonizing the mid-Atlantic islands of the Azores by the late fourteenth century and fishing off the coast of Newfoundland by the fifteenth century, probably in advance of the first Atlantic voyage by the Genoese captain Cristofero Colombo.

But more important than the ships, more basic than the technical knowledge, were the travelers' tales, the rich imaginings, and a growing passion to penetrate the secrets of the universe.

THREE

paris, university of heavenly things

the exaltation of reason and its consequences

Do you think God cares only for Italy?

—FRANCIS OF ASSISI TO CARDINAL UGOLINO,
WHO HAD WARNED THE SAINT
AGAINST PREACHING IN FRANCE

THE MIDDLE AGES ARE A GREAT jumble. As I have put my manuscript together, I have sometimes felt I was not so much writing a book as sewing a gigantic quilt, full of disparate and even clashing remnants: a large patch of ancient Greece, swatches of late antique and early medieval Rome, oddly conjoined strips from maps both geographical and metaphysical, a not-so-blushing virgin, a blushless queen, and (as we shall soon see) a nun who prides herself on being her lover's whore. What on earth do all these things have to do with one another? But to present the Middle Ages otherwise—as a seamless garment—would be to falsify their character and leave the reader grasping at a phantasm.

A medievalist friend of mine once confided that he often daydreamed of living in medieval times. Of course, he added, he always imagined himself a lord of some sort, sitting in his great hall, being served a side of succulent wild boar from his woodland demesnes. He never imagined himself the housechurl who did the serving or the estate serf who had done the hunting and the butchering. Though distinctions between high and low were less acute then than they are in our world, they were sufficiently stark to steer any dreamer's fancies away from the furrowed farms of Europe and toward its castellated hilltops. What appalls a modern dreamer about the Middle Ages is not so much the distance that lay between peasant and prince as that there was seldom any way of shortening that distance: the peasant would always be a peasant, the prince always a prince.

And yet . . . the rigid stratification of social roles was shaken by the rise of the merchant class, the medieval bourgeoisie. Francis of Assisi's youthful plan to "become a great prince" was unrealistic because he took no steps to realize it; but had he taken his father's route, he could have become a great merchant prince. As time went on, wealth vied with nobility for political and social power, and wealth won out often enough, especially as independent cities and towns like Assisi grew into alternative centers of power. But withal, the trader's route to self-improvement was a slippery one. Caravans could be raided by brigands and ships founder at sea. Markets could be cruelly affected by the cosmic vagaries of weather, war, and trade barriers—just as suddenly as markets in our day.

However difficult it may be to characterize correctly the medieval class system, it is even more difficult to grasp medieval thinking, which was broadly metaphorical and analogical rather than *merely* logical and rational. The hagiographical stories that clustered around Francis's life—

that he preached even to birds (who stopped twittering to listen), tamed the ravening wolf of Gubbio, and received in his body the five wounds of the crucified Christ (the stigmata, or piercing of his hands, feet, and side)—were probably taken in a nonliteral spirit by many of the people who first heard them. Interactions with birds spoke of Francis's instinctive resonance with the natural world, the chastened wolf of his ability to elicit good from even the worst of creatures, the stigmata of his thoroughgoing identification with the sufferings of Christ. Did medieval people think these things had actually happened? They might well have considered such a question beyond answering and would instead, like Frida Kahlo, have invoked "the extraordinary beauty of truth."

But because we do not think the way they did, we often misunderstand them. In the historian William Manchester, for instance, we find only contempt for all things medieval. "In all that time," he claims preposterously, "nothing of real consequence had either improved or declined. . . . Shackled in ignorance, disciplined by fear, and sheathed in superstition, [medieval people] trudged into the sixteenth century in the clumsy, hunched, pigeon-toed gait of rickets victims, their vacant faces, pocked by smallpox, turned blindly toward the future they thought they knew—gullible, pitiful innocents who were about to be swept up in the most powerful, incomprehensible, irresistible vortex [that is, the Renaissance] since Alaric had led his Visigoths and Huns across the Alps, fallen on Rome, and extinguished the lamps of learning a thousand years before."

Manchester's libel is peppered with his own unexamined anti-Catholicism, which leads him into one howler after another. (He fulminates against an "infallible" "Vatican," seeming not to know that the doctrine of papal infallibility was virtually unknown in the Middle Ages and that the Vatican did not become the primary papal residence till the union of Italy in 1870.) How he imagines that the Renaissance of the sixteenth century could have arisen from the starved and shrunken medieval culture he describes, I just don't know. As King Lear said (with exquisite medieval logic), "Nothing will come of nothing."

In fact, medieval Europe was far more cosmopolitan and international than it has been since—at least till the establishment and uncertain functioning of the EU. A Frenchman could be king of England; his archbishop of Canterbury might be Greek; a Provençal princess might wed a Spaniard, a German, or a Pole; a man from Umbria might consider himself more French than Italian. But there was a division even then between Europe north and Europe south. The south—Italy south of Lombardy, the parts of France that spoke Provençal, Spain, Portugal, and (to some extent) Ireland, a sort of Mediterranean island misplaced in the Atlantic[a]—was sensuous and sexual. As one went north toward the Germanic tribes, the Saxons, the Franks, the Prussians, the Scandinavians, many pleasures lost their evident appeal, and one encountered more silence, less show, a more rigorous sense of order, both personal and social, and people who had probably never since adulthood taken all their clothes off—and who, if stripped naked, looked like plucked chickens, rather than like the sinuous, sun-loving, copper-colored humans of the south. (Think of the embarrassed white limbs of Adam and Eve in the paintings of Dutch and Flemish masters, as opposed to the expansively easeful biblical nudes given us by Michelangelo and his fellow Italians.) It was partly a matter of climate, of course, and partly of ethnicity. The Mediterranean lands of the old Romans (and even of the old Celts) would remain Catholic; those of the Germanic tribes—unless, like the Rhinelanders, the Schwarzwalders, the Bavarians, and the Austrians, they maintained southern connections—would tend in the sixteenth century to break away and form less ambiguous, more clearly rule-bound and austere societies.

The lands of the Slavs, the snowmen, the

---

[a] The tradition of Irish prudery is of recent origin. Though its roots may be traced in part to the post-Reformation education of Irish Catholic clergy in French institutions tinged by Jansenism (Calvinism in its Catholic manifestation), its most obvious source is the English language itself, learned by the great majority of Irish people only in the nineteenth century—and then in its sexually repressed and respectability-obsessed Victorian form. In any case, it is not of medieval origin. See *How the Irish Saved Civilization,* p. 214n and passim.

toughest peoples of all, lay beyond such distinctions. For in Eastern Europe, whether Catholicism or Orthodoxy prevailed, there flourished a Christianity of inhuman fasts, unending winters, and interminable liturgies, as well as a personal hygiene that included boiling oneself in steam, then rolling in ice. Whether one was naked or clothed, the point was never sensuality but survival. The Czechs, a partly Slavic, partly Celtic people, were an interesting exception.

The great jumble that was medieval Europe should warn the historian against pronouncements too broad, for sprightly—and sometimes garish—exceptions to his generalizations spring up everywhere. As one considers Manchester's depictions of medievals as "shackled in ignorance, disciplined by fear, and sheathed in superstition," one wonders if he ever surveyed the freewheeling spirit of intellectual inquiry that invigorated the great urban universities of the thirteenth century.

If you could walk the streets of Paris in the thirteenth century, you would encounter many familiar sights and sounds. The bustling city, full of impressive architecture, lively commerce and exotic wares, beggars and other casualties of urban life, self-regarding fashion plates, men on the make, and even gawking tourists, would remind you of many a modern city. Though much smaller than any contemporary capital, the Paris of eight centuries ago was a noisy warren of rough and splendid contrasts, a maze of stage sets featuring comic and tragic scenes in alternation, such as only a great city can produce.

But nowhere in this always colorful, often dirty, sometimes sweaty panorama would you feel more at home, more sure of who was who and what was what, than along the city's Left Bank, home to artists, writers, absentminded professors, and unruly students—indeed, the cultural nerve center of medieval Europe. The students, many thousands of them, constituted the largest population group on the Left Bank. They were especially numerous in the Latin Quarter, clustered around the famous rue du Fouarre.[b] They were divided into four principal group-ings: the French, the Norman, the English-German, and the Picard (or students from the Low Countries). Students who didn't fit obviously into one of the other three categories were assigned to the Picard. Since all had different mother tongues, Latin, the language in which the mas-ters gave their lectures, became the lingua franca of student intercourse; hence, the Latin Quarter.

The University of Paris was chartered in 1200, some fifty years after Europe's first univer-sity at Bologna. But whereas Bologna distin-guished itself immediately in the field of law (and thereby ensured that Latin would remain the technical language of law throughout the West), Paris seemed to distinguish itself in everything, if especially in philosophy and other liberal arts. Though we sometimes speak of an-cient "universities" (such as one at Bordeaux in Gaul in the time of Ausonius and another at Glendalough in Ireland in the time of Saint Kevin), those were amorphous, informal, vol-untary associations compared to the structured universities of the Middle Ages, which are the direct ancestors of our own. Students enrolled, paid tuition, and sat for announced series of lectures, which were delivered by salaried schol-ars who were members of specific faculties—medicine, law, theology, the arts—as well as of professional associations. The university itself was a chartered corporation[c] largely indepen-dent of the city and kingdom in which it was housed. The University of Bologna was even run by its students, who voted the members of the administration into and out of office.

Other universities soon sprang up after the

---

b Rue du Fouarre (or Straw Street) still exists, though most of its curved extent has been renamed rue de Dante; and it continues to attract hordes of young people—today to its cluster of comic book shops. It may be found across the Seine just south of the Cathedral of Notre-Dame. A few steps west of rue du Fouarre, once strewn with straw to keep down dust, stands the twelfth-century Church of Saint Julien-le-Pauvre, Paris's oldest surviving building. The winding streets surrounding this little church still speak of medieval matters.

---

c The idea of separately chartered entities began with chartered towns, which provided the models for chartered universities. Medieval craft guilds, which were a combination of professional associations and labor unions, provided the models for university faculties as well as for professors banding together to achieve common goals not directly connected to teaching.

models of these first two: at Oxford, for instance, at Naples and Salerno, at Angers and Toulouse, at Valladolid and Salamanca, and by the fourteenth century at Prague, Vienna, Heidelberg, and Cologne, all of them blossoming from well-established and intellectually busy city schools of earlier centuries. Sometimes a university was born of student discontent, as when some dissident Oxfordians betook themselves to Cambridge and some outraged Bolognese exiled themselves permanently to Padua.

Except at Bologna, students did not rule the roost. Their sheer numbers gave them much power, nonetheless, and their mass movements were rightly feared by administrators, masters, and townsmen, who had come gradually to depend on student patronage for their livelihoods. If the so-called student nations elected to close down a university and take their leave of the city in which they lodged, all their providers suffered, but none more than the local entrepreneurs who offered food, drink, lodging, books, paper, ink, and other services, such as laundry, housekeeping, and whoring. Most feared by administrators and townees alike was any common effort by faculty and student body to wrest concessions or new rights. Such "strikes" were no more unknown in medieval Paris than they were in the Paris of 1968. More common than strikes, however, was the widespread late-night student consumption of cheap and plentiful beer, as well as the deadly combination of drunken student hooliganism and police overreaction. *Plus ça change, plus c'est la même chose.*

At the same time, there were many differences between the medieval university and the modern. Students generally entered the university at age fourteen and stayed for a minimum of eight years. Their basic study was of the seven liberal arts, divided in the Roman manner into the *trivium* (grammar, dialectic, and rhetoric) and the *quadrivium* (the mathematical sciences of arithmetic, Euclidean geometry, astronomy, and musical theory).ᕯ In grammar, one mastered Latin, the continent-wide language of the educated classes; in dialectic, one learned to fashion a logical argument,

ᕯ The medieval course of studies can be traced at least as far back as Julius Caesar's librarian, Varro, who died in 27 B.C. He, however, enumerated nine liberal arts: the seven recognized by medievals plus medicine and architecture—which were dropped from the list by certain early medieval figures, such as Cassiodorus (d. 585) and Isidore of Seville (d. 636).

partly by imitation of philosophers, ancient and contemporary; and in rhetoric, one was taught the refinements of constructing prose, whether oral or written, in such a way as to seize the attention of listeners or readers and to hold their attention through the course of one's exposition. That so much time was devoted to what would today be compressed into a single course with a title such as "Freshman Comp" meant that, unlike contemporary graduates, all the graduates of medieval universities were truly literate and markedly skilled in an impressive repertoire of communication techniques.

Whereas the first six years at university were devoted to lectures by faculty, the last two were set aside to allow the students to show off what they had learned by putting forth specific theses and defending these publicly before audiences that were critical and vocal. University audiences could make a novice lecturer into an overnight intellectual celebrity. Just as peremptorily, they could pack him off to permanent provincial obscurity.

After all this (and a battery of oral examinations), one might be awarded the symbolic laurel wreath of a bachelor of arts degree—though then, as now, there were students who failed to attain a degree, while others settled comfortably into the routine of the perpetual student, still taking courses when their contemporaries had long since taken up professions. An additional year beyond the baccalaureate could win you a master's degree (or license to teach). But if you wished further study in, say, law, medicine, philosophy, or theology, you would need to be able to stay for as much as a dozen years more. Given such daunting prospects (and so many years with little chance of earned income), it is not surprising that the sons of the aristocracy made up a sizable portion of student populations, though there were also scholarships for poorer students, often instituted and administered by local lords or clergy who wished to raise intellectual standards in their home districts.

Like all rich and abiding manifestations of human cultural life, universities took time to develop. We can trace their beginnings to the palace and cathedral schools of the Carolingian era,[c] staffed initially by Irish and English monks, who were the first to implement the *trivium/quadrivium* structure. Their pupils, both noble and poor (for there were scholarship students even then), were educated to take their places, some as lords who could actually read their own correspondence, others as court scribes or bishops' scribes—the two professions that then required literacy and learning. From the ranks of these scribes the higher clergy (bishops, archbishops, and cardinals) would be chosen, but not parish priests, who were required to learn by heart—but not necessarily to read—the words inscribed in the splendidly ornamented books of Latin prayers and rituals.

The collapse of the Roman Empire in the West had devastated European learning, and in the process literacy itself had become endangered. The enormous loss of books in the early Middle Ages (through catastrophes large and small, connected to the fall of Rome and the barbarian invasions) meant that centuries had to pass for basic texts to be rediscovered, recopied, and distributed widely and for libraries to be built up again. But once this had happened, and libraries such as Disibodenberg's were established, creative intellectual life began to percolate once more. Isolated monastic schools, however, could never quite morph into lively centers of learning, for they could not attract the variety of teachers who, in the end, make for intellectual excitement—if only because they are so often in disagreement with one another. For that to happen, cathedral schools in towns and cities had to grow to the point where they could support a larger range of lecturers. A full century before the formal chartering of the University of Paris, the city was already astir with new learning and new masters. And of these masters, none was more celebrated, hated, and sought after than a hot young Breton aristocrat in his early twenties named Peter Abelard.

[c] Charlemagne (or Carolus Magnus), the first Holy Roman Emperor, instigated the short-lived Carolingian renaissance of the ninth century, often referred to as medieval Europe's first renaissance. The renaissance of the twelfth and thirteenth centuries—the subject of this book—is the second. *The* Renaissance of the sixteenth century is the third.

There can be no doubt that Abelard's was the best mind of his age. Not only that, he was exceptionally handsome and utterly self-possessed; he spoke (and sang, for that matter) in an alluring timbre that few could match; and his ready wit was sharp as a short sword. Even as a student in Paris, he had publicly exposed the logical flaws in the propositions of one of his masters and, by sheer force of argument, lured most of the master's students to his own unofficial lectures. The master, Anselm de Laon, was, to be sure, an obfuscating pontificator, and "anyone who knocked at his door to seek an answer to some question went away more uncertain than he came." "He had," recalled Peter much later, "a remarkable command of words, but their meaning was worthless and empty of all sense." Abelard knew how good he was; and if he had a fault, it was the strutting cockiness of a young man who knows he's smarter than everyone else—a quality few can admire, while many pray fervently for his *bouleversement*.

Abelard rooted his thinking in the writings of Plato's student and antagonist Aristotle, only some of which were available in twelfth-century Europe. Plato, not Aristotle, was the Greek philosopher beloved of the fathers of the ancient church and, for that matter, of the whole ancient world. Plato was the one who taught that there was another world, a truer world, in which all the partial goodness, beauty, and justice that we experience in this world is whole and complete; and the fathers saw his description of this "World of the Forms" as a kind of Greek pagan anticipation of the Christian doctrine of the Heaven where God resides. Plato was a radical pessimist who bemoaned the broken incompleteness of our world and of our earthly existence, so much so that one can trace a direct line of development from Plato's antimaterialism and scorn for human flesh to Augustine's doctrine of Original Sin.

Aristotle denied that the World of the Forms was anything but a figment of Plato's imagination.[f] While not denying the existence of the soul—a pagan Greek discovery—Aristotle pointed his students in the direction of this world, the world that could be observed, analyzed, and understood. Aristotle was no idealist like Plato, who believed that ideas were realer than everything we saw, heard, and touched. Aristotle was a rationalist and a materialist. His chief tool for understanding the world was logic, a science he invented; and though many of Aristotle's writings had been lost to the West during the catastrophic destruction of its libraries, some of his writings on logic remained available.

It was the panoply of Aristotelian techniques associated with rational persuasion that Abelard made such brilliant and innovative use of. In his book *Sic et Non* (Yes and No), he would one day show students how to set up an argument for almost anything (Yes) and then demolish it (No) by rational means. This practice would enable a student to feel at home in the world of argument to such an extent that he could finally come to think for himself, to critique the ideas of others—even ideas held sacrosanct by centuries of tradition—and to come at last to his own rational (but firmly held) conclusions. For, as Abelard would write in his famous book, "the prime source of wisdom has been defined as continuous and penetrating inquiry. The most brilliant of all philosophers, Aristotle, encouraged his students to undertake this task with every ounce of their curiosity. . . . For by doubting we come to inquire, and by inquiring we perceive the truth."

[f] In medieval philosophy, this dispute was called "the problem of universals." A universal signifies a unity with reference to some plurality—i.e., "mankind" versus individual men. Any intellectual concept—beauty, goodness, justice, etc.—is a universal, for it stands as a unity against individual beauties, individual persons of goodness, individual acts of justice, etc. The basic philosophical question is what reality these universals possess. Plato believed they had a reality separate from earthly things and existed in the World of the Forms, which was far superior to the shadowy realities of our world because earthly realities were real only insofar as they partook of the existence of their ultimate models in the World of the Forms (the "really real"). This philosophical position is called—paradoxically, from a modern standpoint—extreme realism; Augustine of Hippo was its most outstanding later proponent. Aristotle, the father of moderate realism, believed that universals do exist but only in the real objects of sense experience and that human beings perceive the universal dimension intellectually (i.e., I know my neighbor Sam is an individual; I also know him to be human

and therefore partaking of the universal, humanity). Thomas Aquinas would in the thirteenth century become the most important proponent of the Aristotelian position. "Everything," said Thomas, "that is in the intellect has been in the senses." Though it was to the Aristotelian school that Abelard attached himself, he was ingeniously anticipating Aristotle's solution, since Aristotle's writings on this subject were not available in the West till after Abelard's time. Other positions are possible, such as nominalism, which contends that universals are but words. A fairly concise discussion of this mind-scrambling business may be found in *The New Catholic Encyclopedia,* XIV, 322ff— though you are advised to read at your own risk.

Uh-oh. Rational inquiry begins with doubt? Such as doubting, say, the revealed truths of the Christian religion? Though Abelard never directly challenged central truths, such as the Trinity or Christ's divinity and saving mission, he brazenly announced solutions to knotty theological questions that left conservatives shocked to their marrow. He rejected Augustine's claims on behalf of Original Sin, committed by Adam and Eve and inherited by all mankind. How could we inherit a sin that we had no part in committing? (We may, like the heirs of a bankrupt, he admitted, inherit the punishment.) He denied that Christ died to pay for our sins, as if God the Father either required such ghoulish restitution or permitted Satan to exact it. Christ, asserted Abelard, died—in an act of supreme generosity and identification with the human condition—out of love for us and to make us more loving. The young philosopher exonerated the Jews from the charge of deicide, a favorite in the canon of medieval prejudices. Since they had no idea that Jesus was God, the Jews cannot be accused of wishing to murder God, only of proposing for execution a man they considered a rebel against Jewish religious authority. As Jesus himself had said of all his executioners, "They don't know what they're doing."

It would take more than eight centuries and the perpetration of unspeakable horrors before the Catholic Church—during the quasi-miraculous event of the Second Vatican Council—would conclusively adopt Abelard's reasoning in respect to Jewish guilt for the death of Christ. As for Original Sin, it is chiefly because Pierre Teilhard de Chardin, the ever-gentlemanly twentieth-century Jesuit paleontologist, distanced himself from this Augustinian position that his works of genius, offering a unique combination of scientific and theological insight, remain under a Vatican cloud. And though the idea that Christ died to repay his Father for human sin is still a favorite theory of many (especially evangelical) Christians, it is a doctrine no one can make logical sense of, for, like the Calvinist theory of Election, it necessitates a sort of voraciously pagan Father God steeped in cruelty and, in the case of Jesus's horrific death, his son's blood.

At the age of twenty-five, Abelard set up his own Left Bank school on Mont-Sainte-Geneviève, which would soon provide the nucleus for the University of Paris. In 1113, when he was not yet thirty-five, he was invited to teach at the prestigious cathedral school of Notre-Dame de Paris, where his sensational lectures were sold-out, standing-room-only successes. There he also undertook a private tutorial for the niece of one of the cathedral canons, a man named Fulbert. The niece, Héloïse, was an extremely beautiful and intellectually accomplished teenager; and Abelard, the consummate scholar, who had previously seemed impervious to any temptation but learning and literature, fell deeply in love with her, as did she with him. "In looks she did not rank lowest," Abelard would report smugly at a later date, "while in the extent of her learning she stood supreme." Thus does the consummate scholar convey to us that he loved Héloïse especially for her mind, while giving himself away completely in his subsequent description of their union:

> We were united, first under one roof, then in heart; and so with our lessons as a pretext we abandoned ourselves entirely to love. Her studies allowed us to withdraw in private, as love desired, and then with our books open before us, more words of love than of our reading passed between us, and more kissing than teaching. My hands strayed oftener to her bosom than to the pages; love drew our eyes to look on each other more than reading kept them on our texts. To avert suspicion I sometimes struck her, but these blows were prompted by love and tender feeling rather than

anger and irritation, and were sweeter than any balm could be. In short, our desires left no stage of love-making untried, and if love could devise something new, we welcomed it. We entered on each joy the more eagerly for our previous inexperience, and were the less easily sated.

Here in the second decade of the twelfth century we meet a couple whose sensibility is as modern as our own, as rational as the wryest critic writing in *The New York Review of Books,* as flagrant as the lovers in a buzz-worthy contemporary novel. Little if anything separates us from them.

The punishment visited upon them, however, must bring any reader up short, reminding us that Abelard and Héloïse lived in a very different time and place from those most of us inhabit. Their steamy affair was the subject that all Paris was talking about. The lovers had thrown caution to the winds to such an extent that songs Abelard had written to Héloïse began to be sung everywhere—though undoubtedly in haunts not frequented by Fulbert, so it took a while for the uncle to catch on. Once he did, he attempted to keep the lovers apart, which drove them to such indiscretion that they were finally found in bed together. The sight of Héloïse's growing belly impelled Abelard to send her to his sister in Brittany, where Héloïse gave birth to a son, whom she named Astralabe.

Abelard then sought out Fulbert, made a clean breast of it, and promised to marry Héloïse. Abelard's *apologia* for himself relied heavily on the language of Ovid and the troubadours: "protest[ing] that I had done nothing unusual in the eyes of anyone who had known the power of love." The word he uses for love is *amor,* the Latin equivalent of Greek *eros,* meaning sexual desire. The usual word used by medievals (as by ancient Romans) to indicate nonsexual love was *caritas,* the Latin equivalent of *agape,* the Greek New Testament's word for love that does not seek its own aggrandizement. In the ancient world, there was no connection between the two loves, for one was self-seeking, the other disinterested. But by Abelard's day the new romanticism had al-

ready succeeded in blurring the difference between the two words,[9] so it may be that
Abelard hoped to recruit old Fulbert to the
newly laundered banner of *amor*. If so, he had
badly misjudged his man.

Abelard's only stipulation to Fulbert was
"that the marriage should be kept secret so as
not to damage my reputation." In those days,
a master of the cathedral school, even if he
was not an ordained priest (which Abelard was
not), was expected to live as a celibate because
the school was revered throughout Europe for
the severity of its standards. Fulbert "agreed,
pledged his word and that of his supporters, and
sealed the reconciliation I desired with a kiss."
Abelard then set out for Brittany intending to
bring Héloïse back to Paris "to make her my
wife."

But here he ran into what was for him an
entirely unanticipated difficulty: Héloïse was unwilling to marry. Unlike Abelard, she did not
believe that Fulbert was genuinely satisfied with
the arrangements nor that any "satisfaction
could ever appease" him. Second, she believed
that philosophers had no business marrying,
since they belonged to "all mankind," and that
she could win no honor from such a marriage.
She foresaw clearly "the unbearable annoyances
of marriage and its endless anxieties . . . What harmony can there be,"
she asked, "between pupils and nursemaids, desks and cradles, books or
tablets and distaffs, pen or stylus and spindles? Who can concentrate on
thoughts of Scripture or philosophy and be able to endure babies crying,
nurses soothing them with lullabies, and all the noisy coming and going

9   The popular medieval
hymn *"Ubi caritas et amor,
Deus ibi est"* (Where *caritas*
and *amor* are, there is God)
displays this blurring of
meanings. There is an
innocence to Abelard that
probably blinded him to
Fulbert's more primitive
thought patterns. This
flower-child aspect
certainly evidences itself
in the name the lovers
bestowed on their child.
An astralabe (now, more
commonly "astrolabe")
was an analogue computer
invented by the ancient
Greeks, and improved by
the Arabs, to measure the
altitude of stars and other
heavenly bodies. In the
twelfth century, thanks to
Arab mariners, Western
Europeans had begun to
use it to plot the course
of seagoing vessels and to
make vast improvements
in astronomical (and
calendrical) predictability.
To name a child Astralabe
was to suggest that he was
destined to be a very
modern (and starry)
trendsetter. It brings to
mind the avant-garde rock
musician Frank Zappa,
who named his daughter
Moon Unit.

of men and women about the house? Will [you]," she questioned Abelard, "put up with the constant muddle and squalor which small children bring into the home?"

She proposed an unheard-of solution: she would stay out of her uncle's reach in Brittany, where Abelard could visit her whenever he was free. As Abelard was to recount it later, she insisted that "the name of friend [*amica*] instead of wife would be dearer to her and more honorable to me—only love [*amor*] freely given should keep me for her, not the constriction of a marriage tie, and if we had to be parted for a time, we should find the joy of being together all the sweeter the rarer our meetings were." A no-strings arrangement, which Abelard in his earnestness refused. So Héloïse gave way to his wishes, prophesying, however, that "we shall both be destroyed. All that is left to us is suffering as great as our love has been."

They were wed in secret, after which Fulbert and his friends began to spread news of the marriage, breaking "the promise of secrecy." Fulbert then began to abuse Héloïse verbally and physically, so Abelard spirited her away to the convent of Argenteuil, where she had once gone to school. Fulbert, certain that Abelard intended to rid himself of Héloïse and leave her forever with the nuns, managed to enter his lodgings while he slept. There, with the help of kinsmen and servants, he held Abelard fast and castrated him. As the sun rose, news of the atrocity spread through Paris like wildfire, and "the whole city gathered before [Abelard's] house," lamenting, crying, and groaning. Their "unbearable weeping and wailing" so tormented the poor philosopher, lying in a pool of his own blood, that "I suffered more from their sympathy than from the pain of my wound, and felt the misery of my mutilation less than my shame and humiliation."

Fulbert seems never to have been held to account for his act of retribution, perhaps because Abelard never pressed charges, more likely because Fulbert was too well connected to be brought to justice. But, as Abelard informs us, "the two who could be caught"—his own treacherous servant and one of Fulbert's men—were blinded and castrated, probably by students of Abelard. All that was left to the tragic couple was the lifetime of suffering Héloïse had foreseen. Héloïse became a famous abbess, Abelard a monk and an even more famous philosopher, theologian, and writer than he was already[b]—but also a public thinker dogged by insistent accusations of heresy.

His chief tormentor would be Bernard of Clairvaux, sponsor of Hildegard of Bingen and would-be censor of Eleanor of Aquitaine, who now makes his third appearance in this book. Bernard was the self-appointed Grand Inquisitor of twelfth-century Europe, a sham saint capable of complete chastity as well as of undying jealousy and hatred. How he loathed Abelard for his former freedom of body and his continuing freedom of mind. How he wished him only further ruin—all of course under the deceptive umbrella of Bernard's scrupulous monitoring of theological orthodoxy. "Faith believes," proclaimed Bernard with a sneer. "It does not dispute."

His persecution, following his very nearly public castration, shook Abelard's famous self-confidence. "God," Abelard came to believe, "had struck me in the parts of the body with which I had sinned." At his life's end, Abelard even begged forgiveness for any inadvertent heresy he might have fallen into. "Logic," wrote Abelard in his final "Confession of Faith," "has made me hated by the world. . . . I do not wish to be a philosopher if it means conflicting with Paul [the first-century missionary apostle and author of many New Testament letters], nor to be an Aristotle if it cuts me off from Christ." A sincere statement, but still the confession of a broken spirit whose fire has been quenched.

Héloïse was someone else altogether. More Roman Stoic than medieval Christian, more feeling woman than merely cerebral philosopher, more astringent realist than pious believer,

[b] We have lost Abelard's songs to Héloïse in the days of their courtship (though some may have been incorporated anonymously into the famous collection *Carmina Burana*). Besides his works of ethics and theology, his later liturgical songs, his letters to Héloïse, and his autobiography (called *Historia Calamitatum* and usually appended to the letters), he left an intriguingly modern account entitled *Dialogue Between a Philosopher, a Jew, and a Christian*.

she nonetheless kept both her religious vows and her promises to Abelard. Having no alternative, she became an exemplary, cool-headed nun, but one who never forgot who she really was and what she really felt. Many years after the parting of the lovers and their claustration in separate monastic communities, they embarked upon an intense correspondence. Héloïse's letters, in particular, are so unlike any other medieval expression left to us that many scholars for many years upheld the theory that they were modern forgeries. But they are written in an excellent, allusive twelfth-century Latin that would be nearly impossible to fake; and since no one has been able to offer a consistent theory on how they came to be if they are not by Héloïse, the scholarly tide has turned at last and named her as their author.

Her first letter begins with a salutation that is both technically correct and utterly atypical of her time (and just as atypical of most other times, as well):

> To her lord, or rather father; to her husband, or rather brother;
> from his handmaid, or rather daughter; from his wife, or rather sister:
> to Abelard, from Héloïse.

She upbraids her former lover in no uncertain terms for having failed to write to her for so many years, for forgetting her and leaving her comfortless, despite "the love I have always borne you, as everyone knows, a love which is beyond all bounds . . . God knows," she goes on,

> I never sought anything in you except yourself; I wanted simply you, nothing of yours. I looked for no marriage-bond, no marriage portion, and it was not my own pleasures and wishes I sought to gratify, as you well know, but yours. The name of wife may seem more sacred or more binding, but sweeter for me will always be the word friend, or, if you will permit me, that of concubine or whore. . . . God is my witness that if Augustus, Emperor of the whole world, thought fit to honor me with mar-

riage and conferred all the earth on me to possess for ever, it would be dearer and more honorable to me to be called not his Empress but your whore.

What she asks for now is that Abelard write to her so as to fortify her courage and help her persevere in an arid life she would never have chosen freely. So it is her letter that initiates the famous correspondence that follows, one in which Abelard does his best to explain himself and to make up, as well as he can, for his long silence. "And so," writes the abbess,

> in the name of that God to whom you have dedicated yourself, I beg you to restore your presence to me in the way you can—by writing me some word of comfort, so that in this at least I may find increased strength and readiness to serve God. When in the past you sought me out for sinful pleasures your letters came to me thick and fast, and your many songs put your Héloïse on everyone's lips, so that every street and house resounded with my name. Is it not far better now to summon me to God than it was then to satisfy our lust? I beg you, think what you owe me, give ear to my pleas, and I will finish a long letter with a brief ending: farewell, my only love.

The correspondence took place over five years or so, containing many queries from Héloïse, ever the eager student, and many instructions from Abelard, and ending in all likelihood about the year 1138. Abelard died early in the next decade at the Cluniac monastery of Saint-Marcel, near Chalon-sur-Saône, at the age of sixty-three, probably of Hodgkin's disease. Afterwards, Héloïse sought the favor of Abelard's body from Peter the Venerable, the holy abbot of Cluny. Peter had admired Abelard, calling him "the Socrates of the Gauls, Plato of the West, our Aristotle, prince of scholars," and was happy to oblige Héloïse, who buried her husband in a tomb in her Convent of the Paraclete, which

Abelard had founded and turned over to her and her nuns. At the same time, Peter the Venerable promised Héloïse that he would try to get a good cathedral job ("a prebend") for Astralabe—the only mention we possess of Astralabe's continuing existence and of his mother's continuing concern for him. When she died some twenty years later, the nuns buried her with Abelard, her "only love"; and though their bones have been disinterred several times over the eight and a half centuries that have intervened between them and us, they lie together to this day, close to the entrance of Père-Lachaise, where sympathetic Parisians still leave flowers on their grave.

D espite Abelard's intellectual brilliance, his handsome exterior and theatrical temperament worked against the wide acceptance of his novel ideas. But in the thirteenth century at the University of Paris, then in full swing, a man of very different aspect and temperament, though just as innovative and even more dependent on Aristotle, succeeded in baptizing Aristotelian thought in a manner that gained wide acceptance and, in the end, even lasting papal approval. That man was Thomas Aquinas, a slow-moving, seldom-speaking great lump of a friar,[i] who gave off no flashes of brilliance and even appeared to casual observers to be a bit of a dimwit.

Thomas (Tomasso d'Aquino in his native Italian) was the youngest son of Landulf of Aquino, an important nobleman whose lands lay between Naples and Rome in the northern reaches of the Kingdom of Sicily, then ruled by the Holy Roman Emperor, Barbarossa's Hohenstaufen grandson and Thomas's second cousin, the astonishing Frederick II, known as Stupor Mundi (the Stupefaction of the World). Landulf sired at least six other sons and five daughters, most of whom

---

i "Friar" (from *frere*, or brother, in both Old French and Middle English) was the normal designation for a man of one of the wandering orders, such as the Franciscans, not vowed to remain in a particular place and sing the hours of the church's office (or official prayer).

grew up to take prominent places in the world. Thomas's mother, Teodora of Chieti, Landulf's second wife, was a Lombard, but in his veins flowed Norman, German, and Italian blood as well. His ancestry was, in fact, typically continental; and the males of his family, like their fellow knights throughout Europe, were skilled in war and poetry. Their particular war was waged almost continually on behalf of the emperor against the pope, rendering their lovely hill country of Roccasecca and Montesangiovanni full of peril.

Thomas gave evidence from an early age that he would rather handle a book than a sword. Indeed, so visibly did he shirk the school of chivalry, of horse and target, lance and armor, that Landulf and Teodora resolved quite early in his life to give him to Monte Cassino, the great Benedictine abbey in their neighborhood. With the monks, Thomas advanced from discipline to discipline with amazing speed, despite his heavy gait and growing girth. But physical prowess was so lacking in the boy that even his handwriting was embarrassingly awkward. In later life, it would become, as the manuscripts left to us bear witness, as unintelligible as a doctor's prescription.

By the time he was eighteen, the imperial-papal war had reached Monte Cassino itself, so the monks-in-training were removed to the University of Naples in the Kingdom of Sicily to complete their studies. There, under the tutelage of Peter of Ireland, the teenage Thomas was introduced to Aristotle through the recently translated commentaries of the Hispano-Arabic philosopher Averroës. The surviving works of Aristotle had never been lost to the Muslim world (thanks to Arabic-Byzantine connections); and in the relatively tolerant atmosphere of Arabic Spain, all these were gradually translated into Latin in a collaborative Muslim-Jewish-Christian effort. Thomas Aquinas was the first medieval Christian to have such access to all the surviving works (in Latin translation) that he could use them freely to construct his own philosophy.[j]

The members of Thomas's family, unimpressed by his original interest in an ancient

[j] Latin translations from Arabic, as well as original Latin works making use of Arabic—and often of Hebrew—words, begin to appear

in Europe as early as the mid-tenth century. Such Oriental influences also figure in the works of Gerbert of Aurillac, who was one of the first to introduce "Arabic" (actually Indian) numerals to replace the clumsy Roman system, which required the use of an abacus even for many simple calculations. (In 999, Gerbert became the first French pope, dying in office four years later.) Another early route by which Greek learning reached the West was that of Sicily and southern Italy, which long retained their Greco-Arabic culture. Salerno, in particular, which was a medical center from at least the ninth century, provided the medieval world with continuous, if flickering, illumination by Greek science. The great irony in all this cultural borrowing was that as Greek works in translation became generally available to Europeans, Islam, which had served the role of cultural conduit, was in retreat throughout Europe.

Greek philosopher, were thrown into confusion by his decision to leave the Benedictines and join the Dominicans. The Dominicans, like the Franciscans, were not vowed to stability but were known as mendicants (or wandering beggars), because they depended not on the abundance of abbey lands but on handouts from the faithful. Since the Aquinos could never have made Thomas a soldier, they had expected to make him in due course the abbot of Monte Cassino, a distinguished figure appropriate to their heritage. No lord or lady could bear a beggar in the family. The more soldierly Aquinos were dispatched to kidnap Thomas on his way to Bologna, whither he was wending in the company of John of Wildeshausen, master general of the Dominican order, and other friars en route to their annual general chapter. Thomas was confined to the family castle at Roccasecca, where he demonstrated such tenacity of purpose that Donna Teodora gave in at last and released him to rejoin the friars.

Thomas was fortunate to study at Cologne with the foremost Aristotelian of the day, Albert the Great, a German count who had joined the Dominicans. Albert's famous exposition *De natura rerum* (On the Nature of Things) was a landmark attempt to reestablish "natural philosophy"—or science, as we would call it today—in the Aristotelian spirit of observation, analysis, and conclusion. Simple people, amazed by what he seemed to know about the processes of nature, feared him as a sorcerer. He became Thomas's advance man, informing one and all that this seeming dolt, teased by his fellow students as "the Dumb Ox of Sicily," was a quiet genius who would outshine them all: "You call him a Dumb Ox; I tell you this Dumb Ox shall bellow so loud that his bellowing will fill the world." Following Thomas's ordination to the priesthood (while only in his mid-twenties), Albert recommended him for a teaching post at the University of Paris.

Thomas would spend much of his working life lecturing and writing at Paris, but with a significant interval in Italy, much of it spent setting up a school at the Dominicans' glorious complex of Santa Sabina on the Aventine Hill. Wherever he was, he read, lectured, wrote, and, as his obligations multiplied, dictated. Though he was able to read much more of Aristotle than had been available to Abelard, and though (as he remarked gratefully), "I have understood every page I ever read," Thomas's philosophical positions hardly differ from those of the earlier Parisian lecturer. The difference is in the tone, seldom contentious, never contemptuous, always serene and reasonable and so tranquilly analytical as to be magisterial. It is a tone that allays his readers' prejudices, calms their fears, and shores up their confidence. "So far as I can see" is his bland, oft-invoked phrase, even though what follows may contain a novel proposal or a conclusive rejection of some widely held notion.

In this way, Thomas eventually—by the wide circulation of his voluminous writings after his death—won over almost the whole of the Christian world to his philosophy. In the wake of Thomas Aquinas, medieval Christendom gave up its dread of non-Christian pagan philosophy and adopted most of the philosophical positions of Aristotle, as sorted through Thomas's careful sieve. The gloomy old Platonism of the early fathers of the church—Plato and his disciples (such as Plotinus) being the only Greeks previously exempted from general condemnation—was set aside somewhat and invoked less and less frequently. For Thomas did not believe that we lived in the gloom of a cave, tied to a decaying mass of matter, and that everything we perceived was illusion or trickery. He believed we lived in our bodies, created good by a good God, and received true perceptions through the media of our five senses, which like clear windows enabled us to form generally accurate impressions of the world as it is. He replaced the shadows of Plato's Cave with the sunshine of everyday reality.

Not only had God made us and made us good—and here Thomas's philosophy slid into his theology—God had deigned to share our humanity in the person of Jesus. Our bodies were not despicable carrion but temples of the Holy Spirit, the same Spirit that brooded over the face of the deep at the world's creation, the same Spirit that descended from on high to consecrate Jesus at his baptism in the River Jordan, for ours was the same physical humanity that Jesus shared, our senses the same five with which he had perceived the world. The Son of God's Incarnation had blessed and elevated all matter. With such thoughts as these did the medieval schoolmen (or scholastics) move the Christian worldview away from its previously pessimistic meditations on material corruption and human depravity and toward a worldview that was happier, more incarnational, and more appropriately Judeo-Christian.

Whether or not Augustine and the other ancient fathers would have consented to such propositions no longer mattered. They were far enough in the past, and Thomas's voice strong enough in the present, that his moderate realism carried the day, becoming in time the sturdy philosophy on which the Catholic Church would rest its theological structure, a happier edifice altogether than what had served it in earlier centuries. And yet, this considerable change in emphasis still linked the medieval with the ancient world, for a Greek was still at the bottom of the whole thing. When Chesterton, that sly exaggerator, calls this vast embrace by which medieval believer was linked to ancient philosopher "the great central Synthesis of history," he cannot be far wrong, for surely there is no other synthesis with longer grasp or deeper roots.

For all his balanced and capacious mind, much that Thomas had to say seems hugely irrelevant today. Modern readers find many passages baffling and wearisome. So many of Aristotle's distinctions, which Thomas brought over wholesale into his own system, impress us as pretty useless. What contemporary scientist could possibly do much of anything with the distinctions of substance (or essential nature) and accident (or appearance, inessential quality)? And yet it was from just such meditations on incarnate reality that medieval science would take its uncertain first steps.

What is a thing in itself? Is it even possible to understand anything in itself, or do we understand it only through the medium of universal categories? What is any object, and how is it related to the whole—to the rest of reality? These are questions the Presocratic philosophers had asked and which in the time of Thomas Aquinas continued to receive Greek answers.

Though Thomas distinguished carefully between natural reality and supernatural, he found that his (and Aristotle's) philosophical categories could be useful instruments for dealing with matters of faith. Thus, substance and accident were distinctions useful for the study of the Christian Eucharist. All such matters as the Eucharist, the Trinity, the Incarnation were mysteries inexplicable. Yet the mind could not be stopped from considering them, turning them over as if they were specimens in a laboratory, and trying to make some human sense of them. In the mystery of the Eucharist, ordinary bread and wine became Christ's body and blood, so that our bodies might feed on him and our souls be nourished. But when the priest pronounced the words of consecration used by Jesus at his Last Supper—"This is my body"; "This is my blood"—what happened? The elements did not change their appearance. No, said Thomas, the accidental appearances of bread and wine remain, but the substance, the essential nature of the elements, is metaphysically transubstantiated into Christ's body and blood.

The ancient fathers of the church, men from Clement to Augustine to Gregory the Great and beyond, had felt no need to pick apart such mysteries so clinically. They preferred to guard them, then leave them in the realm of mystery. But by the time of Thomas a great shift had already occurred. Centuries of eucharistic enactments—liturgies, masses, viaticums, communion services, eucharistic benedictions, expositions of the Blessed Sacrament, Corpus Christi processions through the streets—

had introduced into inquiring minds a series of insistent questions: what is going on here? what is its meaning? is anything happening and, if so, how? Many were as dissatisfied with Thomas's (and the church's) explanation as would have been Aristotle himself, who taught that an accident could not exist if it did not adhere to a substance. For there is no floating whiteness in our world, only the white picket fence. And since the accidents of bread and wine could hardly be said to adhere to Christ's body, was not this church teaching logical nonsense? Such a question pushed the questioner back to ancient Presocratic inquiries: what is this thing? what is its nature? what is that thing? what is everything? what is the world?

Thomas Aquinas died before he reached fifty, as pious a priest as ever lived and more industrious than any other, leaving behind twenty-five packed volumes of Latin (in the definitive Parma edition of 1873). Yet he stopped writing in his last days because, he said, "Everything I've written seems to me like so much straw compared to what I have seen." What he had seen we don't know but we probably have some hint of it in his eucharistic hymns, some composed at the invitation of the pope and showing a hidden side of Thomas, deeply devotional and surprisingly poetic. His hymns are untranslatable, their Latin too pithy and witty. The greatest one, the soaring *"Pange lingua"* (Sing, My Tongue), is still sung throughout the world each Maundy Thursday but never sounds quite right in English. Another, *"Adoro te devote, latens Deitas"* (Faithfully Do I Adore Thee, Hidden Deity), is almost as challenging to translate, though Gerard Manley Hopkins made a laudable attempt:

Adoro te devote, latens Deitas,
Quae sub his figuris vere latitas:
Tibi se cor meum totum subjicit,
Quia te contemplans totum deficit.

Godhead here in hiding, whom I do adore
Masked by these bare shadows, shape and nothing more,

See, Lord, at thy service low lies here a heart
Lost, all lost in wonder at the God thou art.

Visus, tactus, gustus in te fallitur;
Sed auditu solo tuto creditur:
Credo quidquid dixit Dei Filius:
Nil hoc verbo veritatis verius.

Seeing, touching, tasting are in thee deceived;
How says trusty hearing? that shall be believed:
What God's Son has told me, take for truth I do;
Truth himself speaks truly or there's nothing true.

In cruce latebat sola Deitas,
At hic latet simul et humanitas:
Ambo tamen credens atque confitens
Peto quod petivit latro paenitens. . . .

On the cross thy godhead made no sign to men;
Here thy very manhood steals from human ken:
Both are my confession, both are my belief,
And I pray the prayer of the dying thief. . . . [k]

In this poetic pondering, those old, reliable senses of ours are found to be deceived by the silent but overwhelming mystery of God. Behind the meditation unanswered questions surely press upon us—matters psychological, metaphysical, theological, and scientific. But the hymn removes the obscuring veil of centuries from the medieval mind, showing us a humble but questing spirit that must soon advance into unknown territory.

k   "The dying thief" is one of two criminals crucified on either side of Jesus. In Luke's Gospel, the thief asks Jesus to remember him "when you come into your Kingdom." Jesus replies: "I tell you solemnly: today you will be with me in Paradise."

FOUR

oxford, university of earthly things

the alchemist's quest
and its consequences

*He fed them with corn fat
and filled them with
honey from the rock.*

—INTROIT, CHOSEN BY THOMAS AQUINAS,
FOR THE FEAST OF CORPUS CHRISTI

THE LONG JUDEO-CHRISTIAN HISTORY of God's interventions in human affairs— from the feeding of the Chosen People in the parched Sinai desert to the feeding of the baptized people of Europe with *Corpus Christi,* the Flesh of God's Son— suggested to the medieval mind that reality was not pedestrian but fabulous, that is, replete with incredible marvels. Medieval lives may have been, by our standards, prosaic and predictible, but medieval imagination, the lens through which medieval men and women viewed the world, gave its viewers a more lively and grand account of reality than anything we would dare assay.

Nonetheless, the wave that emanated from Thomas Aquinas intellectualized Europe beyond any surge previously known, drawing the attention of all to the primacy of human reason in the struggle to come to terms with human experience. Not even God's revelation, filtered through scripture and church, could replace reason's role in tackling and settling questions—since even God's revelation must be approached, absorbed, and digested by human reason. Just as the five senses are the mind's windows on the world, the individual mind's reasoning capacity must be for each one of us the final interpreter of the extraordinarily diverse and often confusing data that the senses supply us with. Such a philosophy must necessarily reduce the role of revelation and of church in the lives of those who subscribe to it, for it is the human mind, and it alone, that ultimately sits in judgment on the meanings of the scriptures and the pronouncements of the church, as on all else. "Reason in a human being," reasoned Thomas analogously, "is rather like God in the world." Just as it is God who animates the world and its myriad manifestations and enables them to function, so reason animates the human being and enables him to function. Reason, therefore, is what gives human beings their link to divinity, for it is the possession of reason that makes us most like God.

Though the new intellectualism necessarily confined religion somewhat, it hardly eliminated it. Thomas, like all his colleagues, was an orthodox believer. He might, for the sake of a particular disputation, take an atheistic or heretical position, but he never adopted such a position as his own. He, too, found reality fabulous—and far too serious for intellectual clowning. "Three things are necessary," he wrote, "for a human being's salvation: to know what he ought to believe; to know what he ought to desire; and to know what he ought to do." Reasonable, yes, and respectful of rational knowledge above all else, but sober and focused on what truly mattered.

The unicorn, a symbol of Christ, about to lay his head in the lap of a virgin. The holly tree behind the unicorn is also a symbol of Christ. From a fifteenth-century French tapestry.

There was, however, a nonphilosophical form of knowledge far more appealing to the mass of human beings who hardly had time or aptitude for the endless disputations of the schoolmen: pictures, whether actual pictures or word pictures. From the twelfth century onward, an explosion of storytelling and a riot of color and form begin to invade street corner, church, castle, and library to the delight of ordinary people, who could find little or no delight in Thomas's tight reasoning. The famous series of stained-glass windows (in every cathedral and abbey church) that tell the stories of the Old Testament and the life of Christ, so often called "the Bible of the poor," were not the only visual feasts. There were tableaux, verbal and visual, that went beyond the scriptures to speak more theoretically, if always appealing as much to the eye and the ear as to the mind.

One of these was the story of the unicorn, who purifies water with his horn and can be captured only if he lays his head in the lap of a virgin. He is of course Christ, who lays his being in the womb of the Virgin and cleanses the world of its impurities. Another was the story of the pelican, who was believed to tear her breast with her beak to feed her young. She, too, was Christ, who nourishes us through excruciating but self-inflicted suffering. Both stories were told and retold in the illustrated books known as bestiaries, which purported to explain the symbolic significance of all God's creatures.

In the twelfth-century church of San Clemente in Rome, the brilliant mosaic apse over the main altar presents us with a view of reality that is both cosmic and eucharistic; and there is no sight in all of Rome more worthy of contemplation. The central image is of the crucified Christ, mildly accepting his suffering and death, his face full of peace. Perched on the four extremities of the dark, red-rimmed cross are twelve white doves, symbolic apostles, rapt in contemplation though about to fly off to the ends of the earth. Jesus's mother, Mary, and the Beloved

The twelfth-century apse of San Clemente, Rome.

Disciple stand in mourning beneath the arms of the cross. But spiraling forth from the foot of the cross, where it is watered by the blood of Christ, a stupendous acanthus bush curls outward and upward, encircling nearly a hundred separate images. These include flowers of many varieties, an oil lamp, a basket of fruit, beasts wild and tame, and people of all kinds involved in all kinds of labor. Each figure has a special meaning: a caged bird, for instance, represents the Incarnation, whereas wild birds flying upward are souls freed by death on their way to union with God. The humility of many of the figures is meant to remind us that not only have we been redeemed, but so has the whole world and everything in it. The spiraling branches of the acanthus embrace even two pagan Roman gods, Baby Jupiter, formerly king of the gods, and Baby Neptune, formerly king of the deep, who rides a slippery-looking dolphin. Even the ancient pagans have been redeemed, and their mythologies are usable by us, so long as we reduce them to less fearful and more apposite dimensions.

Most tender of all are the depictions of ordinary medieval life, shepherds with their flocks and herds, farm children helping their parents, a lord and a lady watching the proceedings, a tonsured monk giving food and water to a colorful bird, and a bosomy lady in white, wearing flow-

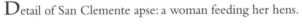

Detail of San Clemente apse: a woman feeding her hens.

Detail of San Clemente apse: one of two stags
drinking from the streams of water that flow from
the acanthus bush below the cross of Christ.

ing sleeves and an enormous brooch (neither of which would have
found approval with Bernard of Clairvaux) while feeding her excited
hens. One soon notes how many of these images are of creatures nourishing creatures or of creatures taking nourishment on their own, as
in the case of two stags drinking directly from streams that flow from
the root of the acanthus. "As the hart panteth after the water brooks, so
panteth my soul after thee, my God," we are meant to recall in the words
of Psalm 42.

To appreciate the impact of this mosaic it is nearly necessary to attend a mass celebrated at the altar below the apse. As the ritual of the
mass unfolds beneath the cosmic wildness of the apse, we reflect that we
are all caught up in the universal mystery of Christ, who has redeemed
us and all of creation, even the humblest humans and the humblest
things, so that he might come to us as bread.

It may strike the reader that a meditation on the meaning of the Eucharist is an extremely odd way for science to rise from the ashes of the Dark Ages, but that is more or less how it happened. Not only the mysterious bread and wine but the mysterious pelican, the mysterious bear, the mysterious lion, the mysterious stars, and even the lowly ant (whose economic thrift is a lesson in how to conduct our lives)—all

Detail of San Clemente apse: symbolic animals and objects, as well as scenes of various medieval people at their labors (including the woman feeding hens, lower left), all within the curled branches of the acanthus bush that is nourished by the blood of Jesus.

these and many more natural phenomena presented themselves to the medieval observer first of all as God's creations, as gifts descended from Heaven to us below. But at length the desire to interpret their meaning, to understand what they were there for, was refined—under the persistent influence of philosophers like Abelard and Aquinas—by Aristotle's logic and Aristotle's stress on the importance of natural observation. And so, in its rudimentary essentials, science may be said to have risen in the medieval world in a cloud of Christian imaginings, but borne aloft on an air current of new respect for reason and observation.

Nowhere in Europe did the new scientific sensibility stride more boldly into view than at the University of Oxford in the time of Roger Bacon. Though Oxford was then one of the newly chartered European universities, it had like Paris existed as a center of learning for longer than anyone could remember. Bacon was already a student at Oxford when Thomas Aquinas was a boy, for he was a decade older than Thomas (and would survive him by eighteen years, dying in 1294 when he was in his late seventies). Bacon's first model of the inquiring scientist was Oxford's broadminded chancellor Robert Grosseteste, later bishop of Lincoln, just about the first European to employ controlled experiments, using data that could be measured, quantified, and cross-checked mathematically. Bishop Grosseteste's range was as broad as his industriousness was deep: in addition to philosophical tracts and commentaries on many of the books of the Bible, he wrote groundbreaking treatises on the tides, solar heat, colors and the rainbow, meteors and comets. His Latin translation of Aristotle's *Nichomachean Ethics* and his commentaries on other works of Aristotle, such as the *Physics,* advanced the work of both general philosophers and those specialized philosophers who would come to be called scientists.

If little remains today (at least beyond the bourne of Merton, the university's oldest college) of the Oxford of Bacon's time, the town must already have had some of the feeling of antiquity that Matthew Arnold loved, "so venerable, so lovely . . . steeped in sentiment as she lies, spreading her gardens to the moonlight, and whispering from her towers the last enchantments of the Middle Age." It certainly boasted many of the miniature delights that Hopkins enumerates in his vision of medieval Oxford: "Towery city and branchy between towers; / Cuckoo-echoing, bell-swarmed, lark-charmed, rook-racked, river-rounded . . ." It was far less bustling than Paris and far less international, but the very insularity of its "folk, flocks, and flowers," its polished brasses and painted doors, its happy conjunction of town and countryside, gave Oxford its own well-swept, tucked-in charm. Though Latin was the only language officially permitted to students, we know that Chaucerian English—that wonderful mishmash of Anglo-Saxon and French—often resounded through the quads, if only because of the punishments meted out to any scholar who lapsed into his mother tongue. (He was, upon a second offense, obliged to eat his dinner alone in a corner of the refectory.)

Like Thomas Aquinas, Roger Bacon studied under Albert the Great and taught for a while at Paris (when Aquinas was there), but it is with Oxford and its heralded spirit of no-nonsense practicality and experimental positivism that he will ever be associated. Bacon took the great Dominican's enshrinement of reason and brought it a step further. "Reasoning," he wrote, "draws a conclusion and makes us grant the conclusion, but does not make the conclusion certain, nor does it remove doubt so that the mind may rest on the intuition of truth—unless the mind discovers it by the path of *experience*." Bacon then imagines a man coming upon the phenomenon of fire for the first time. The man might by reason arrive at the conclusion that fire burns, injures, and destroys. But this reasoning would not in itself tell him all we know of fire. He would need to put his hand in it, or, if not his hand, "some combustible substance," and "prove by experience what reasoning teaches. But when he has had the actual experience of combustion, his mind is made certain and rests in the full light of truth. Therefore," concludes Bacon axiomatically, "reasoning does not suffice, but experience does!"

Experience, by way of observation and experiment, beats unaided reason every time. Reason is necessary; we cannot function without it. But only experience can confirm what reason proposes. Albert had already taken a turn in this direction, declaring that in many matters *"Experimentum solum certificat"* (Experiment—or experience—alone gives certainty). But though Albert was for his time a great botanist, cataloguing and accurately describing a staggering profusion of trees, plants, and herbs, it would fall to his English pupil to embark upon seas of experience previously uncharted.

We know that Thomas was a fat friar and Francis a bone-thin ascetic, that Hildegard was a sickly nun and Eleanor a radiant queen. Of Roger we have no description at all, and he seems at times in his surviving writings so much a sprite, a will-o'-the wisp, that he would be too quick for anyone's pen to capture on a page. Realizing the need for accurate translations from foreign tongues, he compiled extensive grammars of the Greek and Hebrew languages and attempted, though never completed, a grammar of Arabic. But more important than these tremendous accomplishments (which would have been for most men the work of a lifetime or two), Bacon was the first medieval Christian to set forth an entire system of natural knowledge, based wholly on observation and experiment.

He experimented with lenses and mirrors; he seems to have invented a telescope and perhaps, as he is credited in Umberto Eco's *The Name of the Rose,* eyeglasses. He demonstrated that white light can be broken up into the spectrum of colors by passing it through glass beads. (Four and a half centuries ahead of a similar experiment that Isaac Newton would one day perform, Bacon alarmed his students by the uncanny magic of bringing a rainbow to earth.) His writing on the subject of the human eye remained the standard text till Johannes Kepler would take up optics and visual theory in the year 1600. Bacon declared that the speed of light, though enormous, was finite. But since this phenomenon cannot be observed by the naked eye and since it would take many more centuries to establish it as scientific fact, no one is sure how he came by his insight. He created astronomical tables far more accurate than anything previously conceived; and he urged the pope to reform the calendar, a reform that was accomplished by Pope Gregory XIII only in the late sixteenth century (and that produced what remains our calendar to this day, despite occasional, usually religious, objections).[a]

He was the first systematic geographer since ancient times, describing Europe, Asia, and much of Africa after doggedly collecting information from travelers; and he recognized that the earth was a sphere. (But then, so did virtually everyone in the medieval world. The stuff about "flat-earthers," medieval churchmen who condemned as heretics all who claimed that the earth was round, was a calumny invented by two fabulists working separately: Antoine-Jean Letronne, an anticlerical nineteenth-century Frenchman, and Washington Irving in the same century in his unreliable biography of Columbus.) Bacon, in particular, wrote as clearly and dispassionately as did the ancient Greeks on the "curvature of the earth."

Bacon's *Opus maius* is an enormous encyclopedia of all medieval knowledge in the arts and sciences. He created a general systemization of chemical knowledge; and his description of the composition and manufacture of gunpowder is the earliest known in the West: "One may cause there to burst forth from bronze [ordnance] thunderbolts more formidable than those produced by nature. A small quantity of prepared matter occasions a terrible explosion accompanied by a brilliant light. One may multiply this

[a] Medieval Christians used the Julian calendar, promulgated in the reign of Julius Caesar in the first century B.C. This calendar, because of an astronomical miscalculation, was about eleven minutes longer than the actual solar year. Bacon was aware of the discrepancy, which had grown to ten days by the time Gregory XIII resolved to correct the problem. Though the pope suppressed ten days of the year 1582, the role of the papacy was by then in dispute across Europe. It took Protestant England, for instance, almost two additional centuries to accept the Gregorian reform. The Orthodox Church has never accepted it, which is why major Christian feasts are normally celebrated later in Orthodox lands than in the West.

phenomenon so far as to destroy a city or an army." He even predicted the inventions of the steam engine and internal combustion: "Art can construct instruments of navigation such that the largest vessels governed by a single man will traverse rivers and seas more rapidly than if they were filled with oarsmen. One may also make carriages which without the aid of any animal will run with remarkable swiftness." In addition to foreseeing the coming of automobiles and steamships, he made plans, despite incredulous responses from his contemporaries, to construct a flying machine in which he believed men would one day travel.

For all that, Bacon was in some respects more medieval than the philosophers Abelard and Aquinas. For despite his status as "the first man of science in the modern sense" (in the accurate description of the British historian of science Charles Singer), Bacon was also an astrologer who raised his eyes to the heavens and an alchemist who searched beneath the earth—like the Alexandrian mathematicians who were his true forebears, a reader of stars and their significance and a practitioner of "this cursed craft," as the alchemist's assistant in *The Canterbury Tales* names the dark art of mining base metals for the purpose of changing them into gold. To appreciate how a great scientist could also be a magus and sorcerer, we must consult what we have already learned about the medieval worldview.

All early societies and civilizations believed that patterns in the heavens were predictive of life on earth and that the stars controlled our destinies. Such ideas entered the medieval world indirectly by way of the ancient civilizations of Egypt, India, and China and more directly by way of Greece, Rome, and, during the twelfth-century recovery of additional Greek texts, Arabia. These heavy influences were countered, to some extent, by the inconstant condemnations of the church, which could never approve wholeheartedly of astrology because it seemed to erase the moral contribution of the human will in decision making. Augustine of Hippo, in particular, had heaped scorn on the whole business. But it would take the elaboration of a solidly based science of astronomy in the time of Galileo and Shakespeare (both born in 1564) to render the claims of astrology incredible—at least among well-informed people.

Shakespeare's famous lines "The fault, dear Brutus, is not in our stars, / But in ourselves" are unlikely to have been expressed so definitely much before his time. In Bacon's time, what appears to us a confusion of astrology and astronomy was still unresolved. It was indeed Aquinas, rather than Bacon, who gave the first push toward separating the two. Aristotle, like all ancient philosophers, thought the universe eternal. Aquinas knew it had been created by God.[b] Building his exposition on an earlier one by the seminal Jewish philosopher Moses Maimonides, Aquinas argued that though Aristotle's analysis was logically correct, God had in fact created all things from nothing, choosing in his overflowing generosity that there be Something—the original mystical miracle—rather than nothing. Once the eternality of the universe was done away with, the inexplicably independent power of the stars was doomed to follow. One cannot logically believe in both free will and a provident God and yet continue to hold to belief in separate arbitrary powers.

Even deeper in the subconscious of medieval Europe than its superstitious reverence for the stars was its pagan nightmare of a world of shapeshifters, where anything might turn into anything else. German stories of a prince turned into a frog or a revolting beast by an evil witch vied with Celtic stories of druids who turned themselves into ravens and children who in their sorrow turned into swans. The prehistoric Irish wizard Tuan Mac Cairill celebrated his ability to turn himself into just about anything:

[b] May no one use this passage to bolster an argument for "intelligent design." I am describing medieval science in the process of its being born—at a time when it was not yet absolutely separated from philosophy and theology. Science, as Bacon and others understood, must confine itself to experiment, observation, calculation, confirmation, and similar procedures. There is no way of devising a controlled experiment with God as its object, so God cannot be subjected to scientific proof—or disproof. Simply put, God cannot be made the subject of science. Despite this, it should be obvious that the Judeo-Christian prejudice in favor of a Creator (and of a beginning for time and for the universe) provides a much better *prelude* to the scientific enterprise than did the eternal universe of the Greeks.

A hawk to-day, a boar yesterday,
Wonderful instability! . . .

Among herds of boars I was,
Though to-day I am among bird-flocks;
I know what will come of it:
I shall still be in another shape!

Knowing nothing of science in our modern sense, people of the centuries before Abelard believed that anything might become anything else—and that anyone might become anyone else (as can still happen so easily on a blind date).

But this prejudice in favor of shapeshifting melded well with Aristotle's theory that four elements—earth, air, fire, and water—were the building blocks for everything in our world. If everything was composed of these four in different proportions, it must be possible to make one thing into another by recombining the elements in a new balance. Thus, both the surviving manuscripts of Greek science and the underground imaginings of European paganism encouraged a predisposition toward finding alchemy credible. Within even the most orthodox forms of Christianity, one can find evidence of this predisposition. For who was a greater alchemist than the priest who changed bread and wine into the body and blood of Christ? Who were greater quarriers of hidden gold than the faithful who harvested the grain and baked the bread, who grew the grapes and trod the winepress, decanted the brew and consumed the sacrament?

The medieval alchemists never succeeded in finding their "philosopher's stone," by the powder of which they believed base metals could be turned into gold and youth could be restored. This powder, they theorized, would prove an elixir (from the Arabic, *al-iksir*, thence from the Alexandrian Greek *xerion* for "healing powder"—thus demonstrating the ultimate paternity of this idea in the late antique civilization that rose from the mud of the Nile Delta). As the American historian of science Robert P. Multhauf has described the philosopher's stone, "a substance capable of inducing a chemical transformation solely by its presence, and that in small quantity, its meaning comes very near to that of the modern term 'catalyst' "—not in itself a crazy idea. At any rate, the alchemists' patient experiments did succeed in isolating alcohol in the twelfth century and nitric, sulfuric, and hydrochloric acids in the thirteenth. Their bizarre laboratories, filled with urns and tubes, vials and vessels, lights and mirrors, fire and smoke, became, therefore, the forerunners of our chemistry labs, and they our protochemists. In later centuries, German and Low Country chemists—such as Botticher, van Helmont, and Glauber—still searching for the philosopher's stone, will stumble on the manufacture of porcelain, the nature of gas, and the composition of many chemicals.

Why did the alchemists connect gold with eternal youth? Gold, they perceived correctly, is different from any other earthly substance. Unlike all other metals, which rust or gradually corrode, gold cannot be damaged by heat or by any other natural process. In the words of Terry Jones, the English comedian-turned-medievalist, "It can be hammered to one-thousandth of the thickness of a sheet of newsprint, and drawn into a wire finer than a human hair, and remains quite unchanged. In a mortal world, gold is incorruptible." And if it is incorruptible, it may possess the ability to restore to human beings the incorruptibility that was lost when God banished Adam and Eve from eternal Eden, sending them into our world of death and decay.

It is easy, from the perspective of the twenty-first century, to dismiss an early scientist such as Bacon. It is easy to dismiss Richard of Wallingford, born around the time of Bacon's death, a student at Oxford—by then Europe's chief center for the study of the mathematical disciplines of the quadrivium—who later in life when he was abbot of the Benedictine motherhouse at nearby Saint Albans wrote the first medieval treatise on trigonometry and invented the first astronomical clock, a sort of mechanical astrolabe, despite the hideous deformations that leprosy was causing in his face and hands. It is easy to dismiss the fourteenth-century French cosmologists Jean Buridan and Nicholas Oresme, who were the first to realize that the earth rotates on its axis. It is easy to dismiss the enterprising Italian physicians Hugh of Lucca, Roland of Parma, William of Saliceto, and Mondino da Luzzi, who incorporated into their studies the recently recovered medical treatises of Hippocrates and Galen (whom we met previously in late antique Alexandria) and who added considerably to the knowledge of anatomy, especially because of their daring in dissecting human corpses. They all made mistakes; and their preference for a unified vision of reality, their refusal to be confined to discrete disciplines, often led them down blind alleys.

But their insistence on the essential unity of human knowledge remains the real philosopher's stone, still sought by modern scientists with the same zeal with which it was sought by Roger Bacon. Albert Einstein's attempts to uncover a "grand unified theory" that would explain the universe is one with Bacon's encyclopedic efforts. "It was characteristic of the medieval Western thinker," remarks Singer, "that, like the early Greek thinker, he sought always a complete scheme of things." Once again, we hear echoes of Chesterton's "great central Synthesis of history," a synthesis that began with the Greeks, that medieval philosophers—including natural philosophers, or scientists—married to a Judeo-Christian worldview, and that flowed naturally into the thought of even the greatest theoretical physicist of the twentieth century.

FIVE

padua, chapel of flesh

the artist's experiment and its consequences

*Both the man of science and
the man of art live always
at the edge of mystery.*

—J. ROBERT OPPENHEIMER

AND THE PURSUITS OF BOTH, WE may say, are inevitably informed by what‑ ever philosophical outlook they may have attached themselves to. In reading the works of Roger Bacon, one cannot go far without running into his Plotinian assump‑ tions—his belief that the basis of the world is mystical but that our ultimate focus must be on the other world, the unchang‑ ing one, for ours is a sorry world of decay. If he was influenced in practical ways by

Aristotle—as was every philosopher of the thirteenth century, for Aristotle was in the air they breathed—his ultimate loyalty was to the Christianized version of Plato that Augustine of Hippo had served forth so forcefully.

In midlife, Bacon entered the Franciscan order, approximately a half century after Francis had founded it; and his attachment to a neo-Franciscan mind-set is a notable aspect of his later work. Francis's original idea that his followers should own nothing but live as perpetual beggars had proved difficult, almost impossible, to abide by as time went on and as the order's duties called it to administer educational and medical institutions of various kinds. An enduring split opened up within the order between literalists and absolutists, on the one hand, who came to be called Spirituals, and those, on the other, who were more practical and relativist and who came to be called Conventuals. (Roger's affinity was with the Spirituals.)

But this split, which at times sank even to violence and threatened the dissolution of the order, was as nothing compared to the gulf that opened between the followers of Saint Francis, the gentle, ill-educated Italian poor man, and the followers of Saint Dominic de Guzmán, the well-educated but militant Spanish nobleman who transformed himself into a riveting preacher against heretics. Dominic had founded his order not as a model of evangelical poverty but as an assault engine; and his followers, Dominicani, came to be satirized as *"Domini canes,"* dogs of the Lord, snarling and relentless in their pursuit of heretics.

The universities of Paris and Oxford, to which both orders supplied faculty, were periodically convulsed by waves of faculty discord, much of it Dominican versus Franciscan. Of course, non-friars—masters who were either diocesan priests or clerics in minor orders (and therefore free to marry)—could take a dim view of all friars, whether Dominican or Franciscan,[a] and even assert that no friar had any business teaching at a university. To hell with these peace-disturbing *routiers;* let them return to the roads where they claim to belong.

In the second half of the thirteenth century, the Franciscans became more and more suspicious of the renaissance of Greek-inspired philosophy that was emerging in their midst. Taking refuge under Augustine's banner, they came to see Aristotle's thought as a sometimes useful but awfully dangerous instrument that assigned far too much value to unaided reason. The muddled human mind, damaged by sin, wanders too easily astray, so reason requires God's illuminating revelation to keep it on the straight path. Indiscriminate reading of Aristotle and his commentators—so many of them Muslims, Jews, and heretical Christians—can lead only to disaster. Thomas Aquinas, in the course of his short life, had no such qualms either about Aristotle or about the central philosophical (and scientific) value of reason, whether aided or unaided by revelation. His writings formed the Dominicans' blueprint for teaching, and "Thomism" became their rallying cry, as dear to Dominicans as it was fraught with peril to Franciscans.[b]

For his positive positions on Aristotelian thought and the value of reason, operating independently, Thomas, that most considered and undemonstrative of men, gained a posthumous reputation as an unreliable radical. In 1277, on

a The words we now distinguish as *cleric* and *clerk* once referred to the same sort of person, one who could read and write and was therefore capable of acting clerically—as secretary to a man of importance, whether secular lord or bishop. For clerics in minor orders—those who had been ordained to simple tasks such as bell-ringer and acolyte but not to the diaconate or priesthood—ordination changed little in their lives, except that they could petition to be tried for a crime in ecclesiastical, rather than in the harsher secular, courts. The church preferred that all masters be ordained, at least to minor orders, because this gave the church greater control over university instruction. In addition to the diocesan clergy, attached to cathedrals, churches, and universities, there were monks abiding in monasteries, only some of whom were ordained as clerics. The others were called "brothers" and had no more clerical status than nuns or "sisters." Friars, who were not confined to monasteries, were free to travel. Besides the Dominicans or Blackfriars (founded in 1216) and the Franciscans or Greyfriars (1223), the most prominent friars were the Carmelites or the third anniversary of Thomas's death, Étienne Tempier, bishop of Paris, solemnly condemned 219 "Aristotelian" propositions as heretical and grounds for the excommunication of anyone who was found to hold them. Tempier's list largely consisted of propositions from the loonier liberal fringe of the neo-Aristotelian movement, but included in the list were a score of propositions drawn from the works of Thomas Aquinas. This condemnation was enthusiastically seconded by Robert Kilwardby, archbishop of Canterbury and himself a Dominican. So we may say that, in the short run, Thomism lost.

In the very long run, however, things would turn out rather differently. Thomism never disappeared from university circles because the dons could never stop arguing over it—and a vigorous episcopal condemnation so often foretells future success. Less than fifty years after his death, Thomas Aquinas was raised to the altars as a canonized saint by Pope John XXII, who found the Franciscans repulsive. (With their one habit each and their bare feet trailing street offal in a time before the invention of sanitation departments, you could certainly smell the Spirituals coming long before they made their appearance.) In 1879, Thomas's philosophical and theological writings were finally accepted by Pope Leo XIII as the official teaching of the Catholic Church. But this late papal approbation was something of a Pyrrhic victory, for the pope who proposed it viewed Thomism principally as a weapon to be used against the rising

Whitefriars (1226) and the Augustinians or Austinfriars (1256). A friar might be an ordained priest but was more likely to be a simple "brother."

b Though in this controversy the Dominicans come off with far less mud on them than the Franciscans, the Dominicans are covered in historical shame because of their support for and staffing of the Holy Inquisition and their embarrassing enthusiasm for burning heretics. During the late Pope John Paul II's millennial year of apologies, the Dominicans somehow failed to apologize for their inhuman persecution of the Albigensians and many other "heretics." Franciscans also played their part in these sadistic rituals, which ended often enough in the victim's being burned at the stake, surrounded by splendidly costumed clerics and courtiers prancing in procession; but in the fourteenth century the Inquisition burned several innocuous Franciscan Spirituals. The object of the Inquisition was always the ferreting out of *Christian* heresy—that is, till the infamous Dominican Tomás de Torquemada, Grand Inquisitor in Spain from

1487 to 1498, initiated the persecution of thousands of Muslims and Jews on generally trumped-up charges.

☾ What Thomas Aquinas's encyclopedic masterpiece, *Summa Theologica* (Sum Total of Theology), did for the thirteenth-century Hans Kung's 700-page masterpiece of summation, *Christ Sein* (*On Being a Christian*), has done for our age, raising the hackles of defensive conservatives everywhere but welcomed gratefully by any Christian who appreciates the need for a new synthesis. The Swiss theologian's reliance on ponderous Germanic theoreticians, especially Kant (and such neo-Kantians as Hegel, Marx, Freud, and Heidegger), may one day appear—inevitably—as useless as does Thomas's reliance on Aristotle, but for us Kung's analysis remains fresh and unlikely to reach its expiration date anytime soon.

---

political and social liberalism of nineteenth-century Europe. By the time Leo gave his seal of approval (more than six centuries after Thomas's death), many Thomistic categories, strategies, and interpretations had outlived their usefulness and grown archaic, unwieldy, and irrelevant to contemporary concerns.☾

Thomas, the Dominican figure with the most enduring historical influence, nonetheless takes a backseat to Francis, whose influence was never narrowly intellectual but broadly cultural. Hard as it would be to imagine the likeness of *any* Dominican being used as a contemporary ikon, everyone still knows the identification of the simple cinctured figure with arms extended who stands in so many modern gardens, usually in the middle of the birdbath. Francis the gesturer, *le jongleur de Dieu,* God's tumbler (as he was called in his lifetime), continues even in our day to enthrall imaginations. When I find myself in New York—that most contemporary of cities—in early October, I seldom fail to attend the spectacular chanted celebration of Francis's feast day at the Cathedral of Saint John the Divine, complete with a stately main-aisle procession of animals small and large, domestic and exotic—an ox, an ass, rare birds, insects, and reptiles, a camel, a horse, sometimes even an elephant—the great mock-Gothic church resounding (below the celestial sounds of Paul Winter's *Missa Gaia*) with the earthly cries of all the New York pets whose owners have brought them to be solemnly blessed for the coming year.

Whereas Thomas impressed intellectuals, Francis has always captivated ordinary people, and I suspect he always will. The gentle presence of Assisi's Little Poor Man so reverberates through contemporary attitudes toward nature, ecology, and the animal kingdom that it needs no further elaboration here. What the reader is less likely to be aware of, however, is Francis's lasting impact on the arts, especially on the plastic arts, theater, and (believe it or not) film. To appreciate this impact, we must return to the moment—which we studied earlier in the apse of Santa Maria in Trastevere—when Western art moved to separate itself from static Greek formalism and began to become its irrepressibly lively self.

The moment was not really a moment, more like a century. This "moment" of movement began in anonymous demonstrations of happiness, such as the famous "smiling angel" of Rheims or the almost comically contented face of the Trastevere Christ greeting his mother in Heaven—so far removed from the humorless angels (who saw nothing

The famous smiling angel on the facade of the cathedral at Rheims.

Jesus as Pantocrator (All-Ruler), in an eleventh-century Greek mosaic that dominates the ceiling of the monastery church at Daphni.

funny about anything) and the scowling, all-powerful Pantocrator (All-Ruler) Christs who had previously dominated Greek and Roman apses. But in the disposition of figures, the Trastevere apse follows the old Byzantine model. The figures (except for Christ and Mary) are not related to one another: they stand as abstractions against a cold gold background. They have no context but the gold that surrounds them, no identity but their particular form of dress, no individuality but the symbols they hold in their hands. Expressionless, they stare down at us, a panel of heavenly judges.

Francis knew nothing technical about the arts, at least nothing beyond a rudimentary appreciation of the new lyricism of his time. Though his prayers did indeed bear the imprint of the troubadours, he never attempted to make a mosaic, to paint, or to draw. Nor is there any record of his writing or directing a mystery play or even putting on the plainest of one-acters. But he understood the importance of gesture—of corporeal expression that speaks beyond words—and so he was able to do something that would profoundly affect both plastic and performance arts, that took the new lyrical sensibility and combined it with a barely born ocular sensibility, and that brought both to a fruition never before dreamed.

In the generation after Francis, the most notable Franciscan was the Italian master Bonaventure, a contentiously conservative figure at the

University of Paris, who as general of the order attempted unsuccessfully to prevent Roger Bacon from publishing his discoveries. He also, after collecting many eyewitness accounts, wrote a biography of Francis, an account full of marvels, not all of which we need take literally. It contains, however, a particularly instructive narrative of the Great Gesturer at Christmastide:

> Now three years before his death it befell that he was minded, at the town of Greccio, to celebrate the memory of the Birth of the Child Jesus, with all the added solemnity that he might, for the kindling of devotion. That this might not seem an innovation, he sought and obtained licence from the Supreme Pontiff, and then made ready a manger, and bade hay, together with an ox and an ass, be brought unto the place. The Brethren were called together, the folk assembled, the wood echoed with their voices, and that august night was made radiant and solemn with many bright lights, and with tuneful and sonorous praises. The man of God, filled with tender love, stood before the manger, bathed in tears, and overflowing with joy. Solemn Masses were celebrated over the manger, Francis, the Levite of Christ, chanting the Holy Gospel. Then he preached unto the folk standing round the Birth of the King in poverty, calling Him, when he wished to name Him, the Child of Bethlehem, by reason of his tender love for Him. A certain knight, valorous and true, Messer John of Greccio, who for the love of Christ had left the secular army, and was bound by closest friendship unto the man of God, declared that he beheld a little Child right fair to see sleeping in that manger, Who seemed awakened from sleep when the blessed Father Francis embraced him in both arms.

If this translation gives some sense of Bonaventure's credulous piety and of his tendency to wrap the founder of his order in unearthly light, it also has about it the sort of emotional ambience we still seek out at Christmas. There is no reason to doubt that John of Greccio gave this

Francis of Assisi's first *presepio* or *crèche*. Fresco by Giotto in the basilica at Assisi.
Note the reduced size of ox and ass, meant perhaps to minimize
their importance in this scene.

narrative to Bonaventure, though we needn't believe that the wooden
Babe in the manger came alive at Francis's touch, only that John in the
unearthly illumination of Christmas night believed that was what he saw.

There is some slight evidence that Italians before Francis may have
been known to fashion a wooden *bambino* to lay before the altar at the
midnight Christ-mass. But leading an ox and an ass into the sanctuary

was an original idea. With it began the tradition of the *presepio,* or Christmas *crèche,* the practice of arranging a tableau of live creatures, both animal and human, near the Christmas altar, to portray the story of the first Christmas night. Eventually, the tradition divided in two, giving us a *crèche* of statues on display throughout the Christmas season and a pageant of live actors, usually children, to dramatize the Christmas story separately. But leave it to Francis to lead large live animals into the church and even to insist on real hay.

Bonaventure is intent on telling us many things: that Francis first sought the pope's permission for his innovation (most unlikely), that Francis acted as deacon, chanting the gospel of Christmas and giving a tender sermon[◊] (most likely), and that all was radiant and solemn, tuneful and sonorous (more or less, no doubt). But the biographer seems not to have noticed the import of what Francis was doing. Francis must have asked himself several questions before directing this wonderfully excessive display: what did the stable look like? what was it like to give birth to a child there "betwixt an ox and a silly poor ass"? what did the baby look like? what did the baby feel? As Francis had told his friend John, "I wish to make a memorial of that child who was born in Bethlehem and, as far as is possible, behold with bodily eyes the hardships of his infant state, lying on hay in a manger with the ox and the ass standing by." Though Bonaventure fails to name them, it's possible, even likely, that Francis on this or another occasion brought in a nursing mother to play Mary and a man to play Joseph, perhaps children to

[◊]   Francis allowed himself to be ordained deacon but never priest, a status to which he refused to aspire despite pressure from the church's hierarchy, which took his refusal as a sign of humility. But Francis always considered himself a layman; his refusal to take the least step toward becoming part of the hierarchy (for priests can become bishops but deacons cannot) may have been dictated more by his quiet disapproval of priestly displays of power than by simple humility. Deacons, however, are permitted to proclaim the gospel in church and to preach on its text. The text of the Christmas midnight mass gospel is Luke 2:1–14, which takes us from the scene of a pregnant Mary and her husband Joseph, setting out from Nazareth for Bethlehem "to be taxed" by the Roman occupiers, through the birth of Jesus in the stable at Bethlehem, to the appearance of an angel who informs local shepherds of the miraculous birth and is then joined by a heavenly choir singing "Glory to God in the highest and on earth peace, goodwill toward men."

play angels. Eventually, of course, there would be shepherds, wise men and their train, and a whole menagerie that included sheep, a cock, and even camels.

This archetypal tableau, presented to the people of Greccio in the vale of Rieti on Christmas night in the year 1223, announced the end of the ikon and the beginning of realism. No more would the visual artist make a kind of Christian idol to be bowed before and held in awe. No more would traveling companies offer merely symbolic dramas with actors brought onstage to illustrate virtues and vices, as in the medieval drama *Everyman*—who is never any particular man.^c The wholly new question to be asked was historical, emotional, particular, and human: *what would it have been like to be there?* This question, never asked before, was still being asked at the end of the Second World War by men like Vittorio De Sica and Roberto Rossellini as they set aside fancy-dress filmmaking and artificial indoor sets and went out to the broken streets, peeling stairwells, pitted walls, and piteous disorder of Rome to direct the first films of Italian Neorealism, gathering ordinary people—non-actors—to play many parts. In the town of Greccio on Christmas night in 1223 were born the arts as we still know them.

T he story is told by Giorgio Vasari, the sixteenth-century Florentine artist and architect whose *Lives* of other artists is more famous than any of his surviving paintings and buildings. One day, probably in the late 1270s, a man was riding from Florence to Vespignano. He was Cimabue, the greatest artist of his day, whose tender brushstrokes had already departed, if a little tentatively, from the still-dominant Greek tradition. Cimabue passed a field where a boy of ten was watching sheep for his father. But this boy was no mere shepherd, for he was watching the sheep with a pointed stone in one hand while drawing a likeness of a sheep on a larger

---

℮ Of course, such symbolic dramas continued to be staged. *Everyman* itself is later than Francis. But Francis opened up new possibilities.

Sixth-century Byzantine Virgin and Child in the Church of Sant'Apollinare Nuovo, Ravenna.

stone, "a flat, smooth slab." Cimabue dismounted to take a closer look and was amazed by the drawing he saw. Here was a ten-year-old peasant who was a talented artist. At Cimabue's invitation, the boy, Giotto di Bondone, went to work in Cimabue's Florentine studio. By his late teens he was painting panels for local churches. By about the age of twenty Giotto could be found on a scaffold at Assisi in the nave of the just-completed basilica, painting frescoes to adorn the lavish new church dedicated to Assisi's new saint. Though Francis would have decried such attention to himself (he had, after all, asked to be buried among convicted criminals), we can only be grateful that the basilica that rose over his bones became the occasion for the astonishing homage that Giotto would render.

Before we allow ourselves to drown happily in the splendor of Assisi, we should take a quick overall look at Giotto's (equally quick) development from sketching shepherd to assured painter. Whatever his sheep may have looked like, the artistic models that surrounded the boy Giotto were all severely Greek.ᶠ He would have been familiar with the standard apparitions that

ᶠ Greek ikons had flooded into Italy especially in the eighth and ninth centuries, as ikon artists and ikon-venerating monks migrated there to escape persecution by Greek ikonoklasts. Ikonoklasm (or image breaking) had the backing of many of the Byzantine emperors, who had come to believe that Islam's rejection of human images found favor with God and was therefore responsible for Muslim military successes.

Cimabue's Madonna and Child with Angels and Prophets,
painted c. 1260 for the Church of the Trinity, Florence, and
now in the Uffizi Gallery.

Giotto's wryly realistic Madonna of Borgo San Lorenzo.

loomed everywhere in thirteenth-century Italy. Two images, in particular, were omnipresent: Virgin and Child Enthroned and Christ Crucified. No matter where you went, they pretty much seemed the same, awesomely rigid images to be looked up to and invoked. In Cimabue's scarce surviving works, we can trace his break with this ikonic tradition. His Virgin, at least when contrasted with its Greek model, is sweet and smiling, his Child actually childlike. Giotto goes further: though his earliest (probable) madonna—a badly damaged study in tempera on a wooden panel—may be a bit stiff, she looks like a real woman, someone who might actually show up this afternoon at the parish church of Borgo San Lorenzo in Florence, where the panel is still displayed. The teenage Giotto's model was no Greek ikon but a local mother; and from her watchful expression we can still surmise that she had mixed feelings about serving as model for this brutal-looking boy.

For Giotto, the creator of so much beauty, was himself no beauty. Giovanni Boccaccio, the daring Florentine satirist who was Giotto's younger contemporary, reminds us that "amazing genius is often found to have been placed in the ugliest of men"—and that Giotto was one of these, a man of bottomless humility, who "always refused to be called 'Maestro,' even though he was the master of all living artists and had rightfully acquired the title. And this title which he refused shone all the more brightly in him in that it was eagerly usurped by those who knew far less than himself, or by his own disciples. But for all the greatness of his art, neither was he physically more handsome, nor had he a face more pleasing in any way, than Messer Forese da Rabatta"—whom Boccaccio has previously described as having "a small, deformed body, and a flat, pushed-in face." No doubt Boccaccio is exaggerating slightly for the sake of his narrative, but we learn from other witnesses that Giotto had an excessively broad face and a short, stout, barrel-chested body and that he always maintained the manner of a modest man—not the usual way with artists then or now.

Giotto's subsequent madonnas, the virgins of his mature art, go even further in the direction of realistic portrayal. His *Ognissanti Madonna,* now in the Uffizi in Florence, has an insouciant air—her lips parted in a half smile over her white teeth, her young breasts pointed and pressing against her nearly translucent white dress—that would have been impossible to any painter before him. This madonna's expression is reserved but earthy and almost amused.

There is never anything amusing about crucifixion, but even in this subject we may trace Giotto's development. The severe Greek ikon gives way in Cimabue's curvilinear treatment to a more supple, more balletic, less exalted sense of the human body. Giotto, in *his* crucifixions, how-

Giotto's *Ognissanti Madonna* (Madonna of All Saints),
now in the Uffizi.

Cimabue's
Crucifixion at
Arezzo.

Thirteenth-century
Greek Crucifixion.

Giotto's Crucifixion in the Scrovegni Chapel, Padua.

ever, eschews all artistic swish: here is a good man dying on a cross, surrounded by his few suffering friends. That's all. Don't show off, *artista*.
Don't even reach for anything like gory sensationalism. Pity, that's all.
Pity and profound reverence for human suffering. And silent contemplation. However innovative, however magisterial his work becomes,
Giotto's reverent humility makes all his art into prayer. He is, in the
truest sense, Franciscan.

Giotto, throughout his adult life a Franciscan tertiary—a lay (pre-
sumably married) member of the Franciscan order—must have felt
deeply his vocation to portray the life of Francis in paint on the walls of
the upper church in Assisi's new basilica. Still working formally under

the tutelage of Cimabue, who had been given the commission to oversee the decoration of the upper church, Giotto was allowed, it would appear, complete freedom over the series of twenty-eight frescoed scenes that would adorn the lower walls—a quiet admission, perhaps, by Cimabue that his student had already surpassed him. The result would be a necklace of scenes so detailed and complete in their physicality that Europe had seen nothing like them since the long-ago death of classical fresco art.

The technique of making a fresco is excruciating in its demands on the artist, for the scene must be painted rapidly on wet plaster (*fresco* meaning "fresh" in Italian). The artist can sketch out for completion only as much of the scene as he can confidently cover in one day's light, for by the time the sun returns the next day the wall will already be too dry. The advantage of such a technique is that the pigments fuse with the wall itself during the drying process, becoming more permanent and, in their effect on the viewer, more substantial and profound, for the colors take on a vivid depth and eternality impossible on a wooden panel. The disadvantage, in addition to the anxiety of racing against time, is that there is no going back, no possibility of correcting a mistake at a later date.

In Giotto's frescoes, Francis at all times wears his golden halo—without which detail the friars of the basilica would undoubtedly have been unwilling to pay for the paint. But in other ways there is scant allowance for otherworldliness. The three-dimensionality of the figures is unlike anything seen since ancient times, thanks to careful gradations of color, which turn darker toward the edges of each figure. To thirteenth-century eyes, each figure in these scenes might as well have been a hologram, for it seemed to pop out and become as rounded as in life, "making it," as Boccaccio claimed, "so much like its original in Nature that it seemed more like the original than a reproduction. Many times, in fact, while looking at paintings by this man, the observer's visual sense was known to err, taking what was painted to be the very thing itself." Though at first glance the scenes made by Giotto and his assistants—of whom we can identify at least four—look to us like paintings of the late

Renunciation of Worldly Goods by Giotto, Basilica of Saint Francis, Assisi.

thirteenth century, we can with a little effort come to see them with the eyes of Giotto's contemporaries.

The saint is often seen in profile—an absolute no-no in Byzantine ikonography and a startling innovation in Giotto's time—and in physical association with other human beings, giving, taking, talking, confronting, thanking. He is never alone and exalted, always on the same level as others, always engaged with them. His is a life of encounters, for as Martin Buber said, "All real living is meeting." In Giotto's fresco cycle, we meet a real saint in motion, living a real life on the same plane as everyone else. Each scene is enclosed within painted architectural elements—elaborately executed trompe l'oeil marble corbels—that enhance the impression of three-dimensionality, the impression that we are looking at these scenes through a series of open windows, leading us into another man's life, allowing us to spy on him and gain some insight into his inner self. We have for so long been used to such depictions that it requires some concentration for us to appreciate again the thunderous revelation that these frescoes were in their time.

Though it is not possible for us to linger here over each of the twenty-eight images, a closer look at four of them will give us sustenance for our continuing Giotto journey. The *Renunciation of Worldly Goods,* the scene in which Francis also renounces his father, is a fine example of Giotto's democratic spirit, for all participants, even the distracted bishop, face one another on the same plane. The father's punishing right arm is restrained discreetly by his neighbor, for violence is always muted in Giotto. The gulf between father and son is black, immense, and uncross-

Dream of Innocent III by Giotto, Basilica of Saint Francis.

able, relieved only by Francis's hands petitioning the dimly distant hand of God far above the town. All the figures are framed by the actual buildings of Assisi, domestic and secular on the left, public and sacred on the right—pink, yellow, white, and blue, demonstrations of Assisi's pride in its mercantile adornments as against the nakedness of the humble saint.

In the *Dream of Innocent III,* the pope lies in his private chamber, the carefully detailed curtains that surround his sleeping alcove attesting to the reality of the scene (even if he is unlikely to have worn his pontifical robes and golden mitre to bed). He dreams that his cathedral church of San Giovanni in Laterano is falling down, held aloft only by the strength of the Little Poor Man of Assisi. It was because of this nightmare that Innocent resolved in the morning to give his approval to Francis's peculiar experiment of the Lesser Brothers (or Friars Minor). The dramatic center of the scene is the stressed young face of Francis, all calm concentration and determination to succeed, his thick right wrist supporting the entire building.

A personal favorite of mine is the *Exorcism of the Demons of Arezzo,* not so much for the demons (who, it must be admitted, are wonderfully individualized in their high dudgeon), nor even for Francis, kneeling humbly in prayer behind the official exorcist and giving the exorcism wings, as it were. What attracts me here is the detailed recital of Arezzo's glorious architecture, caught as if in

Exorcism of the Demons of Arezzo by Giotto, Basilica of Saint Francis.

Saint Francis Mourned by Saint Clare by Giotto, Basilica of Saint Francis.

a freeze-frame, just as it was in Giotto's day, rising in aspiration above the city's walls, a colorful fantasy of medieval skyscrapers. Either the exorcism failed to rid the city of all its demons or they crept back sometime later (perhaps through the infernal cleft that spreads so ominously under the walls), for lovely Arezzo morphed into an enthusiastic center of Italian fascism in the 1930s, later serving Roberto Benigni as the setting for his comic and touching holocaust film, *La vita è bella* (*Life Is Beautiful*).

The last scene we shall examine in this cycle is *Saint Francis Mourned by Saint Clare,* a fresco in which Giotto's assistants probably had a hand. It is a pity that the face of Clare is ruined, but the stance of her body leaves no doubt as to her attitude. Francis, even dead, seems more alive

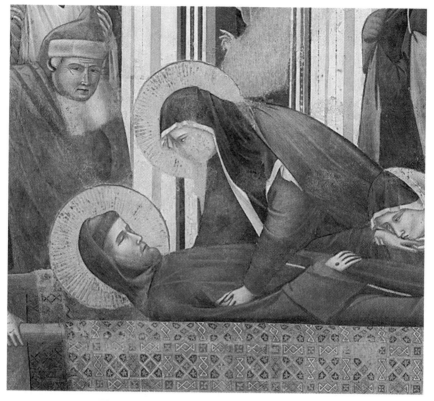

Detail of *Saint Francis Mourned by Saint Clare.*

than any of the grieving onlookers, and the inclination of his head to Clare's, and hers to his, resolves all ambiguity: here was a mighty friendship. Francis often warned his followers that they should not be surprised if he turned up one day with children of his own. This was taken by pious interpreters like Bonaventure to mean that Francis was conscious in his holy humility that even a saint could fall into the most despicable of sins. I rather think he meant that, though he had been given his life's commission by God and had to follow it, he was a man like other men and would much have preferred to take a wife, know fleshly intimacy, and love the children of his body. Here his bier is laid out before San Damiano, the chapel he had restored and later turned over to Clare and her sisters; and his face in Giotto's depiction still gives off an aura of the romantic masculinity that might have taken him to a far more ordinary, more obvious, more human way of life, rather than to weary death at forty-five. He married a concept, whom he gallantly called Lady Poverty, but he gave every evidence of being a man of tangibility, who constantly ran his fingers over the world of the senses and loved everything those fingers touched.

Though death anchors the foreground of the fresco, this is, as the Veronese critic Francesca Flores d'Arcais calls it, "one of the most animated scenes in the cycle . . . The nuns pour out of the church in a fluttering of veils with the vivacity of an airy flight of brown swallows," volatile, unstable testaments to chastity. The men of Assisi in their "brightly colored clothes," purchased, for all we know, from old Bernardone, cluster together weightily in democratic fraternity, their heads bobbing. They are the people from whom Francis sprang, the men he might have remained among and been one of. Beyond them a boy— a child like the one Francis and Clare never had together—climbs a tree to get a better look. But Francis and Clare occupy the lower center of the picture, as they occupy the minds of every viewer, medieval and modern. Here, at this nearly breathing still point between Francis and Clare, "is a feeling" as Flores d'Arcais puts it, "of intense rapport."

As Francis brought new tangibility to the life of the spirit, Giotto restored a like tangibility to art. But the Francis cycle at Assisi was almost a finger exercise compared with what came next.

In the first decade of the fourteenth century, Giotto, now in his mid-thirties, was invited to execute a commission in Padua by Enrico Scrovegni, an ambitious and very wealthy merchant-banker. Ser Scrovegni had recently purchased the ruins of the ancient Roman arena in his city, and there he intended to build an imposing palace for himself with an adjoining chapel. Would Giotto decorate the chapel? It was to be a relatively small, private family chapel, but Scrovegni had big plans for it: he

wanted an artistic jewel that would wow his friends, intimidate his enemies, and last forever. He got what he wanted.

Padua (Padova to Italians) hosts the second oldest university in Italy,
nearly a century old by the time Giotto finished his chapel, and its streets
and cafés have long echoed with the lively clamor of student laughter
and student despair. The city boasts some of the largest and best-
proportioned piazzas in Italy, as well as a twisting fantasy of domes and
towers—the breathtaking Basilica of Saint Anthony of Padua, dedicated
to the Portuguese Franciscan who died several decades before Giotto was
born and became one of Christendom's best-loved saints. As many as
five million pilgrims a year still visit his basilica, which is called Il Santo
(The Saint) by all Padovani. Padua, almost impossible to drive into today
because of its latticework of one-way streets and its absence of parking
spaces, may have been only marginally more accessible in Giotto's time,
for it has always been a crowded, not-so-negotiable place, laid out awk-
wardly in the shadow of Venice. But once you succeed in dismounting
your horse or getting out of your car, Padua yields the sort of refreshing
and stimulating encounters that no pilgrim would willingly pass up. Even
today, its principal jewel is not the Scrovegni palace, pulled down in the
nineteenth century, nor even the miraculous apparition of Il Santo, but
the unassuming building of modest proportions called the Scrovegni (or
Arena) Chapel, the sole survivor of Ser Scrovegni's monumental building program.

A visit to the chapel today can be a disappointment, if only because
its present keepers push visitors through with such alarming alacrity. If
ever one needed a generous amount of time to ponder a work of art, it is
in this unique room, some sixty-seven feet by twenty-eight, nearly sixty-
one feet high, roofed by a tunnel vault. The overwhelming impression
on entering is of Deep Blue, somewhat darker and more vibrant than
azure and tending here and there toward turquoise. Not only do most of
the scenes that adorn the walls show this blue as background, the whole
of the dominating vault is painted blue, interrupted by little else than
small gold stars, which seem only to intensify the color. This is the sky,

Interior of Scrovegni Chapel, Padua, with frescoes painted by Giotto.

of course, but not quite the sky at earthly midnight or midday but a sky that seems to have exchanged places with the sea, a sky of cosmic spectacle and mysterious comfort.

On the entrance wall, Giotto has painted a Last Judgment, a fearful enough representation, yet something to contemplate rather than quake under. Unlike the later and more famous version by Michelangelo, this Judgment does not rise up over the altar but is behind us, something to be reminded of on one's way back into the world, not something to crush the viewer here and now beneath its awesome power. Each of the side walls holds four layers of scenes, the highest layer giving us the life of Mary and her parents (as narrated in apocryphal gospels), the second and third layers giving us the life of Christ (as narrated in the four canonical gospels of the New Testament). The lowest layer, just above the choir stalls, contains depictions of the Seven Virtues and Seven Vices, thus echoing gently the scene of Judgment that looms behind us.

The Virtues and Vices, painted as marbleized trompe l'oeil panels, are both charming and (in the case of the vices) comical, but they will not detain us now. The chapel has no apse; its principal focus—if one may speak of focus in a room so plenteous in attractions—is the triumphal arch that frames the sanctuary. The heavenly scene at its height is of God the Father instructing the Angel Gabriel that he is to bring to Mary the news of her impending pregnancy. Just below this scene are two panels on either side of the arch: on the left Gabriel descends to Mary; on the right Mary receives the news. Unsurprisingly, the chapel is dedicated to this Annunciation of the Incarnation.

The richly pleasurable narrative scenes on the side walls, which command the bulk of the chapel's space and send one's eyes in all directions, are "read" by starting at the highest panel on the right, then moving rightward along the length of the top layer on the right-hand wall and then the left-hand wall till one has reached the top panel on the far left, the *Procession at Mary's Wedding to Joseph.* Facing the triumphal arch and taking in the scenes of the *Annunciation,* one then drops down a level, studies the *Visitation* (Mary's visit to her cousin Elizabeth, pregnant

Angel Gabriel appears to Mary, Scrovegni Chapel.

with John the Baptist), and then begins again at the nearest scene on the second level of the right-hand wall, the *Nativity of Jesus.* Making a circuit of the second level rightward along the right-hand wall, then rightward along the left-hand wall, one arrives at last at the *Triumphal Entry of Jesus into Jerusalem* (on what is called Palm Sunday). Facing the arch once more, one turns to read the first of the panels on the third level, the *Last Supper.* This is followed by a reading of all the panels on the third level, as one maintains a rightward direction down the right-hand wall, then up the left-hand wall till the *Descent of the Holy Spirit at Pentecost* is reached, the last panel on the left-hand wall closest to the arch.

I give these directions to emphasize how elaborate is the chapel's plan and how much a successful visit to this shining room will be aided

Mary receives Gabriel's message, Scrovegni Chapel.

by prior study. To examine each scene in detail, however, would take a separate book (and several good ones are already available). All that can be done here is to point out one further complication in Giotto's scheme and in so doing to draw your attention to three of the most compelling sets of scenes.

Though the obvious and most initially rewarding way to approach the chapel is to read its scenes chronologically, using the same order as we would for written text—from left to right and from top to bottom— it is also possible to read the scenes in columns from top to bottom. Often, if not always, Giotto has managed to enrich the meaning of one scene by the supporting presence of another. Take, for example, the *Nativity of Jesus,* in which we see Giotto moving toward a new sense of perspective. Though the rules for attaining three-dimensionality by the use of perspective would not be fully understood till after his time, Giotto takes significant steps in that direction by the dramatic use of foreshortening (the neck of the donkey, the placement of the stable, the half-hidden arm of the shepherd). Most innovative, however, is the charged seriousness of Mary's profile as she stares in love and fear at her

Nativity of Jesus, Scrovegni Chapel.

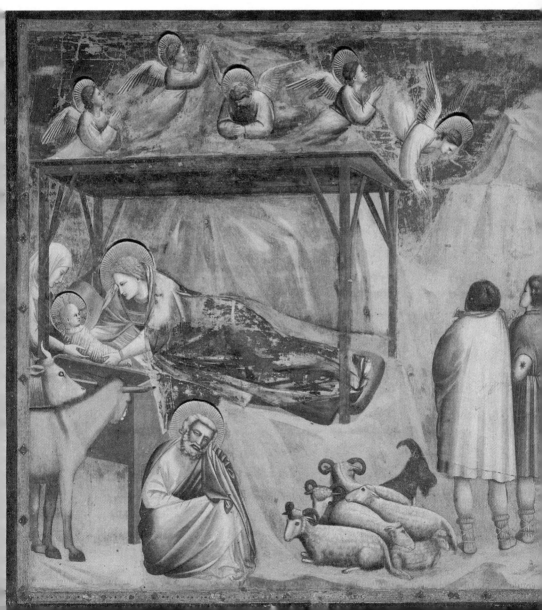

newborn Babe, while the nodding head of Joseph, old and weary, offers such a contrast. The ritualistic placement of the infant between mother and nursemaid has eucharistic significance. "This is his Body," the two women could well be intoning, as they present the baby to one another, to the animals, and to the world. Any doubt that this is Giotto's intent is dispelled by the scene directly below the *Nativity,* which is the *Last Supper,* at which Jesus, just prior to his crucifixion, offered his body as bread to his disciples with the words "This is my Body."

Last Supper, Scrovegni Chapel.

Similarly, the *Marriage Feast at Cana* has eucharistic significance because it was at Cana that Jesus changed water into wine and because every mass is, to an extent, a marriage feast between Christ and the communicant. In support of this, we are given, in the scene just below the *Marriage Feast,* the *Lamentation over Jesus,* in which two women once again hold Jesus, offering him to us as they did at his Nativity. But this time they are holding the head of a fully grown dead man while three other women hold his hands and feet. The grief of the many human mourners is mirrored and strengthened by the mourning of angels in Heaven. Once again, "This is his Body" would provide the appropriate caption.

Marriage Feast at Cana, Scrovegni Chapel.

Such eucharistic messages will become only more explicit as Western art progresses. In Bernardino Luini's remarkable version of the Lamentation, for instance, an early-sixteenth-century painting, the body of Jesus is presented to the viewer even more directly—from an altarlike stone platform covered in a linen cloth, which is the typical covering for a Catholic altar. A startlingly comprehensive exhibition that opened at the Houston Museum of Fine Arts in late 1997 under the title "The Body of Christ in the Art of Europe and New Spain, 1150–1800" demonstrated conclusively that Catholic artists, from before the time of Giotto to well after, have repeatedly made connections between the Word-Made-Flesh—the Babe born at Bethlehem—and the eucharistic

Lamentation over Jesus, Scrovegni Chapel.

body of Christ offered in the mass. The Catholic belief that the mass is not merely a reenactment of the Last Supper but a kind of re-offering of the sacrifice of Jesus's life on the cross at Calvary forms the ultimate theological basis for this visual connection.[f]

But why, if we are not traditional Tridentine Catholics, should we care about this? What is this peculiar theological development to us?

Just as the Catholic Eucharist acted as catalyst for the development of Western science, it provided a basis for the development of artistic realism. The question "What is the Eucharist?" was soon followed by natural philosophers (one day to be called scientists) with the question "What is matter?" The same pondering on this Eucharist sparked in medieval artists a desire to present reality more fully, more accurately. Giotto's Catholicism could conceivably have sent him in a completely different direction—toward, say, fanciful legends about the Holy Grail,[g] toward abstruse symbols and mythical animals like the unicorn, toward more gold and even less realism. Instead, his eucharistic Catholicism, informed by a Franciscan spirit, pushed him toward a nearly scientific quest to reproduce more exactly in art the very things his eyes could see, his hands could touch, his heart could love—and preeminently among these lovable things the human body itself.

Ugly Giotto, lover of the human body and of human interactions. His ugliest subject is neither the crucifixion nor the figure of the dead Christ but the betrayal of Jesus by Judas in the

[f] Since the Thomistic terminology of *substance* and *accident* (based on Aristotelian science) and, therefore, the Thomistic explanation of the Eucharist are no longer serviceable, readers of a speculative bent may find the painfully convoluted probe by the celebrated (and reviled) Dutch theologian Edward Schillebeeckx in *The Eucharist* to be of some help in assessing contemporary approaches to eucharistic theology—but it is not for the fainthearted.

[g] The Holy Grail figures especially in the stories of the Arthurian cycle, though it may have had an earlier origin. It is the ultimate object of quest for the Knights of the Round Table, though only a perfectly pure knight can find it. It seems occasionally to change its shape (and even its function and meaning), but it is generally to be identified with the cup used by Jesus at the Last Supper. It was believed to have been brought to England after Jesus's Passion by Joseph of Arimathea and buried in Chalice Well in Glastonbury.

Betrayal of Jesus by Judas, Scrovegni Chapel.

Garden of Gethsemane on the night before Jesus's crucifixion. Judas, you will recall, had told the temple priests that for money he would identify Jesus with a kiss so that the Roman guard could arrest him. At the picture's center, Judas embraces (in fact, envelops) Jesus, who studies him with sad compassion not very different from the expression of his mother Mary on the night of his birth, for both mother and son can see what lies ahead—the hideous suffering this night will bring in its wake. On the left, Peter severs the ear of the high priest's servant, on the right an armed Roman soldier resolutely steps toward Jesus as soldiers at his back move in for the arrest. The night rings out with activity, torches and clubs are brandished aloft, and a shofar bleats its warning. It is by far

Giotto's most violent and upsetting picture. And Judas is *so* ugly, not because of his physiognomy but because of his expression, the resolute ugliness of someone cruelly set on doing evil.

In the back of the chapel is another face, the face of Giotto himself, painted by one of his assistants. Like Judas, he is shown in profile, the technique that Giotto championed. He stands, however, among the anonymous elect at the Last Judgment. Perhaps if seen full face he would look ugly, perhaps his body if separated from those on either side of him and turned toward us would be displeasing. But Giotto's life has led him to eternal life with God. He has been saved, he's on his way into Heaven; and his contentment, his beatitude, his high expectations for what comes next suffuse his features with a satisfying glow. The opposite of Judas's screwed-up grimace, the face of Giotto, who labored without rest and with such dedication on an immensity of works, both surviving and lost, is just sublimely relaxed.

His work is done. His influence on generations to come, whether direct or indirect, on sculptors as well as painters, on Renaissance and modern artists as well as late-medieval ones—on Pisano, Ghiberti, Donatello, the Della Robbias, Fra Angelico, Masaccio, Piero della Francesca, and Mantegna, on the inevitable trio of Leonardo, Michelangelo, and Raphael, and perhaps especially on that inspired superrealist Caravaggio—will be immeasurable. He, grandfather to them all, can at last let himself off the hook and enjoy his eternal rest.

And that is how life became art.

Giotto in yellow hat on his way to Heaven, *Last Judgment,* Scrovegni Chapel.

Campanile di Giotto, Florence.

Giotto's Carraia Bridge, now destroyed, Florence.

SIX

florence, dome of light

the poet's dream
and its consequences

*Dante and Shakespeare divide
the modern world between them;
there is no third.*

— T. S. ELIOT

THOUGH ASSISI CONTAINS THE WORK of Giotto best known to the world and Padua the crown of his achievement, Giotto left his charmed handiwork in other places as well: Rome, Rimini, and Naples for sure, Bologna and Arezzo most likely, and especially Florence, where he decorated the still-extant, if much abused, Peruzzi and Bardi chapels of Santa Croce and carried out many

Cathedral of Santa Maria del Fiore, in Florence,
surmounted by Brunelleschi's dome; to the right is the
Campanile, designed by Giotto.

other commissions, only some of which remain in our keeping. We
know that late in life he even undertook architectural works: the classi-
cally graceful Carraia Bridge spanning the River Arno (reduced to dust
in the Second World War) and the jocund bell tower that stands beside
Florence's great cathedral and is still known as the Campanile di Giotto.
For in 1334, less than three years before his death, the humble painter
was named chief of public works for the city of Florence and *capomaestro*
(master builder) for the construction of its new cathedral.

Giotto hardly had time to leave his mark on the architecture of the
Duomo di Santa Maria del Fiore (Dome of Saint Mary of the Flower),
as the new cathedral would be called. But the appointment of the greatest artist of his age to be overseer of municipal planning is typical of the

role proud Florence had begun to play along the length of the Italian peninsula—as unfailing magnet for creative genius. From the last decades of the thirteenth century, through the fourteenth and the fifteenth, and well into the sixteenth, Florence—Firenze, originally Fiorenza, the Flowering City as its name indicates—seemed almost continually to be burgeoning like a spring garden, blooming with fresh works of art and architecture. Spearhead of the Renaissance, Florence became in the course of these centuries undisputed leader of European learning in arts and sciences and the first city in seventeen hundred years to lay legitimate claim to the intellectual preeminence of ancient Athens. It was here in 1436 that Filippo Brunelleschi finally completed the dome of the cathedral, largest, highest, and most astounding building in the world of its time— "big enough to cover in its shadow all the Tuscan people"—and set a fashion in architecture that has scarcely run its course; it was here in the last years of the fifteenth century that Michelangelo transformed forever the art of sculpture; and it was here in the last years of the sixteenth century that a group of aristocratic intellectuals resolved to resurrect the art of ancient Greek drama in a new form, which came to be called *opera*.

But already in the time of Giotto, Florentines knew their city to be the navel of the world, unsurpassable in achievements intellectual and artistic. So it is almost unremarkable in such a city that as the teenage Giotto di Bondone was learning to be a painter in the cluttered *bottega* of Cimabue, the teenage Dante Alighieri, perhaps a year or two older than the painting peasant, was learning to be a poet, and an exceedingly architectonic one at that, as he strolled freely through the streets of his native Florence, observing the progress of its many architectural novelties. Like James Joyce, self-exiled from Dublin at the start of the twentieth century, the young Dante committed everything he saw and heard to memory—including his lessons in the liberal arts—and such ecumenical absorption would serve him well when, far from home, he began his masterpiece, *The Divine Comedy,* which would be, as are all works of art to some extent, an exercise in memory. But whereas Joyce was recalling the details of a paralyzed provincial capital, Dante would be remember-

Baptistery of San Giovanni, Florence.

a   When the English version of a phrase of Dante's Italian is taken from Peter Dale's translation of *The Divine Comedy,* as here, it is placed within quotation marks. When there are no quotation marks or when the quoted phrase is not preceded by the Italian original, the translation is mine. Whenever a longer passage is quoted and indented, the translation is Dale's.

ing what was for him the bountiful center of the known world: *"fiorian Fiorenza in tutt' i suoi gran fatti"* ("Florence flowering in feat and deed").ª

The octagonal Baptistery of San Giovanni—*"il mio bel San Giovanni"* (my beautiful San Giovanni), as Dante called the place of his baptism—had stood next to the old cathedral for centuries and had perhaps preceded it, dating possibly to as early as the fourth century. A smaller version of Rome's pagan Pantheon, the

Mosaic of Satan in Hell, Baptistery of San Giovanni, Florence.

baptistery was never left to be just another lovely old building. In the eleventh century, an operation was begun to encase the entire facade in white marble from Luni and green marble from Prato, a fashion that would migrate throughout Tuscany and return at last to Florence, there to enjoy its apotheosis in the white, green, and *pink* of the new cathedral. In the twelfth century, porphyry columns, booty taken by the Florentines in war, were added to either side of the Baptistery's main entrance. In the early thirteenth century, a splendid mosaic pavement was laid within the building; in later years, in fact through the whole of Dante's childhood and early manhood, the vault of the building was being decorated with colorful mosaic images, enclosed in elaborate geometric patterns. In the months preceding Dante's death in 1321, Andrea Pisano would erect a set of gilded bronze doors, illustrating the life of John the Baptist; and in the early fifteenth century, Lorenzo Ghiberti would follow with two additional sets of bronze doors, one set illustrating in exquisite detail the life of Christ, the other principal scenes from the Old Testament, this last so fine that Michelangelo would call it "the Gate of Paradise."

The perpetual drama of Florence—building, adding, embellishing, transfiguring—held the attention of the young Dante, not only in his beloved Baptistery but at so many other sites around the city: the decorative medieval fortress of the Palazzo Vecchio (Old Palace), now the town hall; the nearby grain market, designed by Arnolfo di Cambio and burned to the ground in 1304; the Ponte Vecchio (Old Bridge), spanning the Arno (along with three other handsome bridges), crowded with medieval houses, and reconstructed in the fourteenth century after a flood; the tenth-century churches of Santi Apostoli and Badia Fiorentina, the Benedictine Badia (or Abbey) containing a "rich complex of chapels, gardens, libraries, and shops," which spread out just across the way from the Alighieri family house; and, farther on at opposite ends of the city, the Dominican foundation of Santa Maria Novella and the Franciscan foundation of Santa Croce, both built in the poet's lifetime and at each of which he received instruction in philosophy and theology.

The eleventh-century San Miniato al Monte, surmounting a green hill, affords incomparable views of the city below. One of the most beautiful churches in Italy, it has been a model for many. But for Florentines like Dante it was always a place to recall that "the city is born out of the valley, its monuments enclosed by an amphitheatre of hills," in the words of Marco Chiarini, former director of the Palantine Gallery in the Pitti Palace, "its architecture . . . created by the human mind in imitation of its natural setting."

We all know citizens of such vibrant cities as New York, London, Paris, and Rome (and of many smaller burgs) who would be forever cast down were they to be permanently separated from the city they love. Still, according to R.W. B. Lewis, "Dante associated himself with his native city to a degree almost incomprehensible in modern times. Florence was not merely his birthplace; it was the very context of his being." There are three things everyone seems to know about Dante: that he was a native of Florence; that he fell in love with a girl named Beatrice, with whom he scarcely ever spoke and who became the vehicle for the concluding insights of his great poem; and that he died in exile.

All these things are true, as well as a few others that Lewis relates compactly:

> He was Dante Alighieri, a distinct individual with a classic profile and a sometimes tempestuous disposition. He had intimate friends, like his sportive neighbor Forese Donati; literary colleagues, like the older poet Guido Cavalcanti; and deadly enemies, like Forese's brother Corso. He was the dedicated lover, from a distance, of Beatrice Portinari, until her death at an early age in 1290 [less than a year younger than Dante, she would have been twenty-four], and a few years later he composed in her memory his first major work, the *Vita Nuova,* the story in prose and poetry of his devotion to her from the age of nine. In the course of time Dante became a married man (his wife was another and more sedate member of the Donati clan), with three [more likely, four] children. But he was an ardent personality, and more than once, in pursuit of other Florentine maidens, he lost the straight way, to borrow his phrase at the opening of the *Inferno.* Even in his lifetime, as the first two canticles of the *Divine Comedy* began to circulate (around 1315), he was recognized as the greatest Italian poet, the *somma poeta,* of his age. But he was first and last a Florentine, and indeed, on one level, his masterwork, the *Comedy,* is an expression of his passionate feelings about Florence, his rage against the conspirators who had driven him out, his longing to return.

In the eyes of today's visitor, Florence seems a small polished gem of a city. But in Dante's youth it was, with its population of eighty thousand, the largest city in Europe after Paris, home to Europe's most influential bankers, and issuer in 1252 of the gold florin,[b] which quickly became Europe's leading coin. Florence, run as a capitalist republic by merchant oligarchs, was the principal source for many of the continent's most desirable luxuries—silks, tapestries, jewelry, embossed leather—an altogether more powerful nucleus than it would later be. What happened here commanded the attention of everyone.

Unfortunately, what happened here in Dante's lifetime—an endless feud among the city's leading families—was not atypical of city life in medieval Italy. Dante came from a well-established (if second-tier) family of landowners. He had lost his mother when he was seven and his father when he was still in his teens. He took an early and prominent role in the life of his city, first as a soldier in arms, then as a municipal official. It was this prominence that would bring him to grief when the tides of political power shifted.

The main fight was between the Guelphs and the Ghibellines, two families to begin with, and, later, factions that drew to their sides other families and associations of partisans, till they had drawn towns, cities, provinces, and whole countries into their blood-soaked conflict. The names of the parties altered somewhat depending on the vernacular in which they were invoked: in Germany, where they had originated, the Guelphs were the Welfs; in the Norman tongue of Britain and Ireland the Ghibellines were the Fitzgeralds. Though the conflict had religious and political dimensions, it was always at base a struggle of willful and unyielding factions whose professed ideologies shifted and blended as circumstances required. The feud, which began in the reign of Frederick Barbarossa and grew out of his project to reassert imperial rule over Lombardy, lasted a century and a half, petering out only halfway through the fourteenth century, as the Black Death stalked Europe. The official line was that the Ghibellines were sup-

[b] The gold florin, which weighed 54 grams, was called *fiorino* (little flower) by the Tuscans in allusion to the figure of a lily stamped upon it, though this may also have been an allusion to Florence itself.

porters of the emperor, the Guelphs of the pope—but only *più o meno* (more or less), to use modern Italian's most characteristic phrase.

Florence was a Guelph city, which after many humiliations had managed to expel its Ghibellines soon after Dante's birth. Though Guelph by familial, civic, and religious loyalties, Dante nonetheless attempted to play fair. When in 1300 he was elected a prior of Florence— one of seven priors who, working together, were the highest civil authority—he ruled as harshly toward errant Guelphs as toward fugitive Ghibellines. But by this time, the Guelphs were fighting among themselves, divided into two factions, White and Black. After a sixteen-year-old White lost his nose, sliced off by one of the Blacks in a street fight, Dante and his fellow priors banished the ringleaders on both sides. That mutilation—"the destruction of our city," as one chronicler termed it— and the subsequent banishments would prove Dante's undoing as a Florentine.

One of the banished Blacks—Corso Donati, a relative of Dante's wife—determined to have his revenge and fled to Rome, where he found an abundance of coconspirators, including the reigning pope. Boniface VIII, who had just proclaimed the first Holy Year to coincide with the turning of the century (and to rake lots of pilgrim gold into papal coffers), was one of the vilest men ever to sit on the throne of Saint Peter, a cleric wholly concerned with his own power and aggrandizement, who took to parading about in the costume of an emperor ("I'm pope! I'm Caesar!" he shouted) and who remodeled the papal crown into the novelty of the triple tiara, symbolic of his vaunted authority as high priest, king (of the Papal States), and emperor over the emperor. These last two roles were justified by a spurious eighth-century document, known as the Donation of Constantine, in which the first Christian emperor had supposedly made donations of vast tracts of land in central Italy to the papacy and had awarded to the pope "the privileges of our supreme station as emperor and all the glory of our authority." Boniface's overriding ambition was to establish clerical, and particularly papal, control over every aspect of European life. "Outside this [Catholic] Church," he shouted in the historic bull *Unam sanctam,* "there is neither salvation nor remission of sins," and "it is altogether necessary to salvation for every human creature to be subject to the Roman Pontiff."[c] Needless to say, this was not a bull the reigning emperor found agreeable.

Boniface was also a man who enjoyed involving the papacy in wars and skirmishes. In June 1301, he sent off a formal request that Florence supply him with two hundred horsemen to help with a small war he was waging to deprive the notorious Margherita degli Aldobrandeschi, the Red Countess of Tuscany, of her lands south of Siena, the rival city that served the Ghibellines as their Tuscan stronghold. It's true that Margherita was quite an act, having (among other things) urged her lover to murder his wife, which he did. But Dante wisely advised the Council of Florence to sit on its hands. *"Nihil fiat"* (Let's do nothing) is the phrase of Dante's that echoes down the ages, an awfully good maxim for so many political situations in which violence is urged by some au-

---

[c]   The papal title of "supreme pontiff" is an illegitimate borrowing of the imperial title *pontifex maximus* (literally, "supreme bridgebuilder"), an ancient and mysterious appellation awarded the emperor as head of the Roman college of *pagan* priests.

thoritarian hothead. In the end, the council capitulated to the pope, who never forgave Dante his daring.

Because the popes had long had an on-again, off-again alliance with the French monarchy against the German emperors, Boniface invited Charles de Valois,ↄ the weak-kneed brother of the French king, into Italy, where he soon found himself at Siena plotting an invasion of Florence with Dante's mortal enemy, Corso Donati. The invitation did not mean that Boniface had a high regard for Charles, any more than for any Frenchman. "I'd rather be a dog than a Frenchman," shouted the pope, leaving earnest literalists to wonder if this bull of a pope believed in the soul (or in anything), since he would rather be a soulless dog than a Frenchman whose immortal soul had the possibility of reaching Paradise. Dante was sent by the Florentines, along with two other ambassadors, to plead with Boniface to call Charles off. The pope heard their plea, made no reply, released the other two ambassadors to return to Florence, and detained Dante.

On November 1, Charles entered Florence and occupied it with a large army, all the while making promises to preserve the peace. But soon, with Corso descending on the scene and issuing threats and curses left and right, Charles permitted widespread looting and burning, as urged by the Black extremists. Dante's house was vandalized and his wife and children were forced to flee to relatives. By April, all the White belligerents had been made to abandon the city. In January 1302, Dante was charged by the newly elected Black priors with accepting bribes and diverting municipal funds to his personal use, for which gargantuan fines were assessed against him. Though the charges were fabrications, Dante's failure to appear in person to answer them brought down on him (and on fourteen other former officials) the condemnation of death by burning. Dante, not quite thirty-seven years of age, would never again be able to return to his native city.

ↄ Charles, though never a king, was always trying to become one. He auditioned successively for the role of king of Aragon, king of Sicily, emperor of Constantinople, and Holy Roman Emperor but never got a part. "*Fils de roi,*" his countrymen said of him, "*frère de roi, oncle de trois rois, père de roi, et jamais roi.*"

Dante in red in a fresco in the chapel of the Bargello, Florence.

Released at last by the pope and making his way back to Florence, Dante had reached Siena by the time he had news of the charges against him. He lingered in Tuscany awhile, allying himself briefly with the Ghibellines of San Godenzo, then with those of Forlì to the east. But within a few months, despairing that any good could come of these associations, he took off north to Verona, where he found shelter and welcome in the shadow of Bartolomeo della Scala, *"il gran Lombardo"* (the great Lombard), as Dante would call him and from whom he received *"lo primo tuo refugio e 'l primo ostello"* ("first refuge and first lodging"), words that carry a warm exhalation of relief after trials too chilling and too many.

Though Dante would remain forever grateful to the great Lombard, the Veronese refuge was short-lived. During the winter of 1303–4, Bartolomeo died and was succeeded by his antipathetic brother Alboino. Dante was on the move once more. In leaving Verona, he was also cutting himself off from his connections to the White Guelphs. He had first come to Verona as their emissary. Now, finding his party *"malvagia e scempia"* (evil and stupid)—never a winning combination—he resolved to set off on his own, *"parte per te stesso"* (a party of one). Anyone who has ever come to find his fellow partisans as dismaying as the opposition will understand the abiding loneliness that enveloped Dante.

There is a portrait of Dante in profile in the chapel of the battlemented Bargello, the massive "Palace of the Captain of the People," official residence of the *podestà,* and Florence's oldest surviving government building, constructed a decade before Dante's birth. Dante may be found among the blessed in Heaven in the fresco of the Last Judgment on the altar wall. Though the fresco was made sometime after Dante's death, there is every reason to believe that if it was not painted by Giotto himself it is from the hand of one of his assistants, at any rate someone who had known Dante, the citizen of Florence, but never saw him again after his banishment. The fading Dante on the chapel wall is a tall, thin, handsome man in his mid-thirties, clean-shaven, dignified in rich, dark-red velvet, and learned (for he carries a book). He has a strong, well-defined jaw; thin, firmly closed lips; and the aquiline nose of the ancient Romans. Many of the contented *beati* around him are smiling sweetly, looking here and there, as people will. Dante stares straight ahead, serious, intense, meditative, resolute. The portrait is a just one, according well with everything else we know about the man.

But the years to come would not be kind to Dante. For several years we have incomplete information on his whereabouts. He stays at Arezzo, Treviso, Padua (where he runs into Giotto, then at work on the Scrovegni Chapel), Bologna, Venice, the Lunigiana, and Lucca, and with several different hosts in the Casentino Valley. We lose track of him from time to time, but always he appears to be wandering in or near Tuscany, circling Florence, hoping. For ten years after the death sentence of 1302, Dante will almost never spend as much as a year in any one place; often enough his stay will be far shorter. He will learn, as one of the characters in the *Commedia* will tell him, the bitterness of exile:

> "Tu lascerai ogne cosa diletta
>> più caramente; e questo è quello strale
>> che l'arco de lo essilio pria saetta.
> Tu proverai si come sa di sale
>> lo pane altrui, e come è duro calle
>> lo scendere e 'l salir per l'altrui scale.
> E quel che più ti graverà le spalle,
>> sarà la compagnia malvagia e scempia^c
>> con la qual tu cadrai in questa valle."

<hr>

℃ This phrase, which I earlier translated literally as "evil and stupid," Dale, partly to keep with his rhyme scheme, translates as "venomous and foul."

> *"And everything you loved most dearly there*
>> *You shall abandon. This opening shaft the bow*
>> *Of banishment will shoot into the air.*
> *How salt another's bread is you shall know;*
>> *How hard the step will tread, mount or descend,*
>> *Upon a stranger's stairs where you must go.*

> And what will most of all weigh down and bend
> Your shoulders is the venomous and foul
> Mob that will walk with you to this vale's end."

The young, attractive, enviable presence that almost assaults us from the chapel wall of the Bargello will be transformed during these ten years of wandering into a very different older figure, *"peregrino, quasi mendicando"* (pilgrim, almost beggared), as he tells us, "a ship without a sail and without a rudder, cast about to different harbors and inlets and shores by the dry wind of humiliating poverty." By the time he returns to Verona again—for the youngest of the della Scala brothers, the admirable Can Grande, had become lord of Verona on the death of the antipathetic Alboino—Dante is a stooped, prematurely aged man in his late forties whose large, dark eyes flicker starkly from a dark, thickly bearded face. As E. M. Forster describes him in his magical tale "The Celestial Omnibus," he is "a sallow man with terrifying jaws and sunken eyes." He walks slowly and always looks thoughtful and sad, though his manners are impeccable and his unfailing courtesy to all is a cause for comment. Boccaccio, who will interview many Veronese for his biography of Dante, tells of a cluck-clucking clutch of Veronese ladies who were taking the air one day and were terribly frightened by Dante when he appeared, as if from nowhere, and walked past them. With his gaunt, clouded face and air of sadness, he seemed as if he had suddenly emerged . . . *dal inferno!*

Indeed, Hell was much on Dante's mind during this time, for he had begun his great poem, which he called simply *Commedia* (and which would earn the adjective *Divina* centuries later). It is divided into three parts (called *canzoni,* or song sequences): *Inferno, Purgatorio, Paradiso* (Hell, Purgatory, Heaven), each *canzone* having thirty-three *canti* (songs, lyrics, or, in this case, rounded episodes), with the *Inferno* having an extra introductory *canto,* thus making one hundred *canti* in all. The tightness of the structure cannot be overemphasized, for there is nothing like it, nothing so thoroughly architectural, in all the rest of literature, whether ancient or modern. The *Comedy* is a series of storeys, apartments, rooms, and frames in which everything fits into everything else, all planes leveled, all lines plumb, all corners perfectly squared. Even the novel rhyme scheme is amazing in its completeness. *Terza rima,* Dante called it: aba, bcb, cdc, and so forth, never deviating and never failing to rhyme—and rhyme gracefully and naturally—through its 14,233 lines of eleven syllables each.

If this sounds—to the reader who has never attempted the *Comedy*—like an invitation to dry schematization and considerable pain rather than to the normal pleasures of literature, I plead with you to lay aside your prejudice. The real problem for the English-reading reader lies not in the poem's architectonics, which (once you have been alerted to them) fade imperceptibly into the background, but in the language. Dante's Italian is simple—like its predecessor, medieval Latin—and can be understood by anyone reading a straightforward bilingual translation.[f] But the use of language—the severity of diction, combined with an ambiguous allusiveness—is unlike almost anything in English. There is in Dante some of the music we hear in Milton, but whereas Milton overwhelms us with his gorgeously vibrating organ chords, Dante, poor in resources, sticks to the chastity of chant. There is something of Spenser's *Faerie Queene* in Dante (or rather something of Dante in *The Faerie Queene*), but this comparison is more misleading than helpful, because Spenser's bullheaded politics have grown entirely irrelevant and his elaborate allegory weighs one down after a while and becomes at last a bore. Dante's politics remain universal, his allegory so subtle that one seldom need advert to it; he seems rather to be telling a

[f] There are two complete and admirable translations of the *Comedy* in English, each published in three paperback volumes and each with facing pages in Italian and English: John D. Sinclair's literal (and somewhat archaic) prose translation, published by Oxford, which also offers a splendid commentary, and Allen Mandelbaum's poetic but faithful translation, published by Bantam. Nearly fifty years separate the two translations, Sinclair's published in the late 1930s, Mandelbaum's in the early 1980s. I have chosen—at least in the longer passages—to quote from a less well-known translation by Peter Dale, published in 1996 by Anvil (London), because of Dale's surprising success in approximating Dante's *terza rima* in English, while remaining generally faithful to the Italian. See also Notes and Sources at the back of the book.

poignantly personal story. The only English poet to approach language in a way truly close to Dante's is George Herbert, who can be sweet but severe, confessional but colloquial, realistic but hopeful, symbolic but ordinary all at once. Yet Herbert never attempted anything remotely similar in scale to the *Comedy.*

Enough of comparisons. Let us approach the work, beginning with the most famous first line in all of literature:

Nel mezzo del cammin di nostra vita
    mi ritrovai per una selva oscura,
    ché la diritta via era smarrita.
Ahi quanto a dir qual era è cosa dura
    esta selva selvaggia e aspra e forte
    che nel pensier rinova la paura!
Tant' è amara che poco è più morte;
    ma per trattar del ben chi'i' vi trovai,
    dirò de l'altre cose ch'i' v'ho scorte.

Along the journey of our life half way
    I found myself in a dark wood
    Wherein the straight road no longer lay:
How hard it is to tell, make understood
    What a wild place it was, so dense, adverse
    That fear returns in thinking on that wood.
It is so bitter death is hardly worse.
    But, for the good it was my chance to gain,
    The other things I saw there I'll rehearse.

In his first three lines (literally, "In the middle of the journey of our life / I found myself again in a dark wood / where the straight way was lost"), he alerts us to three things: he is thirty-five, halfway to his allotted "three score years and ten"; this, though his personal story ("I"), will have universal meaning ("*our* life"); he is lost. The verb form *ritrovai* can mean "I found" or "I found again." To find oneself lost is paradoxical but also the beginning of a realistic assessment of one's position. Because *mi ritrovai*, considered by itself without the phrase that follows, suggests "I found myself again," there may even be a slight hint, here at the very beginning of the work, that Dante will in the end find his way out of the savage (*selvaggia*) darkness.

This first canto, Canto I of the *Inferno*, is set on Good Friday 1300, the same year that Dante was elected a prior of Florence and the same year the dreadful Boniface proclaimed as the first Holy Year. In 1301, Dante voted in the Council of Florence against aiding the pope in his war; in the same year, Charles occupied Florence, while Dante was detained at Rome. In early 1302, Dante was condemned to death in absentia and banished. The tumult of these three years—and Dante has an endless fascination for threes and their multiples—forms the personal backdrop of the *Comedy*: they are the years of Dante's life when "all changed, changed utterly."

Dante, writing nearly a decade later, is looking back on his former self, the intense young man with prospects in view, whom we met on the wall of the Bargello. The *Comedy* is an allegory because it presents Dante, its main character, on a pilgrimage through Hell, Purgatory, and Heaven, a pilgrimage not unlike the one the Holy Year pilgrims made to Rome. But whereas they visited an earthly city—and one where, as Dante (thinking of Boniface, who sold church offices for a price) says, "Christ is bought and sold the whole day long"—Dante will journey to the world beyond the veil, even to the heavenly city itself. The great poem is a comedy because it ends well. But in the course of a largely painful journey, Dante the poet has so universalized the sufferings of Dante the man that his personal story can serve as a template for the lives of all readers in every age.

After a night spent in fear "in the lake of the heart," Dante sees beyond a hill the rays of the sun—"the beams of the planet that leads men straight on every road"—and heads east, only to have his way blocked by three beasts escaped from Hell: the spotted leopard of lust, the hungry lion of pride, and the lean she-wolf of avarice. They represent his (and everyone's) temptations. In flight from them all, he runs smack into the ancient Roman poet Virgil, who is Dante's principal model, *"lo mio maestro e 'l mio autore,"* as Dante most touchingly addresses him. "You are he from whom alone I took the beautiful style [*lo bello stilo*] that has brought me honor." Beautiful style, most surely. Dante's studious attention to Virgil's felicitous refinements, transferred to the emerging Italian vernacular and widely praised as the *dolce stil nuovo* (the sweet new style), had brought him fame. His early poems, all in the rampant tradition of courtly love, made him preeminent among the *fedeli d'Amore,* the devotees of the god of Love, always in thrall to one mistress or another. But now as Dante meditates on the crisis of his life, his supple poetry, still *dolce,* must stretch itself considerably to embrace the all-encompassing theme of suffering.

There is no way past the she-wolf, so Virgil proposes to guide Dante by another route—through Hell—and what a tour it will be, though much of it so famous that it need not greatly delay us here. In Canto III they move through the entranceway that bears the awful notice ending with the words ABANDON ALL HOPE YOU WHO ENTER HERE. Their first encounters, if they can be called that, are with the Drearies, who, having no place of their own, mill about Hell's entrance, "those who lived without blame or praise," whining wraiths who never truly lived at all, the lukewarm, who are "as hateful to God as to his enemies," the people no one claims. Among them Dante identifies a pope, Celestine V, a silly, weak-willed man who resigned the papacy at the urging of his ambitious counselor, who then engineered his own election—as Pope Boniface VIII.

Next, they cross the river of death on Charon's boat and find themselves in a combination of the Greco-Roman Hades and Limbo, the place where the souls of the good who were unbaptized go after death: the heroes, poets, and philosophers of antiquity, Muslims, et al. (This is also where the "saints" of the Old Testament remained till they, as Christians by anticipation, were rescued by Christ, who, according to the ancient creeds, "descended into Hell" after his death to liberate all the Jewish saints from Adam and Eve to the latter prophets.) Though Dante is openly contemptuous of many of the men who occupied the throne of Peter, he is unquestioningly orthodox, in fact Thomistic,[9] in his theology. The problem of what happens to good pagans after their deaths may be the only point on which Dante appears uncomfortable with standard Catholic doctrine: he accepts the prevailing theory of his time—that, because the pagans were never saved by Christ through baptism, they lack the capacity for seeing God and must be kept somewhere apart from Heaven[b]—but it goes against the grain; and in the *Paradiso* he even manages (with courageous inconsistency) to sneak a few pagans into Heaven.

9 In Cantos X and XI of the *Paradiso*, Dante will meet Thomas Aquinas, who praises many fellow theologians, including those condemned for heresy and those with whom he disagreed. In Heaven, their differences have been harmonized. The high praise by Thomas, a Dominican, for Francis of Assisi is paired (in Canto XII) with the praise by Bonaventure, a Franciscan, for Dominic. All these are indications of the loathing Dante came to have for partisanship.

b No one seems to believe this anymore. The nub of the old argument, that baptism was absolutely necessary for salvation, has been more or less nuanced away. See page 130.

Sinclair puts it well when he writes, "The relation of the virtuous pagans to the Christian scheme of salvation was a matter of acute and peculiar difficulty for Dante. With his deep conviction of the divine ordering of secular history (represented mainly by the story of Troy and Rome [as told in Virgil's *Aeneid*]) as a kind of parallel and complement of sacred history (represented by the Old and New Testaments and the Church), with his strong sense of the unity of humanity and of all its spiritual values, and with his profound reverence for all that was best in what he knew of pre-Christian paganism [especially Thomas's version of Aristotle], the exclusion of the virtuous heathen from salvation, inevitable as he conceived it to be, put a great and painful strain on his mind." Dante's solution here is to give the good pagans "a noble castle" in Limbo, "seven times encircled by high walls and defended all around by a lovely stream," and "a meadow of fresh verdure, where there were people with serious eyes which do not dart about and with great authority in their demeanor: they spoke seldom and with gentle voices."[1] For unbaptized pagans, they're doing well—and they don't know what they're missing.

It's only after Limbo that the real Hell begins. The Drearies, clustered near the entrance, are betwixt and between; the good pagans in the First Circle exist in a sort of Greek Elysium. But in the Second Circle of Hell, where the Lustful are confined, there is real, if mitigated, suffering. It should be borne in mind that anyone who repents before death will not be found in any of Hell's circles; only the unrepentant are here—in the case of the Lustful, usually those who had no time to repent. They are blown about like small birds on fierce gusts of wind. Virgil points out Semiramis, Cleopatra, Helen of Troy, Paris, Tristan, "more than a thousand shades, naming them as he pointed to each, whom love had parted from our life."

Dante recognizes a pair of lovers, bound together, who "seem so light upon the wind," and speaks to them kindly as they are borne near him. They are Paolo Malatesta, who had been the dashing Captain of the People of Florence when Dante was an impressionable teenager, and his mistress Francesca da Polenta of Ravenna. Dante certainly knew members of her family and may even have known her. Like all Italians of the time, he knew her story. She had been married for ten years to the crippled son of the lord of Rimini but fell in love with Paolo, her husband's younger brother. At the time, she had a daughter of nine; Paolo was married, with two children. While they were making love, the cripple surprised and murdered them both.

Dante's kind speech evokes a kind response from Francesca, blown about above him:

[1] We can see in this description the sort of dignified, slow-moving demeanor that was prized by Dante and his contemporaries. A loud voice, abruptness, calling attention to oneself, excessive demonstrativeness were all indications that one should take one's place among the fishmongers.

"O animal grazïoso e benigno
  che visitando vai per l'aere perso
  noi che tignemmo il mondo di sanguigno,
se fosse amico il re de l'universo,
  noi pregheremmo lui de la tua pace,
  poi c'hai pietà del nostro mal perverso."

"O living creature, gracious and kind to bear
  The black fumes, and visit us who stained
  The earth with blood when we were living there,
If the King of all the universe remained
  A friend to us, our prayer would be your peace,
Because you pity our fate perverse and pained."

Dante, full of sympathy for their torment, is moved to tears by Francesca's words. He asks her then, "how love gave her to recognize her dubious desires"—in other words, how did she and Paolo come to sleep together? She answers with one of the *Comedy*'s most famous sentences: *"Nessun maggior dolore / che ricordarsi del tempo felice / nella miseria"* (No greater sorrow [is there] / than to recall the happy time / in misery). She goes on to explain that one day she and Paolo were reading together. It happened that the book was an engrossing Arthurian romance of Guinevere and Lancelot:

"Per più fïate li occhi ci sospinse
  quella lettura, e scolorocci il viso;
  ma solo un punto fu quel che ci vinse.
Quando leggemmo il disïato riso
  esser basciato da cotanto amante,
  questi, che mai da me non fia diviso,
la bocca mi basciò tutto tremante."

> *"Several times the reading changed our tone*
> *And color, drove our eyes to meet; just one*
> *Defeated us, one moment on its own.*
> *When we had come to where the kiss was won*
> *From such a lover with that fondest smile,*
> *What he, who never goes from me, had done*
> *Was tremblingly to kiss my mouth. . . ."*

Dante, himself a *fedele d'Amore,* a well-known writer of courtly love poetry, and (we may confidently surmise) an adventuring philanderer, knew just how such a temptation could overpower anyone. All the while Francesca spoke, the silent Paolo wept (*"l'altro piangea"*). It was too much for Dante; he grew so faint that he dropped to the ground as a dead body drops (*"caddi come corpo morto cade"*).

The poet never has another word to say about this couple, locked in their eternal embrace as they are blown about by the wind. But there are at least two unspoken thoughts here: sexual sins are the least of all, deserving of the most forgiveness and the most lenient punishment; and Dante, fainting, here repents of his own sexual adventures, which certainly during his lonely exile have been sins of adultery, and resolves to lead a better and more *honest* life. Native discretion and a sincere regard for the reputation of his long-suffering wife, still lodged uncomfortably at or near Florence, keep him from saying anything explicit. But in Dante's poetry his most foundational thoughts are often implied and left for the reader to intuit, and his strongest impulses are subtly dissolved in the color of the atmosphere and the scent on the wind.

Honesty is the hidden key to understanding Dante's *Inferno*. It is dishonesty the poet has come to hate most of all—the dishonesty of popes and politicians, of Guelphs and Ghibellines, of Whites and Blacks. It is dishonesty, which always begins with dishonesty to oneself, that has made such a mess of the world. In his tour of the world of sin—which is what the journey to Hell really is—Dante is trying with all his prowess to get things straight, the things that really matter. He is drawing, in all its latitude and longitude, as accurate a map of the moral universe as he can make. He has taken on this enormous task for all of us, but first of all for himself. He needs to know what is really true so that he can reorient his life and sail to his appointed end. He is tired of going rudderless. It is this new moral dimension in the middle-aged man that transforms his poetry from courtly love sweetness to ultimate seriousness. Dante retains the quick and playful sensibility that any great poet possesses. He has not lost his sense of ambiguity, his irony, his subtlety. But none of these things is an end in itself any longer, a bauble to pleasure a prince or to dazzle a crowd. All is now in service to his ultimate end.

Hell, as Dante conceives it, is an upside-down cone formed from concentric circles, something like the cone of a great volcano. It is largest at the top, where the Circle of Limbo is, a little smaller in the Second Circle, to which the Lustful are confined. The Third Circle, the Circle of the Gluttons, is smaller still—and so on, till one reaches the depths of Hell and the most confined circle of all. In each circle, the punishment fits the crime: the Lustful perpetually blown about, as they were in life; the Gluttons perpetually prostrate in a stinking sewer.

Sinclair has given us a lucid outline of "The System of Dante's Hell," which I reproduce here with some revisions.

Incontinent:	At the Entrance:	Drearies		
	First Circle:	Good Pagans		
	Second Circle:	Lustful		
	Third Circle:	Gluttons		
	Fourth Circle:	Avaricious and (its opposite) Prodigal		
	Fifth Circle:	Angry and Sullen		
	Sixth Circle:	Heretics		
Violent:	Seventh Circle:	First Division:	Violent Against Others	
		Second Division:	Violent Against Self	
		Third Division:	Violent Against God, Nature, Art	
Fraudulent:	Eighth Circle (*Malebolge*):	Simply Fraudulent:		
			First Pit:	Panders and Seducers
			Second Pit:	Flatterers
			Third Pit:	Buyers and Sellers of Church Offices
			Fourth Pit:	Sorcerers
			Fifth Pit:	Buyers and Sellers of Political Offices
			Sixth Pit:	Hypocrites
			Seventh Pit:	Thieves
			Eighth Pit:	Fraudulent Counselors
			Ninth Pit:	Makers of Discord
			Tenth Pit:	Falsifiers
	Ninth Circle (*Cocytus*):	Treacherous:	*Caina*	Treacherous to Kindred
			Antenora	Treacherous to Country and Cause
			Ptolomea	Treacherous to Guests
			Judecca	Treacherous to Lords and Benefactors

Those who have sinned through incontinence (or lack of self-control) are the least guilty. They will never leave Hell, but, Dante learns from Virgil, their torments will lessen with time. Though heretics sin against truth, they may believe what they say, so they too are less guilty. The violent, likewise, lack self-control, though the consequences of their actions are far worse than those of the simply incontinent. But it is the Eighth and Ninth Circles of Hell, where those who have been dishonest and deceptive are incarcerated, that especially describe Dante's vision of evil at work in the world.

The circles of Hell are fairly crammed with the once rich and powerful, especially with kings and other titled personages and with members of the higher clergy. The clergy are also well represented among the avaricious of the Fourth Circle. "These tonsured ones were clerics without doubt," Virgil explains to Dante, "And cardinals and popes in whom the sin / Of avarice brings its worst excess about" [Dale's translation]. For Dante, as for all other thinking people of his time, the worldliness of churchmen and their constant craving after wealth and power were the most destructive forces loose in the world.

In the Third Pit of the Eighth Circle, this circle called *Malebolge* (Evil Pits), Dante finds the simonists, those who bought and sold church offices for personal gain—"who prostitute the things of God for gold and silver." These are buried headfirst in apertures of solid rock from which only their feet and calves stick out, the rest of their bodies buried deep in the flames of Satan's oven. Though the *Comedy* is set in 1300, when Boniface was still on the papal throne, Dante sees that a flaming orifice has already been prepared for him. At the moment, it houses Pope Nicholas III, who died in 1280. Soon it will welcome Boniface (who died in 1303), as Nicholas is pushed farther down below him. One day, it will claim in his turn Clement V, the French pope who moved the papacy from Rome to Avignon at the behest of Philip the Fair and who was reigning as pope when Dante wrote the *Comedy*.

Dante is positively delighted at the prospect of so many terrible popes receiving their due at last and chortles expectantly: "Are you there already, *there already,* Boniface?" He then turns on the current occupant of the hellhole and delivers a mini-homily: "Pray, tell me now, how much money did our Lord ask up front from Saint Peter before he gave the keys [to the Kingdom of Heaven] into his charge? Surely, he asked nothing but 'Follow me,' nor did Peter or the others take gold or silver from Matthias when he was chosen [to replace Judas]. . . . So, stay where you are, for you are punished well. You are the shepherds," Dante goes on, that Saint John the Divine had in mind when he foresaw the Whore of Babylon fornicating with all the kings of the earth[j]—the very image Martin Luther will apply to the corrupt papacy a little more than two centuries later. "You've made a god of gold and silver, and what's the difference between you and the idolaters but that they worship one and you a hundred? Oh, Constantine, how much evil was given birth, not by your conversion, but by the Donation the first rich pope had from you!" As already noted, the so-called Donation of Constantine was a forgery, used by the papacy to prop up its legitimacy in Europe, but Dante could not have known this. How much more righteously he would have railed had he known.

Dante may be circumspect about his own peccadilloes, but not about his satisfaction in seeing his tormentors punished nor in seeing those responsible for the chief political ills of the medieval world receive their eternal comeuppance. He is a medieval man and has no need to feign the pious sympathy occasionally evinced by our contemporary media figures. If he feels like chortling, he'll chortle.

The last and deepest circle of Hell is called *Cocytus* after the river of Greek Hades whose name means "Lamentation." *Cocytus* is an eternally frozen place where Satan himself is confined. Its four rings are named for the historical and mythological characters Dante considers most treacherous: *Caina,* for instance, for Cain, the world's first murderer—and of his brother, at that—*Judecca* for Judas, whose head lies inside one of Satan's three enormous mouths, in

j Dante's New Testament references are to Matthew 16:19 (in which Jesus gives Peter "the keys to the Kingdom of Heaven"); Acts 1:26 (the choosing of Matthias); and Revelation 17 and 19 (descriptions of the Whore of Babylon).

the eternal process of being crushed by Satan's jagged teeth. Though mountainous in stature, Satan is almost as much a figure of pity as of terror: "With six eyes he was weeping and over three chins dripped tears and bloody foam."

The deeper circles of Hell will satisfy any schoolboy with a taste for comic gore, so full are they of body parts, human excreta, and every extreme of degradation. In Cantos XXXII and XXXIII, Dante encounters a couple who are the moral opposite of Paolo and Francesca. Whereas those two lovers are bound together for all eternity by their mutual love, Count Ugolino and Archbishop Ruggieri, both of Pisa, Florence's western neighbor, are frozen together in mutual hatred. Ugolino succeeded in betraying everyone, first his fellow Ghibellines, then the Guelphs with whom he subsequently allied himself. Exiled from Pisa, he was invited back by the archbishop, who promised to effect a reconciliation between Ugolino and his many enemies. But on Ugolino's return, the archbishop had him clapped in irons, along with his two sons and two grandsons. Imprisoned in the tower of the Gualandi, the count and his family were at length left to starve to death after Archbishop Ruggieri gave instructions that the tower be locked to all and its keys thrown into the Arno. When the fastness was at last reopened and the dead removed, it was found that Ugolino had feasted on his (already dead?) progeny before dying himself. "Hunger," he explains to Dante, "soon had more power than grief." Now he feasts on the head of Ruggieri:

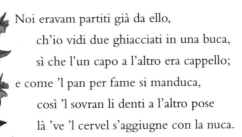

Noi eravam partiti già da ello,
    ch'io vidi due ghiacciati in una buca,
    sì che l'un capo a l'altro era cappello;
e come 'l pan per fame si manduca,
    così 'l sovran li denti a l'altro pose
    là 've 'l cervel s'aggiugne con la nuca.

We'd left him [another traitor] when I noticed, frozen hard,
    Two in the same hole, so cramped, one head
    Seemed, for the other one, a cap or guard.

> But, as when hungry one would chew at bread,
>   So in that neck he sank his teeth to gnash
>   Just where the brain into the nape is led.

The subsequent *canzoni*—the *Purgatorio* and the *Paradiso*—though meant to have equal weight with the first, do not invade the imagination and constrict the heartbeat as does the *Inferno*. Eternal damnation, after all, commands one's attention as can few other themes. And, besides, as C. S. Lewis put it dryly, "The joys of heaven are for most of us, in our present condition, an acquired taste." All the same, the sequence on Purgatory makes a splendid sequel to damnation, for, unlike Hell, Purgatory is a place of punishment that is also a platform of hope.

The denizens of Hell have chosen their sin over all else; it is because of this unwavering choice that they are unable to rise. The citizens of Purgatory, on the other hand, though hardly models of moral life, struggled while on earth—in some part of themselves—to overcome their attachment to their sin. For this reason they will rise to glory—one day, and in certain cases that day remains a long way off. But, cautions Dante to the reader:

> Non vo' però, lettor, che tu ti smaghi
>   di buon proponimento per udire
>   come Dio vuol che 'l debito si paghi.
> Non attender la forma del martìre:
>   pensa la succession; pensa ch'al peggio
>   oltre la gran sentenza non può ire.

> I'd never wish you, Reader, ever to grow
>   Fearful of a good purpose, because you learn
>   How God decides what debt we undergo.
> Ignore the pain; think what such pain will earn.
>   Think that at worst it cannot stretch or spread
>   Beyond the great Day of Judgement's sure return.

"Non attender la forma del martìre: / pensa la succession" ("Ignore the pain; think what such pain will earn") is advice for thinking not just about Purgatory but about one's life in this world. For Purgatory—a time of trial with glory at the end—is but a second chance at life, a second lifetime of suffering for sure, but this time with Paradise securely in reach. Purgatory was the mitigating invention of medieval theologians who felt that there must be a place of purgation beyond death where the great mass of humanity—those not evil enough for Hell nor pure enough for Heaven—could atone for their unatoned sins. "In Dante's vision," writes the insightful Peter S. Hawkins, "the point of purgatory was not so much to 'serve time' in a place of temporal suffering as it was to enter a process of transformation, to become someone new. In short, the poet took what was popularly imagined as an upper chamber of hell and turned it into an extended passage to heaven."

Purgatory is also a passage of social leveling. Having encountered many popes in Hell, Dante meets more in Purgatory. One of these, atoning for the sin of clerical avarice, is Adrian V, to whom Dante kneels in reverence and whom he addresses using the honorific plural, *voi*. Adrian beseeches him to stand. "Straighten your legs, brother, and stand up straight," urges the pope. "Make no mistake: I, like you and all the others, am just a fellow servant of the one Power." All are brothers and fellow servants, all earthly titles and social differentiations are ultimately meaningless. Dante, democratic townsman and impoverished wanderer, possesses far greater insight into the human condition than cloistered Hildegard was capable of.

In Heaven, where Dante meets his great-great-grandfather, the crusader Cacciaguida, the ancestor bemoans the introduction into Florence of differences in affluence, rank, and power and recalls (in a famous passage) a simpler, more virtuous Florence of times past:

"Fiorenza dentro da la cerchia antica,
    ond' ella toglie ancora e terza e nona,
    si stava in pace, sobria e pudica.

Non avea catenella, non corona,

   non gonne contigiate, non cintura

   che fosse a veder più che la persona."

"Florence, within its ancient bounds, from where

   She still hears tierce and nones [monastic hours of prayer],

     reposed as yet

   In peace, sober and chaste, serene and fair.

There was no bracelet then, no coronet;

   No embroidered gowns; no girdle's sway

   That strikes the eye before the person met."

It is the lure of avarice, of a gluttonous desire for more than one needs—and at the expense of others—that has brought upon Florence all the fraudulence and treachery that have issued in its bloody wars and shameful divisions.

These brief incursions into the *Purgatorio* and the *Paradiso* must content us here. The *Commedia* is too great and too grand to be commented on by a shelf of good books, let alone by a single chapter in a book of many things. I leave it to you, the reader, to continue the awesome pilgrimage *"parte per te stesso"* (a party of your own), using this chapter only as a feeble introduction.

If you visit Florence, enter the baptistery to see the layered mosaics of Hell, Purgatory, and Heaven that surely served Dante as inspiration. But then enter the cathedral and look upward at Brunelleschi's amazing dome of light, suspended in space, it seems, without earthly supports over the cathedral's crossing. There you will be reminded of the stupendous ode to the Light of God with which Dante closes the *Commedia*. Though the dome was not raised till more than a hundred years after Dante's death, there can be no question that Brunelleschi, in this summation of all European architecture, ancient, medieval, and even modern, had Dante's closing pages in mind, the dream of seeing God:

Oh abbondante grazia ond' io presunsi
    ficcar lo viso per la luce etterna,
    tanto che la veduta vi consunsi!
Nel suo profondo vidi che s'interna,
    legato con amore in un volume,
    ciò che per l'universo si squaderna. . . .
A quella luce cotal si diventa,
    che volgersi da lei per altro aspetto
    è impossibil che mai si consenta.

O Grace abounding, in which I dared prolong
    My look, and in eternal Light immerse,
    Till power of vision waned at beams so strong.
Within its depth I noticed intersperse,
    By love within a single volume bound,
    The scattered leaves of all the universe. . . .
And, at that Light, a man becomes so he
    Could never turn from it to other sight,
    For that is past all possibility.

Remember always that, as Dante wrote in a letter to Can Grande della Scala, he intended the *Comedy* "to remove those living in this life from the state of misery and to lead them to the state of happiness." He meant his poem for you, Reader, as much as for anyone, for his was a profound faith that one can actually be transformed by *the experience of reading* and that one's desire and one's will may be moved not by the cheap, winking lights of worldly success but, as Dante names it in the last line of the *Commedia*, by *"l'amor che move il sole e l'altre stelle"*—the Love that moves the sun and the other stars.

SEVEN

Ravenna, city of death
the politician's emptiness
and its consequences

*Sound, sound the clarion, fill
the fife,
Throughout the sensual world
proclaim,
One crowded hour of glorious life
Is worth an age without a name.*

—SIR WALTER SCOTT

HOUGH PRINCES AND PRELATES would no doubt agree about the thrill of being part of an exciting age, rather than one "without a name," often enough the price of that "one crowded hour of glorious life" proves steep for individuals who fail to rise to the level of high priest or monarch. Dante's life, though certainly full of color and incident, was—from his exile in 1302 to his death nineteen years later at the age of fifty-six—a life of personal suffering. And that suffering was engendered by the warring prelates and princes whose reckless pursuit of their own wealth and power made life such a misery—and such a prematurely shortened misery—for so many.

In the *Comedy,* which is Dante's map of the moral universe, those who treated others unjustly—by grasping at what was not theirs and by lying and dissembling so as to grasp even more—are tormented in the hereafter, just as they so carelessly tormented others in this life. Only in this way can Dante, or anyone else, for that matter, imagine that justice will finally be done. The ultimate expression of the moral economy of the West may be glimpsed in the symbolic scales by which Christ—in many medieval paintings of the Last Judgment—weighs sinners in the balance and assigns them their eternity, thus assuring the discriminating Justice of which the world is incapable and which is the gift of God alone.

On the night of September 13, 1321, Dante died at Ravenna, having migrated two years earlier from Verona to this unique city on the Adriatic. What brought him here we can't be sure, though Petrarch tells us he had grown weary of the hilarity of Can Grande's court, filled with mounting numbers of tedious jesters, bibulous buffoons, and fawning courtiers. We know that in his last two years, he had the generous patronage of Guido Novello, Ravenna's lord, and was able at last to invite his family—wife, three sons, a daughter, grandchildren—to join him. He was, moreover, surrounded by admiring fellow poets and professors in this hushed and ancient settlement that can feel more like a mausoleum than a city. His correspondence with other European intellectuals had become extensive; and the *Commedia,* now complete and circulating in abundant manuscript copies, was already bringing him praise and fame far beyond that of any other medieval writer.

Thanks to Guido Novello's generosity, the economic future of his beloved sons was at last secure. His daughter entered a convent at Ravenna and took the name Sister Beatrice—which suggests an unusual closeness to her father and an understanding of his singular psychology, rather than any slight to her mother. Dante ventured forth occasionally on diplomatic missions for his lord. Returning from one of these—a mission to Venice—he chose to make the journey by land rather than by sea. Crossing the pestilent marshes that surround Ravenna, he contracted malaria, reached his home, and died.

More than this we do not know, but we may take the few facts we have as hints that Dante, having found the supernatural peace he hymns in the *Paradiso*, also found familial peace and human happiness in his last two years. No other European city outside the territories of ancient Greece is remotely like Ravenna, designated in 401 as the capital of the Western empire by the Eastern emperors and built with Oriental munif-

Sixth-century mosaic frieze
of the emperor Justinian and his court, San Vitale, Ravenna.

icence in the last centuries of their Italian influence. Today, it rivals anything that remains in Constantinople itself; and its grand domed monuments are an eerie if faithful tribute to Hellenic Christian sensibility. However much of a power center Ravenna may have been in the fifth and sixth centuries, by Dante's day it had become the sepulchrally quiet coastal town one comes upon today. If Dante was looking to escape the mad hubbub of a well-connected fourteenth-century court and spend time reacquainting himself with the members of his immediate family, all the while in the shadow of great works that enabled him to muse on power past, he could have done no better than move to Ravenna.

Sixth-century mosaic frieze of the empress
Theodora and her court, San Vitale, Ravenna.

The octagonal basilica of San Vitale, in particular, is like nothing else in Western Europe—except that Charlemagne imitated it slavishly in building the imposing cathedral in his capital of Aachen (or Aix-la-Chapelle), hard by Germany's present border with France. It is instructive to note that the great barbarian monarch imagined that Greek-inspired architecture could lend increased legitimacy to his claim to be Holy Roman Emperor. But San Vitale, the original, possesses in its choir and apse a sumptuous series of mosaics that Charlemagne's artists were incapable of imitating. Among religious subjects from the Old and New Testaments are two striking processional friezes of the Byzantine court, one of the emperor Justinian with his train of officials, soldiers, and clergy, another—answering the first on the opposite wall—of the empress Theodora with her train of clergy and ladies-in-waiting. It is impossible to decide which of these overbearing imperialists one would more fervently wish to avoid, he as debauched and brutal as the most depraved *mafioso,* she as cold and cruel as an ice queen. The mosaicist knew the faces he depicted here and took the risk of telling the truth about them, rightly calculating that no one with power to hurt him would catch his drift.

By the time Dante could have beheld these two, he had finished the *Commedia*; and it would be idle on our part to speculate whether his confrontation with these images would have altered his favorable depiction of Justinian.[a] Dante was desperate to achieve a just society—in theory, if not in fact. In order to remedy the sad state of things political, one must first, he reasoned, have a model in mind of what a just society would look like. In such a society, he theorized, justice

a Dante's wrongheaded assignment of Justinian to Heaven was possible because he knew so little about the man, and what he thought he knew had been so thoroughly corrupted by legendary invention. Similarly, he places Bernard of Clairvaux in Heaven, whereas I would exclude him, despite his undoubted importance, on account of his insufferable self-righteousness. Dante knew far less than we do about the life (as opposed to the pious writing) of Bernard. Bernard had been canonized in 1174, almost a century before Dante was born; and Dante, despite his bad opinion of many popes, took with all seriousness the act of papal canonization. Dante's assignments to the afterlife are spot on whenever he actually knew someone (e.g., Boniface VIII) but less accurate for those he knew only by their medieval reputations.

would be universal and applied to all equally. The only power capable of creating such a society was located in the ancient tradition of universal empire. An enlightened Roman emperor, freed from the political interventions of a corrupt papacy, would be the ticket to a better society. For Dante, in his profound meditation on the state of humanity, had come to the conclusion that men and women could not find within themselves the strength to lead truly moral lives if they were forced to live in evil conditions, surrounded by random violence and rank injustice. They needed more supportive environments "in which," as Peter Maurin would insist in the twentieth century, "it would be easier . . . to be good."

Dante, however, had no access to Procopius's scandalous account of their imperial majesties' joint reign, the *Anekdota* (Secret History), which was unavailable in his day in the West—or even in the East, for that matter, for it had been written in secret in the reign of Justinian and passed surreptitiously for centuries from one Greek reader to another— and saw the light of day only in the seventeenth century at Lyons, but with notable omissions that the French editor considered too indecent for publication. "My teeth chatter," wrote Procopius, "and I find myself recoiling as far as possible from the task; for I envisage the probability that what I am now about to write will appear incredible and unconvincing to future generations." Even in our day, the murderously shameless lives of the imperial couple, as revealed by Procopius, one of history's earliest and most engaging gossip columnists, must give a reader pause.

We, however, shall not pause, except to note that it was Justinian's rationalization of the many accrete contradictions in Roman law and his promulgation of a universal *Corpus Juris Civilis* (Body of Civil Law) that so impressed Dante. Nor was this a negligible achievement, for it is upon Justinian's consolidations of Roman law that a majority of the world's legal systems (outside China and the English-speaking world) are still based. But Dante would have been less impressed had he known of Justinian's passive indulgence of his wife's kinky sexual preferences and programmatic cruelties and his endless persecutions of whole populations, as well as of individuals, and his pitiless interventions in non-Roman societies, profound resentment against which paved the way for the triumph of Islam around the Mediterranean.

We end (well, almost end) as we began—in a Greek city. If this book's Alexandrian Prelude may appear artificial to the reader who first opens to it, I hope its importance may seem more persuasive by book's end. The matrix of the Western world, the form that gives it shape, is a Greek matrix, the shape of reason, thought, mind, rational inquiry. Its contents, however, flow into this ancient Greek mold from ancient Jewish and early Christian sources and are matters not of mind but of beating heart, moral action and interaction, and fleshly experience. It is in the course of the Middle Ages—and particularly in the twelfth, thirteenth, and early fourteenth centuries—that the contents of the mold jell for the first time to produce an early version of our modern world. It is not a finished version—and perhaps there never will be a finished version. It is, to use a word I relied on heavily in the Introduction, an incarnation; and more recent incarnations will be studied in the volumes still promised in this series.

But this "great central Synthesis of history," remarked upon by Chesterton, is indeed a synthesis of elements that are, in some degree, opposites. It is not possible to imagine the words of Plato with which the Prelude began escaping from the mouth of any Jew or Christian (or even from any agnostic or atheist who has lived his life in Judeo-Christian society). For a post-Greco-Roman, of whatever variety, the soul (if there is a soul) takes into the otherworld (if there is another world), not its education and culture, but the moral character it has formed over the course of its earthly existence. The modern man or woman, however snobbish, cannot compete for snobbery with an ancient Greek. None of us believes our education, our culture, our *mind,* to be of such supreme importance. Who-we-are, our final identity, as Dante impresses on us compellingly, is composed not of what we know but of how we have acted toward others. No matter who you are, you cannot re-assume an ancient Greek, or even an ancient Roman, identity. That possibility was forever blotted out when the Romans became the Italians—that is, when they took on a Christian mind and heart, a Christian orientation, a Christian identity, however inchoate, incomplete, unresolved, and even self-contradictory that identity must always be in every age.

No more is it conceivable that any ancient Greek could have spoken the great Torah-based sentiment expressed by Thomas Aquinas at the outset of Chapter 4. The idea of any god worth a candle feeding his worshipers with corn fat and honey (from the rock, yet!) would strike a refined Alexandrian as *so* primitive and quaint. God, the highest expression of the Spiritual, cannot be concerned with stinking matter in any of its guises.

We are the fortunate inheritors of two profound traditions that cannot be entirely reconciled but must compete with one another down the ages in a never-ending tug-of-war. Science could never have asserted its sensible self within Judeo-Christian society had it not been for the goad that Greek reason provided. Feminism, on the other hand, might well have asserted its relevance without classical influence of any kind, for there was within the Greco-Roman world hardly a whit of feminism anywhere. Artistic realism in its many forms is probably best understood as the result of a combination of Greek natural philosophy (and its obsession with measurement and accuracy) and Christian incarnationalism (and its primary project of finding truth in flesh).

The jumble of the Middle Ages derives to a large extent from the ambiguities of our dual heritage; and the difficulty of making general statements about medieval European culture derives from the same persistent ambiguities. The division of the medieval political establishment into an interlocking puzzle of competing nations, at the threshold of asserting their separate identities, adds to the difficulty. In order to trace consistent themes through so much jumble (and to keep this book to reasonable length), I have been forced to omit or reduce in scope many subjects I had intended to consider. The absent Marjorie Kempe, Hrotswitha, Meister Eckhart, Duns Scotus, William of Ockham, and Dame Julian of Norwich spring to mind, as well as the barely mentioned Maimonides and unnamed poets of the English tradition from Caedmon to William Langland. Chaucer has only a small speaking part, a sorry omission, since I have always thought that the medieval experience I would most wish to have would be to attend a party with him in London during Christmas week. Whole regions—the Iberian, the Scandinavian, and the Eastern European—have been nearly omitted, and vast subjects, such as politics, warfare, torture, and disease, have been given short shrift. Even major incidents in the lives of major characters—such as the politically motivated suppression of the Knights of the Temple (or Templars) by the first Avignon pope or the relationship of Henry II and Thomas Becket—have had to be left out or reduced to a footnote.

Some of the subjects a reader might have expected to find in a book like this were covered in *How the Irish Saved Civilization*, which ends with the Viking raids of the ninth century, or will be found in the next volume in the series. One of these, the Inquisition, belongs much more to the Renaissance than to the medieval period, when it was relatively tame in its effects. Similarly, the European mistreatment of Jews escalates in Renaissance-Reformation times from relatively benign inattention or generally passive contempt to far more active and frequent persecution.[b] In this volume, I have not gone much beyond the early fourteenth century, after which a rise in violence, especially in northern Europe, and in death by contagion (the Black Death, or bubonic plague) throughout the continent began to alter Europe irrevocably by wiping out a third to a half of its population. The Great Plague in particular was, as the highly regarded Princeton historian William Chester Jordan calls it, "the death knell of medieval European civilization."

b Recent findings by Jewish scholars—for instance, Daniel Baraz, *Medieval Cruelty: Changing Perceptions, Late Antiquity to the Early Modern Period,* and Norman Cantor in many works—support this view. Cantor's *Encyclopedia of the Middle Ages* contains several informative entries, especially "Jews in the Middle Ages."

The reputation of the Middle Ages for thuggish cruelty is largely (if not wholly) undeserved. The humanist intellectuals of the Renaissance who established the category "medieval" intended that it should characterize an age that had neither the accomplishments of the classical period nor those of their "modern" age. All the libelous adjectives hurled by prejudiced historians like William Manchester or even by immensely clever writers like Mark Twain (in *A Connecticut Yankee in King Arthur's Court*) have their origin among those Renaissance humanists.

Like those humanists, we may pat ourselves on the back for our vast advance in knowledge and for our political enlightenment. In science we have ventured to the heart of material reality, progressing so far as to split the atom, which means that there are men in our world who could obliterate life in whole cities, countries, and continents. Soon there will be more such men, since we are doing such an abysmal job of nuclear arms reduction and control. "More than fifteen years after the end of the cold war," exclaimed Mohamed ElBaradei, director general of the United Nations nuclear monitoring agency, in his Nobel Peace Prize acceptance speech, "it is incomprehensible . . . that the major nuclear weapon states operate with their arsenals on hair-trigger alert." The existence around the world of twenty-seven thousand nuclear warheads, many poorly secured, offers the quite thinkable prospect of "devastation of entire nations in a matter of minutes." Dante imagined that Hell was buried deep inside the earth; today he might wonder if it was rising to the surface. What we face here, of course, is not a scientific challenge but a political one.

We have no Roman emperor, good or bad, to bend to. We have no pope to whom we need pay the slightest heed. Dante believed that the pope should be confined to religious matters and that the realms of church and state should be basically unmixable. If he could have thought of such a thing, he would have approved of our modern secular idea of the political separation of church and state.

Dante also believed that only a great and good emperor, a man of universal understanding, could bring peace and justice to his realms. The kind of emperor he had in mind was more an institution than a single person. If he could have thought of such a thing, he would have found the United Nations, with all its flaws and limitations, closer to his ideal than would be any conceivable monarch.

What preoccupied Dante most of all was the acquisitive, dissembling, violence-prone politician, whether clerical or lay, who could lie to himself and lie to others—creating "a vast tapestry of lies," as Harold Pinter called it in *his* Nobel Prize speech—give orders to torture the helpless and banish the innocent while on his way into church, hold men prisoner indefinitely without charging them, execute them boldly and self-righteously, persecute religious and ethnic minorities, refuse to acknowledge the mercenary motives of his closest advisers, abrogate international treaties, pollute whole ecosystems while pretending to do otherwise, and declare his vicious wars just, necessary, and blessed by God. Especially to be feared was the man who did all these things and got away with them because his earnest good looks and earthy sincerity concealed his real intentions from many observers and because he was too powerful to be stopped. Such a man was Philip the Fair, unscrupulous, suspicious, envious, and rigid, who succeeded his father to the French throne in 1285, who regularly blackened the reputation of anyone who dared oppose him, and who fancied himself the "most Christian" of Christian kings.

SOME MAJOR MEDIEVALS

IN THE ORDER OF THEIR BIRTH

CONSTANTINE THE GREAT	c. 280–337
AUGUSTINE OF HIPPO	354–430
BENEDICT OF NURSIA	c. 480–547
JUSTINIAN I	483–565
THEODORA I	500–548
GREGORY I THE GREAT	c. 540–604
CHARLEMAGNE	742–814
ALFRED THE GREAT	849–899
PETER ABELARD	1079–1144
BERNARD OF CLAIRVAUX	1090–1153
HILDEGARD OF BINGEN	1098–1179
HÉLOÏSE	1101–1164
ELEANOR OF AQUITAINE	c. 1122–1204
FREDERICK I BARBAROSSA	c. 1123–1190
HENRY II PLANTAGENET	1133–1189
MOSES MAIMONIDES	1135–1204
INNOCENT III	c. 1160–1216
FRANCIS OF ASSISI	1182–1226
ALBERT THE GREAT	c. 1200–1280
ROGER BACON	1214–1292
BONAVENTURE	c. 1221–1274
THOMAS AQUINAS	c. 1225–1274
BONIFACE VIII	c. 1235–1303
GIOVANNI CIMABUE	c. 1240–1302?
MARCO POLO	1254–1324
DANTE ALIGHIERI	1265–1321
GIOTTO DI BONDONE	1266–1337
PHILIP IV THE FAIR	1268–1314
GIOVANNI BOCCACCIO	1313–1375
GEOFFREY CHAUCER	c. 1340–1400
CATHERINE OF SIENA	1347–1380

love
in the ruins

a dantesque reflection

*If the world grows too worldly,
it can be rebuked by the
Church; but if the Church
grows too worldly, it cannot be
adequately rebuked for
worldliness by the world.*

—G. K. CHESTERTON

AND IF THE CHURCH GROWS too evil? Who shall rebuke it then?

The story this book has had to tell is the story of the (often overlooked and belittled) Catholic contribution to Western civilization. In this story, power-mad popes and greedy kings make only cameo appearances. The main subject is what it has been in each volume of the Hinges of History: "the story of the great gift-givers, those who entrusted to our keeping one or another of the singular treasures that make up the patrimony of the West."

Dante prayed for a reformed Catholic Church in which clergy would be unable to insert themselves directly into the political process. We, by reformation, enlightenment, revolution, and democracy—the movements that rose in the centuries after the story told in this book—have achieved a (usually adequate) separation of church and state. The pope, for instance, now controls only nominal territory and could not raise an army even if he wished to.

But however necessary this was for the health of society, it has not improved the health of the Catholic Church, now caught like a helpless animal in a trap from which there seems no escape. The priestly pedophilia crisis has enveloped almost all of Catholic life, certainly in the United States, as well as in many other countries around the world. The response of bishops, cardinals, and popes has been staggering in its inadequacy. At first, as we all know, they attempted to minimize the extent of the wound that had been inflicted on the church. They hired aggressive attorneys to defend themselves against poor victims;[a] they underreported the numbers of perpetrators; they underreported the numbers of victims; they blamed the media. At last, it became clear that for more years than anyone will ever know, bishops have routinely reassigned priestly predators, allowing them to take advantage of fresh crops of child victims, paying off victims in return for their silence, and keeping everything hush-hush.

Bernard Law—Cardinal Coverup himself—forced to flee office as archbishop of Boston, was even rewarded with the position of archpriest of Santa Maria Maggiore by a grateful Pope John Paul II. Law's new position, which permits him to reside in the most luxurious palace in Rome, also prevents his arrest by secular authorities, for Santa Maria Maggiore is extraterritorial, a fief of

a   This ploy was favored viciously by Edward Egan, the current cardinal archbishop of New York, when he was bishop of Bridgeport, Connecticut. Egan is a clerical insider with almost no pastoral experience. He worked his way up the ladder by adept sycophancy in the Vatican's curial offices. He has had virtually no impact on New York in the years since his appointment, except for his single public act of changing the name of the nineteenth-century immigrant-built cathedral from "Saint Patrick's Cathedral" to "the Cathedral of Saint Patrick."

the Vatican beyond the reach of Italian law. John Paul's successor, Benedict XVI, the former Joseph Ratzinger, has dragged his feet for years on prosecuting (or even investigating) notorious pedophile priests. (See the reference to Jason Berry's *Vows of Silence* in the note below.) The latest Vatican ploy is to blame the crisis on homosexual priests and to devise ways to root them out. This would be comical to anyone who knows a variety of Catholic priests and bishops (since so many are homosexual in orientation, if not in *inter*genital activity), were it not for the further destruction such an inquisition is likely to wreak on an already demoralized priesthood.

Though the U.S. bishops have been forced to create a (more or less) public policy for dealing with these outrages, the Vatican has remained remarkably coy. One cardinal—Dario Castrillon Hoyos, prefect of the Congregation of the Clergy, at a press briefing in spring 2002—even suggested that this was a problem confined to the English-speaking world.[b] The truth of the matter is that the English-speaking world has a tradition of truth-telling in public that is not replicated elsewhere, especially not in Italy, where an admission of forced buggery (like the admission of rape by a woman victim in a Muslim country) would bring such opprobrium on the male victim that he could never hold up his head again but could well expect to be further brutalized. (I love Italy, but I am not in the dark about its limitations.)

Dante bewailed the selling of church offices, describing this practice as "Christ [being] bought and sold the whole day long" in the Rome of Pope Boniface VIII. That was, however, a far less depraved situation than the current one, where, as Dante would be forced to conclude, the twelve-year-old Christ, who conversed with the doctors of the law in the Temple of Jerusalem (in Luke 2:41–52), is made to give blow jobs and rammed up the ass the whole day long by the doctors of the law of the New

[b] Castrillon Hoyos's exact words were "The language used [by the questioner, i.e., English] is interesting. This by itself is an X-ray of the problem." He went on to blame the pedophilia crisis not on the church but on society's "pan-sexuality and sexual licentiousness"; and in Vatican circles the term *anglo sassone* (Anglo-Saxon) is practically a synonym for (to their way of thinking) sick sexual practices. But the cardinal has a history of intervening on behalf of clerical child molesters (see Jason Berry and Gerald Renner, *Vows of Silence: The Abuse of Power in the Papacy of John Paul II,* pp. 232–35).

Jerusalem, while the high priests of the Temple stand guard at the entrances, lest any uninitiated outsiders should discover what is going on. However shocking these words may sound to some ears, there can be no doubt that this is what clerical dissemblers have done to the Jesus they claim to care so much about. For "whatever you have done to the least of these . . . you have done to me" (Matthew 25:40).

At this point, the church seems built not on the Rock of Peter but on sand—the shifting sand of sexually immature priests and of bishops who lie and fawn for a living. It is not so much the vow of celibacy in itself that has brought this crisis about. But enforced, rather than chosen, celibacy, defended by an episcopate of high priests who need fear nothing either from ordinary priests or from lay Catholics, but only from those hierarchs who can bestow or withhold all offices and favors, has brought the church almost to its death throes.

If this church is to survive, it must return to the practices of its apostolic foundations, when celibacy was optional and all clergy—from deacons to bishops (there were no cardinals or popes in those days)—were chosen by the people. A policy of optional celibacy would attract more sexually healthy candidates to the priesthood (rather than the many self-deceivers who are now attracted) and even restore the glory of monasticism. We all need to know that there remain in our harried world symbolic oases of monastic peace; and we all need monks and nuns, whether we know it or not, people who are free from earthly ties and who in great societal perversions, like the fascist regimes of the Second World War, are available to hide political prey from their predators. Popular election of clergy would put responsibility for the church squarely where it belongs—with the church itself, that is, with the Assembly of God's people. The only hope is for an uprising of laypeople who refuse to be disfranchised serfs any longer, led by sincere movements like Voice of the Faithful and Call to Action, which will remove the only power the laity can now claim, the power of the purse, from clerical hands. If this should happen, we will see the political power, which no one gives up willingly, wither. It is only stolen power anyway; it never belonged to the bishops by right. *"Vox populi, vox Dei,"* as even Charlemagne knew. "The voice of the people is the voice of God."

As the preceding chapters have demonstrated, it was not bishops but laypeople who were responsible for the historic glories of Catholicism, given as gifts to the Western world. Of the great figures processing through this book, only a few, like Thomas Aquinas, were ordained, and only one, Gregory the Great, was a member of the higher clergy. The historic role of the higher clergy is to be put in their place by men like Dante and women like Catherine of Siena, who journeyed to Avignon in the fourteenth century to wag her finger under the pope's nose and to remind him of his neglected responsibilities. Without the clear vision and unwelcome advice of such men and women, the church as it is has no chance of acting in the world in succor or in prophecy. (The Catholic Church in the United States may be doomed in any case, unless the episcopate as a whole resigns, divesting itself of its gorgeous robes and walking off the world's stage in sackcloth and ashes. For the bishops who now hold office are surely impostors.)

Like tenants on an eighteenth-century estate, we live amid romantic ruins, a chancel arch here, a crumbling lancet window there, awaiting revenant figures of reformation—the return of energizing, enveloping forces like Hildegard and Francis, Giotto and Dante. We might even find ourselves mumbling a prayer like the one whispered by the anonymous bard who once stood looking at the ruins of Kilcash Castle on the southeast slope of Slievenamon in County Tipperary:

I beseech of Mary and Jesus
That the great come home again
With long dances danced in the garden,
Fiddle music and mirth among men,
That Kilcash the home of our fathers
Be lifted on high again,
And from that to the deluge of waters
In bounty and peace remain.

What is there left to say but "Amen"?

notes and sources

F irst, a word about the title of this book. The "mysteries" are not the
mysteries of modern detective fiction. Our word *mysteries* derives
from the Greek *mystēria,* originally a reference to the secret rites performed in pagan cults, especially the rites of Demeter, goddess of grain,
which were conducted at Eleusis and to which yearly pilgrimages were
organized from Athens. These rites were kept so effectively secret that to
this day no one can be certain what was involved in their execution.
Classical Greek Christians (apart from the whispering Gnostics) were
resolutely opposed to such religious secrets: they wanted everything out
in the open. And yet they called their own rites *mystēria* because they
viewed them with the same exalted, trance-like awe in which the mysteries of Demeter were conducted. *Mystery,* therefore, became the word
in the Christian East for what we in the West would name *sacrament.*
These words once covered more experiences than we might allow for
them today. The worship of the Virgin Mary was a sacramental mystery,
as was the vowing of a nun, as was almost any broadly symbolic action—
Francis presenting himself naked before Assisi's cathedral, Giotto making
a painting of that scene—carried out with ritual dignity.

As has been the case in the preceding volumes in this series, the bib-
liographical notes that follow are not intended as a complete list of
everything I consulted, only of those sources I found most helpful and
which I imagine an enterprising reader might be interested in consult-
ing. *Secondo me,* there is no single work that gives one a more intense and
extensive understanding of the Middle Ages than Sigrid Undset's astonishing three-volume novel *Kristin Lavransdatter,* set in Norway in the first
half of the fourteenth century and covering the life of one woman from
birth to death. It has recently been republished (1997–2000) by Penguin
in a much improved translation by Tiina Nunnally. If an interested reader
were to undertake but one more study of things medieval, Undset is
your woman. Her other medieval novels, *The Master of Hestviken,* a
tetralogy, and *Gunnar's Daughter,* are almost as masterful.

In keeping my bearings, I found two atlases especially useful: Colin McEvedy's *The New Penguin Atlas of Medieval History* (1992), simply laid out and well seasoned by its salty commentary, and Rosamond McKitterick's less focused but quite valuable *Atlas of the Medieval World* (Oxford, 2004), a work of many hands and more than one point of view. Two encyclopedias provided excellent checklists: Norman Cantor's one-volume *Encyclopedia of the Middle Ages* (New York, 1999), up-to-date but oddly selective; and *The New Catholic Encyclopedia,* second edition (2003), a fifteen-volume affair with supplements, whose bias is far more evident in its title than in its generally balanced and exhaustive entries. One of the best new histories of the period is *Europe in the High Middle Ages* (Penguin, 2001) by William Chester Jordan, though three series— *The Short Oxford History of Europe, The Short Oxford History of Italy,* and *The Short Oxford History of France*—are also helpful.

I found especially useful two books on intellectual history. The first of these, *Medieval Foundations of the Western Intellectual Tradition, 400–1400* (Yale, 1997) by Marcia L. Colish, concerns, as its title suggests, the Middle Ages themselves. It is both encyclopedic and balanced. The second, *Inventing the Middle Ages* (Morrow, 1991) by Norman F. Cantor, traces the twentieth-century reaction against the negative view of the Middle Ages that was propagated during the Renaissance. It is selective, quirky, and subjective.

a chaucerian invitation

The Canterbury Tales by Geoffrey Chaucer is widely available in several editions. The murder of Thomas Becket provides the subject for T. S. Eliot's famous play *Murder in the Cathedral.*

prelude:
alexandria, city of reason

The classic study of Alexandria and its spirit is E. M. Forster's *Alexandria: A History and a Guide,* which Lawrence Durrell rightly called "a small work of art." In coming to terms with the reception of Christianity by the Greco-Roman world, I found especially insightful a book from the first half of the twentieth century, *Christianity and Classical Culture* by Charles Norris Cochrane, published in 1940 by Oxford and available still from the Liberty Fund of Indianapolis under their Amagi imprint. But the most impressive work on this period has been accomplished by Peter Brown, who practically invented scholarship for what is now labeled "late antiquity." His many books—from his early and innovative *The Body and Society: Men, Women, and Sexual Renunciation in Early Christianity* (Columbia University Press, 1988) to his recent *The Rise of Western Christendom* (Blackwell, 2003)—have served as invaluable resources; likewise the anthology *Late Antiquity* (Harvard, 1999), edited by Brown, Bowerstock, and Grabar. Other helpful books in this vein include Henry Chadwick's *Early Christian Thought and the Classical Tradition* (Oxford, 1966) and Robert Louis Wilkin's *The Christians as the Romans Saw Them* (Yale, 2003).

For those familiar with biblical languages and the problems of translation, mention should be made of my treatment of Philo's commentary on Genesis. Philo's *psychē zōē,* which I translate as "living soul," is Septuagint Greek. It so happens that the King James Version renders this phrase as "living soul," even though the translators of the KJV were supposedly translating from the Hebrew. But they may well have had an eye on the Septuagint; or if their translation was not informed by the linguistic bias of the Septuagint, it may have been informed by the more generally Grecophile assumptions of Western society.

introduction:
rome, crossroads of the world

Much of the research for this section is dependent on the same sources named in the note on the Prologue. For the lives of early popes, Eamon Duffy's *Saints and Sinners: A History of the Popes* (Yale, 1997) has served me well, as has R. A. Markus's *Gregory the Great and His World* (Cambridge, 1997). The full text of "My Dancing Day" may be found in *The New Oxford Book of Carols* (1998). But it must be confessed that much of the material in the Introduction is a result not so much of my reading as of my experience of contemporary Rome—which is of necessity an experience of historical Rome as well. For readers who wish to explore Italy's dark side, Tobias Jones makes a perceptive, if long-winded, companion in *The Dark Heart of Italy* (Faber, 2003; North Point, 2004).

A second confession: the idea of politicians wearing a miniature electric chair around their necks came to me by way of Lenny Bruce.

One of my early academic readers judiciously cautioned me against my description of medieval mystery plays as "tinseled and tumbledown." While it is certainly true that the guilds invested much money and energy producing these plays, I think they would appear to us, who are so accustomed to sophisticated lighting and complicated electronic tricks, as ramshackle, amateurish, and occasionally tasteless.

one:
bingen and chartres, gardens enclosed

For Hildegard's *Scivias,* I used the translation by Columba Hart (1990) in Paulist Press's most commendable series Classics of Western Spirituality. *The Letters of Hildegard of Bingen* are available in English in a three-volume set from Oxford (1994–2004), translated into English and with a remarkably good introduction and notes and a terrific short bibliography by Joseph L. Baird and Radd K. Ehrman. Included are many letters from Hildegard's correspondents. The bibliography points out notable work on medieval women by Peter Dronke, some of it still available only in German. There are several popular lives of Hildegard, the best one by Fiona Maddocks (Headline, 2001; Image/Doubleday, 2003). *Voice of the Living Light: Hildegard of Bingen and Her World,* edited by Barbara Newman (California, 1998), is more scholarly.

There are several excellent recordings of Hildegard's music. My personal favorite, which contains the Latin hymn quoted in the text, is *11,000 Virgins: Chants for the Feast of St. Ursula* (Harmonia Mundi, 1997, 2003) by the marvelous vocal ensemble Anonymous 4. (The English translation of the hymn is mine.) Likewise, the illuminations found in early manuscripts of Hildegard's works are available in several editions, the most popular being *Illuminations of Hildegard of Bingen* (Bear & Company, 1985), with a commentary by Matthew Fox. Fox's commentary is, however, far more Fox than Hildegard.

In the opinion of some recent scholars, papal approval of *Scivias* is a suspect aspect of Hildegard's biography. See, for instance, Kathryn Kerby-Fulton, "Prophecy and Suspicion," *Speculum* 75.2:224–25, and John van Engen, "Letters and Public Persona of Hildegard" in *Hildegard von Bingen in ihrem historischen Umfeld* (Verlag Philipp von Zabern, 2000), pp. 375–418. One theory in this controversy is that the letter of approbation from Pope Eugene may actually have been written by Volmar. From my point of view, whether Hildegard received papal approbation or just pretended to do so is less important than that, in either case, she wished to be seen as orthodox and as a staunch ally of the reformers.

Similarly, the incident about Hildegard predicting the color of an unborn calf is not meant to demonstrate Hildegard's powers of prognostication, just to remind the reader that she was not above a certain manipulative self-dramatization. After all, how many colors is a calf likely to be?

The classic *Mont-Saint-Michel and Chartres* by Henry Adams is available in several different editions.

It is often claimed that the Christian worship of the Virgin Mary, especially in the image of the Mother nursing the Child, is borrowed from the pagan worship of the Egyptian goddess Isis nursing the divine Horus. But the evidence for this is extremely thin, if not nonexistent; and I remain unconvinced.

two:
aquitaine and assisi, courts of love

For my money, C. S. Lewis's chapter "Courtly Love" in *The Allegory of Love: A Study in Medieval Tradition* (Oxford, rev. 1938) remains the best short treatment of courtly love in English, even if I tend to the opinion that the cult of the Virgin Mary had more to do with the origins of courtly love than Lewis would allow. Newer critical approaches concentrate on courtly love as a literary convention, much to the exclusion of interest in how the convention may have affected behavior or been the consequence of behavior. But just as in our own day the actions of literary and dramatic figures encourage patterns of behavior (and stem from existing patterns of behavior) in the larger culture, I am sure they did so in medieval times. In addition, Lewis's English style offers an adamantine pleasure that few, if any, contemporary critics would be capable of providing.

The (very loose) translations of Ovid are mine, as are the translations of Capellanus and, later in the chapter, of Chrétien de Troyes. When the original language is particularly interesting in itself (and likely to be understood by some readers), I have included it, as in the case of Ovid and Chrétien. When it's just doggerel, as in the case of Capellanus, I haven't troubled you with it.

Alison Weir's *Eleanor of Aquitaine* (Cape, 1999; Ballantine, 2001) is the most up-to-date of recent biographies and possesses invaluable "Notes on the Chief Sources" and an enormous (and enormously helpful) bibliography. There are many recent and excellent studies of medieval warfare and violence, among them *Crusades: The Illustrated History* (Duncan Baird, 2004), edited by Thomas F. Madden; *The Oxford History of the Crusades* by Jonathan Riley-Smith; *Medieval Warfare: A History,* edited by Maurice Keen; and *Chivalry and Violence in Medieval Europe* by Richard W. Kaeuper, these last three all published by Oxford in 1999.

In my treatment of Francis I have relied heavily on Donald Spoto's down-to-earth *Reluctant Saint: The Life of Francis of Assisi* (Penguin, 2002), which is careful never to go beyond the evidence nor to trust in pious legend. But there are so many studies of Francis, old and new, good and bad, skeptical and credulous, that I despair of sorting them out here. For Francis's composition "The Canticle of the Creatures" I used the version in Spoto, which he had from Arnaldo Fortini, *Nova Vita di San Francesco* (Assisi, 1959). For the English translation I also used the version in Spoto, which he had from the three-volume work *Francis of Assisi: Early Documents* (New City, 1999–2001). In the translation, however, I made some small alterations to bring the English closer to my understanding of the Umbrian original.

intermezzo:
entrances to other worlds

The introduction of Chesterton's *Ballad of the White Horse* will no doubt strike some readers as irrelevant, since it is an early twentieth-century, not a medieval, work; and the incident Chesterton gives us—Alfred's vision of the Virgin—has no historical basis. But for me, as in my earlier recommendation of *Kristin Lavransdatter,* there is here a genuine evocation of the feeling and fabric of the Middle Ages that is worthy of our attention.

We now have two contesting schools on the confrontation between Islam and the West: the leftish "Golden Age" school, which emphasizes only the high culture and tolerance of Islam's past (especially in early medieval Spain), and the right-wing "clash of civilizations" school, which declares that no accommodation between Islam and the West is possible. Though each side has its valid points, I belong to neither. And though it is impossible to write about the high medieval period in Europe without reference to Islam, the matter of this book is confined to the lasting contributions of the Catholic Middle Ages to Western society, which means that Islam must remain at its margins.

The travel memoirs of Marco Polo are available in several editions, but the Penguin Classics edition (1958), translated and introduced by Ronald Latham, is still awfully good.

three:
paris, university of heavenly things

The classic study of medieval university life is *The Rise of Universities* (Cornell, 1959) by Charles Homer Haskins, first published in 1923. A persuasive, and far more complex, recent study is *God and Reason in the Middle Ages* (Cambridge, 2001) by Edward Grant. It should be noted that universities arose in the Muslim world well in advance of their rise in Europe, at Fez, for instance, in 859 and at Cairo in 975. Greek texts preserved at these universities, as well as in the Muslim enclaves of Spain and southern Italy, helped prepare the way for the philosophical-scientific renaissance of twelfth- and thirteenth-century Europe.

The medieval philosophers are well limned in Frederick Copleston's monumental *History of Philosophy,* Volume II (Image/Doubleday, 1962), even if Abelard is given short shrift. Copleston's *Aquinas* (1955), available from Penguin, is also outstanding. The classic on this subject is Étienne Gilson's *The Spirit of Medieval Philosophy* (Notre Dame, 1991), first published in 1936. *Aristotle's Children: How Christians, Muslims, and Jews Rediscovered Ancient Wisdom and Illuminated the Dark Ages* (Harcourt, 2003) by Richard E. Rubenstein, a clear, accessible account (despite that misleading phrase about supposedly "Dark Ages"), contains a most readable chapter on the life and thought of Abelard.

A new edition of *The Letters of Abelard and Héloïse* (Penguin, 2003), translated by Betty Radice and revised by M. T. Clanchy, is an indispensable beginning for a study of the two lovers. Constant Mews's *The Lost Love Letters of Héloïse and Abelard* (St. Martin's, 1999) adds detail to their story.

For those seeking a more positive view of Bernard of Clairvaux than is provided by my hasty caricature, the place to begin is the collection of Bernard's writings (1987) in the previously cited Classics of Western Spirituality series.

The differences between Augustine and Aquinas, the two unavoidable figures of medieval philosophy, are many and (sometimes) subtle, just as the differences between their favorite Greeks—Plato for Augustine, Aristotle for Aquinas—are many and (sometimes) subtle. It all goes back to different theories of perception and (attainment of) knowledge. For the Platonic Augustine, God must directly illuminate a human mind if its possessor is to come to know truth; for the Aristotelian Aquinas, the human mind grasps accurately what comes to it through the senses. God's grace only perfects what is already there.

The text and chant for the hymn "Adoro Te Devote" may be found in the *Liber usualis* (Desclee, 1947), pp. 1629–30, along with references to several other eucharistic hymns by Thomas Aquinas. The text and chant for "Pange Lingua" may be found on pp. 811–13 in the section on liturgical texts for the feast of Corpus Christi, all of which were chosen and/or composed by Aquinas. The English translation of "Adoro Te Devote" is included in many editions of the poems of Gerard Manley Hopkins under the title "S. Thomae Aquinatis Rhythmus." Hopkins used a variation on the Latin original, which substitutes *supplex* for *devote* in the first line. It is a later (and inaccurate) version of the original, but it makes no difference to the sense of the translation.

four:
oxford, university of earthly things

To paraphrase T. S. Eliot: No! I am not a scientist, nor was meant to be. My information in this chapter comes largely from four books: Charles Singer, *From Magic to Science,* originally published by Longman in 1928 and reprinted by Kessinger (n.d.); David C. Lindberg (ed.), *Science in the Middle Ages* (Chicago, 1978); David C. Lindberg, *The Beginnings of Western Science* (Chicago, 1992); and Edward Grant, *The Foundations of Modern Science in the Middle Ages* (Cambridge, 1996). The oldest book may be the most accessible.

five:
padua, chapel of flesh

I first came across the connection between Francis's invention of the *presepio* and the tradition of artistic realism in Chesterton's *Francis of Assisi* (Image/Doubleday, 1957), one of his best books. The best "books" to read about Giotto are his paintings, of which there are few in North America: Boston, New York, Washington, D.C. The books I found most helpful are Luciano Bellosi, *Giotto: The Complete Works* (Scala, 1981), a cheaply produced paperback readily available in shops throughout northern Italy and containing an exhaustive list of extant Giottos and their whereabouts; and Francesca Flores d'Arcais, *Giotto* (Abbeville, 1995), which contains an incisive commentary and a lavish, nearly perfect portfolio of reproductions.

six:
florence, dome of light

The bite-sized biography cited in the text, *Dante* (Penguin, 2001) by R. W. B. Lewis, is a trifle muddled, but it ends with a model bibliography. William Anderson's *Dante the Maker* (Routledge, 1980; Crossroad, 1982) is the standard biography in English.

The choice of a translation of *La Divina Commedia* is a thoroughgoing conundrum, for no English translation is entirely satisfying. For sheer readability from start to finish, I would recommend Allen Mandelbaum's *The Divine Comedy of Dante Alighieri* in three paperback volumes (Bantam 1982, 1984, 1986) with facing pages in Italian and English. It is accurate and genuinely poetic. For a prose rendering that adheres closely to the Italian, the obvious choice is John D. Sinclair's (Oxford, 1961), also in three paperback volumes with facing pages in both languages (and using the same title as Mandelbaum's). The translation I use frequently in the text because of its successful imitation in English of Dante's *terza rima* scheme is by Peter Dale (Anvil, 1996), widely available in the U.K. if not here. There are also many articulate defenders of translations by Dorothy L. Sayers and John Ciardi. The best solution, if you can spare the time, is to learn a little Italian and then use one of these translations as a trot while reading Dante's original.

Among many admirable appreciations of Dante, I found most helpful "Life of Dante" by Giuseppe Mazzotta in *The Cambridge Companion to Dante* (1993) and several essays in *Dante's Testaments* (Stanford, 1999) by Peter S. Hawkins.

seven:
Ravenna, city of death

The epigraph is traditionally attributed to Sir Walter Scott because he quotes it in *Old Mortality* (1816), but it is more correctly attributed to the long-forgotten Thomas Osbert Mordaunt (1730–1809) in his poem "The Bee." Procopius's *The Secret History* is published in English translation by Penguin (1966).

postlude:
love in the Ruins

The assertion that "there were no cardinals or popes" in apostolic times, along with the assumption that there were deacons and bishops, needs this further clarification: there was also no separate caste of priests. The only priesthood acknowledged by the primitive Christian community was the priesthood of all believers (1 Peter 2:9), an idea that would be rediscovered at the Reformation.

"Kilcash" appears in *Kings, Lords, and Commons* (Gill & Macmillan, 1959), an anthology of translations of poems in the Irish language from A.D. 600 to 1800 by Frank O'Connor.

acknowledgments

once again, I have many to thank who read the first draft of the manuscript and whose penetrating criticisms were essential to keeping me on the right road. They are: my wife Susan Cahill, John E. Becker, Lauren Broughton, William J. Cassidy III, Michael D. Coogan, John Cullen, Paul Dinter, Mario Marazziti, James M. Morris, Gertrud Mueller Nelson, Gary B. Ostrower, Donald Spoto, Burton Visotzky, and Robert J. White.

Those who toil for my American publishers deserve special thanks: always in the place of primacy Nan A. Talese, but also Kathy Trager, Stephen Rubin, Jacqueline Everly, John Pitts, Rex Bonomelli, Rebecca Holland, Nora Reichard, Ronit Feldman, and Terry Karydes, who is responsible for the smashing design of this book. I am permanently in the debt of Jennifer Marshall, whose intelligent publicity plans have brought my book to the attention of more readers than ever. My debt to the entire Random House sales force is, by this point in the series, ancient and unpayable.

Beyond Doubleday and Anchor, I am particularly grateful to my agent, Lynn Nesbit, and her able colleague Bennett Ashley; as well as Barbara Flanagan, the stouthearted copy editor; Diane Marcus, my assistant; and Andrea Ginsky, research librarian of the Selby Public Library in Sarasota, Florida. In touring various sites I was extremely lucky to have the expert advice of Gertrud Mueller Nelson in Germany, Marion Ranoux in Paris, Malcolm Miller at Chartres, and Rinaldo Piazzoni and Sandra Battisti in Italy. To Vanessa Vreeland I owe special thanks for pointing out the connection between Islam and ikonoklasm and between ikonoklasm and the subsequent flood of Greek images into Italy.

permissions acknowledgments

The author has endeavored to credit all known persons holding copyright or reproduction rights for passages quoted and for illustrations reproduced in this book, especially:

Anvil Press Poetry for the passages from *Dante: The Divine Comedy*, translated by Peter Dale, copyright © 1996 by Peter Dale.

New City Press, Hyde Park, N.Y. (www.newcitypress.com), for the passages from *Francis of Assisi: Early Documents, Volume 1: The Saint, Volume 2: The Founder, Volume 3: The Prophet*, copyright © 1999, 2000, 2001 by the Franciscan Institute of St. Bonaventure, New York.

Oxford University Press for *The Letters of Hildegard of Bingen, Volumes I, II, III*, translated by Joseph L. Baird and Radd K. Ehrman, copyright © 1994, 1998, 2004 by Oxford University Press, Inc.

Paulist Press, New York/Mahwah, New Jersey (www.paulistpress.com), for the passages from *Hildegard of Bingen: Scivias*, translated by Mother Columba Hart and Jane Bishop (in the Classics of Western Spirituality series), copyright © 1990 by the Abbey of Regina Laudis: Benedictine Congregation of the Strict Observance, Inc.

Penguin Group, UK, for the passages from *The Letters of Abelard and Heloise*, translated by Betty Radice (Penguin Classics, 1974), copyright © Betty Radice, 1974.

photography credits

Page 247:   Scala / Art Resource, NY
Page 249:   The Art Archive / San Francesco Assisi / Dagli Orti (A)
Page 250:   Scala / Art Resource, NY
Page 251:   Scala / Art Resource, NY
Page 252:   Scala / Art Resource, NY
Page 253:   Scala / Art Resource, NY
Page 256:   Scala / Art Resource, NY
Page 258:   Scala / Art Resource, NY
Page 259:   Scala / Art Resource, NY
Page 260:   Scala / Art Resource, NY
Page 261:   Scala / Art Resource, NY
Page 262:   Scala / Art Resource, NY
Page 263:   Scala / Art Resource, NY
Page 265:   Scala / Art Resource, NY
Page 266:   Scala / Art Resource, NY (detail)
Page 267:   Cameraphoto / Art Resource, NY
Page 268 (top):   Courtesy Achim Bednorz
Page 268 (bottom): Alinari / Art Resource, NY
Page 270:   Courtesy Achim Bednorz
Page 272:   Courtesy Achim Bednorz
Page 273:   © Alessandro Chiarini / Alamy
Page 277:   © Archivo Iconografico, S.A. / CORBIS
Page 280:   Museo Nazionale del Bargello, Florence, Italy /
                   Bridgeman Art Library
Page 303:   Scala / Art Resource, NY
Page 304:   Scala / Art Resource, NY

Details of the Apse of San Clemente pages 45, 53, 79, 168, 169, 170, 171, 178, and 184: Index S.A.S.

index

Italicized page numbers indicate illustrations.

a note about the author

THOMAS CAHILL is the author of four previous volumes in the Hinges of History series: *How the Irish Saved Civilization, The Gifts of the Jews, Desire of the Everlasting Hills,* and *Sailing the Wine-Dark Sea.* He and his wife, Susan, divide their time between New York City and Rome.

a note about the type

B EMBO WAS ORIGINALLY DESIGNED
by the Bolognese type cutter Francesco Griffo
(1450-1518), who worked for the celebrated Italian
Renaissance printer and publisher, Aldus Manutius. Manutius
commissioned Griffo to design a new typeface for the 1495
publication of a small treatise, De Aetna, by classicist Pietro
Cardinal Bembo about his visit to Mount Etna. The typeface
is named in his honor.

Griffo also cut early italics, music types, and is attributed
with cutting the first roman types with which we are now

familiar. After Manutius' death in 1515, Griffo returned to Bologna where he printed some of his own editions. It is alleged he was hanged for killing his brother-in-law, circa 1518-1519.

During the early sixteenth century the French type founder Claude Garamond used Bembo as his model for his own widely popular typefaces. For this reason Bembo is generally acknowledged to be the foundation and standard for oldstyle typefaces.

This book is set in a digital revival of Bembo, customized by North Market Street Graphics.